THE RIGHT CHOICES ?

A novel by
FRANCES C. YANCEY

I thank my mother who joyfully saw change as an adventure.

I thank my father for instilling the necessity of passionately standing up for your beliefs.

I thank my husband for loving me, sharing my core beliefs and knowing at precisely the same time as me, when it is time to act.

I thank my children for allowing me to see the world through their unique and very special perspectives.

I thank my grandchildren whose needs have given me a second chance to try to raise strong, individual and healthy children.

CHAPTER 1

The baby is coming. My husband is leaving. This morning I almost blurted out the news that I was pregnant. I didn't expect him to be happy, so I waited. I didn't expect him to announce that he was leaving the girls and me. I am stunned; I am numb. Right now I can see the two of us, as if I were watching through a camera. I sit quietly on the bed, folding his clothes, and fitting them into two large, leather suitcases. I endure the harsh words that are flung at me.

As I continue packing, new thoughts are forming. It may be best that he is leaving! I can see myself as my jaw drops open, as I quickly duck my head so he can't see my face. I am sure that if I look at him, he will see something that has been dead in me for so long that I can't remember the last time I held hope in my heart. I know that if he sees that hope, he will do anything to wrestle it from me. As I stare down at my hands, I do not see the socks that I am folding; rather I see my children's faces.

I'll never forget the first time he hit me. I thought he would be happy that I decided to take a course through Athabasca University. I was hoping he'd approve because I wouldn't need to get a baby-sitter for the girls. All of the work necessary for the course would be done at home. He was always after me to do something intelligent so I'd make better conversation with his bosses. He wanted me to impress them so he'd get a promotion.

That was why the punch he gave me was such a jolt. I had done what he wanted - -where had I gone wrong? After he spent the evening punching me in the stomach over and over again, he had the nerve to tell me to register. I tried to comprehend what had happened; wasn't that what I was doing? When he finally calmed down, he towered over me while I cowered in the corner. Then he told me that he had to teach me a lesson; to teach me not to consider anything without consulting him first. Apparently he thought that I was too stupid to make plans. I try to keep telling myself that he is wrong.

Poor little Joan, only six years old, and already she cringes at the sound of her father coming home. Too often his arrival means that obscenities are flung at her: her father yelling that she was too lazy or too stupid to get her chores done. He expects her to have her room as neat as a pin, all of her toys collected from about the house, and to guess if he wants the TV on or off

Now that she knows how to tell time, she anxiously checks the clock as the afternoons wear on. Half an hour before her father is expected home, she falls quiet, and anxiously runs about the house, trying to remember to finish everything that she is expected to do. Some days she puts the TV on, selecting a program that she knows he likes, hoping that it will help make him happy.

The slam of the front door is something I'll never forget. Which husband will it bring? I too have been busy, trying to make a supper that will please him. If I make a casserole, he'll accuse me of trying to show him that I think that he doesn't make enough money. If, instead, I make a fancier meal, he'll accuse me of wasting money. He gets so mad if Suzy's romper has even one little spot on it that he accuses me of being too lazy to do the laundry. Suzy is only two, yet she withdraws the minute her father arrives home. Up until that point, she's a little chatter bug.

Sitting down for supper was torture. The two girls tried to eat as quietly and quickly as possible. At times he acted as a father should; talking to them, showing interest in them. If the girls misjudge his mood and tried to be more open when he wanted quiet, all hell broke loose. I don't know how a father can say such things to his daughters -- his obscenities shock even me. But we can live with the shouting. Last year, the hitting began.

"I lived on my own when I finished high school." I had been planning how to get out of Olds ever since I started high school. At first my jobs were at the college. I worked in the cafeteria, clearing and cleaning up behind students; behind people with dreams. After a year I was promoted to be a cashier. The promotion meant a fifty cent raise. That didn't seem much, but it was the difference between saving fifty dollars a month, and saving seventy-five dollars a month.

I tried to save all my money. My dad wouldn't buy me clothes for school; I had to make them. I taught myself how to sew, and bought only the material I could find on sale. I had a wonderful teacher in grade twelve, and her husband worked at a lab in town. I was good in the sciences, so she convinced him to hire me the summer I finished high school. My salary was twice what I had made at the college. That gave me the push to apply to the University of Alberta, in Edmonton. I hesitated applying, not because of my grades, but because of money.

Two letters arrived on August 14, 1971, that changed my life. The first opened was from the registrar's office, notifying me of my acceptance. I was thrilled, but the thrill was tempered by worry about money. As I held up the second letter, I puzzled over the return address -- it meant nothing to me. Unknown to me, Mrs. Adams had submitted my name for a Janon Labs' scholarship. It was awarded to me, and covered my full tuition for a year.

All of this rolled through my mind as I absently folded clothes that my husband would need so he could leave me. Suddenly I was aware of the silence, and of the curious way my husband was looking at me. I decided I'd better play along and make him feel as if he were dominating me. I managed to shield my hope from him, so he wouldn't steal that from me as well.

He actually made Joan take a bag of his shoes out to the car -- he saved the last humiliation for me. He made me take his suitcases out to the car and pack them in the trunk. He criticized me for not even being able to do that properly. I bit my bottom lip so hard that I thought I'd have blood running down my chin. Joan came out of the house, with Suzy on her hip, and quietly watched as her father, without a word to her, drove off.

She stood for a long while looking down the road. Was she hoping or fearing that he'd return? I gathered Suzy in my arms, took Joan's hand, and led them into a now quiet house. We all settled on the couch without a word and pondered our future.

I'm not sure how long we sat there in silence before Joan blurted out, "He isn't coming back, is he?"

I saw hope in her eyes as she waited for my answer.

"No, I'll never let him in the house."

Poor little thing melted with relief, and then I led her to her bedroom for a nap. She looked ready to collapse. I gave Suzy a bath and tucked her in her crib. I don't know if she needed a rest, but I needed to be alone with my thoughts.

I can't stay in Westlock. All of our friends here are through his work -- he wouldn't let me make my own friends

They wouldn't believe anything that I said about him. Their view of Robert was that of the ideal husband; he provided a good living, he didn't make his wife do all the chores, he always knew where she was and what she was doing.

They thought that was devotion; to me it was control.

CHAPTER 2

I wouldn't be able to make enough money even if I could get a job in Westlock. I want to go far enough away so I don't have to see Robert or hear about him.

Doubt started to enter my mind when I realized that I had a seven year blank on my resume. How many employers would consider expertise in changing diapers, in making play dough, in teaching the children their colours, their numbers or anything that I've been doing all this time, as valuable?

I think I'll have to plan on accepting any sort of job before even thinking about working as a biologist again. I knew I'd have to update my knowledge -- the sciences change drastically in short periods of time.

Of course, some things have stayed the same. Fixing cultures, centrifuging, cataloging, all these are still done. I wrote down all the tasks that I can still do competently and realized that if I could get a job as a lab assistant, I could gradually come up to speed in my field: plant biology.

As I stared at the list I made, early plans came back to me. When I was just finishing university, I wanted to move to Lethbridge and work at the Federal Agricultural Research Station, where a lot of exciting work was being done.

Robert whined so much about the prospect of driving down to see me that I stayed in Edmonton and worked at the university. I assisted students in the labs when I wanted to be teaching the class. I almost decided to go back for my master's degree, but Robert wanted a family right away.

I bowed to his will and worked at the university until I was pregnant.

I thought of Lethbridge again as I wrote down all my options. I had a university friend who lived down there; a strong, kind woman, a doctor. Before I could change my mind, I picked up the phone and dialed the number that I found tucked away in an old address book.

The phone rang as I hoped that she wouldn't be mad that after so many years, that I'd call out of the blue.

Would she even remember me? Robert always told me that I was boring, and stupid. Maybe he was right.

Once I heard her voice, I relaxed, and realized that time hadn't changed her. I thought it best that I just start off with the bare bones of my story and took a quick, deep breath.

"Carol, I feel awful just calling out of the blue like this, but I need your help. I'm not with my husband as of this morning. All that I really know is that I have to leave Westlock. I don't have any of my own friends and I don't think anyone will hire me."

I ran out of breath at that point and came to a screeching halt. She didn't let me down; time hadn't changed her. I think she heard the desperation in my voice.

"Of course I don't mind. It sounds as if this has been a horrible day for you. Why don't you come down and spend some time figuring out what you're going to do? Do you have enough money for the trip?"

That was when I told her it wasn't just me she was saying yes to, but that I came equipped with a two and a six year old.

She didn't pause for a second; she immediately said that was great. "I'll expect you for supper tomorrow. You probably don't want to drive straight through, so why not drive as far as Calgary, and stay with my mom for the night?"

Immediately her mother came to mind. I'd loved it when she visited the residence, for she always brought the whole floor goodies and a positive feeling. It was from her that Carol had inherited her empathy. I immediately said yes. I was quite happy to let someone take over making the plans. I had already made more decisions in one day than I had in seven years.

When I peeked in on the girls, Joan was lying on her bed, not asleep, rather just hugging her panda bear and staring off into space. I sat on her bed and she suddenly blurted out, "I'm glad that daddy is gone mummy. I hate it when he starts shouting at us."

"I do to, Sweetheart, and we don't have to hear it again. Can you get all of your clothes out of the closet, and from your dresser? We're going on a trip after lunch."

Poor Joan, I know I shocked her, but the thought of leaving this house of ugly lies made her happy. She jumped off her bed, and started pulling her nighties and underwear out of the dresser. Laughingly, I told her it didn't matter or not if she was tidy.

When I saw that Suzy was still asleep, I quietly began packing all of her clothes, and just finished as she stirred awake. I took her into Joan's room so she wouldn't be underfoot as I performed the same chores.

I know I made us lunch, what it was, I have no idea. My mind was too busy going over everything that I had packed.

There are so many things that you need to build a new life: birth certificates, school records, immunizations, passports, financial documents, and laughably, my marriage certificate. I looked around the house and didn't see what I was leaving behind. All that was important was that we were leaving

Even a trip such as this requires mundane chores to be carried out. I filled the car up and kept my fingers crossed when I went to the bank machine. I could just picture Robert taking all the money out so I wouldn't have enough to leave, but I guess he still worried about his reputation because the balance hadn't changed. I took a lot. We piled ourselves and our luggage into the car. We took the first step toward freedom.

I don't remember really thinking as we drove on to Calgary. I saw the countryside and enjoyed it. So often a trip had only meant another fight -- without the luxury of going to another room. I even started to sing along with the kids' *Baby Beluga* tape.

I hadn't been in Calgary for a long time, but Carol's mom's house was easy to find. She was so welcoming to us. I know she made us a great supper, and soon after the girls dropped off to sleep. I thought she might want an explanation, but every time I tried to offer her one, she gently turned the conversation to mundane topics. Her quiet and implied acceptance allowed me to let my troubles drift to the back of my brain.

We quietly watched the TV, until the stress of the day finally caught up with me. Once in bed, I thought I'd fall asleep immediately. As I curled up in bed, waiting for sleep to claim me, I suddenly realized that I hadn't once, since that morning, thought about my new baby. I assume that my brain was overloaded, because that was my last thought that night.

Carol's mom was busy cooking up a huge breakfast by the time I came into the kitchen. I felt embarrassed; I had planned to be up early so I could make sure the girls weren't bothering her. Instead, I sat down with them as they proceeded to pour syrup over their French toast and bacon. It wasn't long before they were a sticky mess. What they weren't afraid. They weren't cowering, waiting for their father's footsteps.

I had just started on my second cup of coffee, when Anna whisked the girls off to play in a tub full of bubbles. I heard their shrieks over the sound of the water jets. This was what I wanted, peace for the girls and me. Next thing I knew, the girls came downstairs, dressed and ready to watch *Mr. Dressup*. I used that half- hour to shower, dress and pack. Mr. Dressup was just closing the Tickle Trunk when I finished packing the car. We said good-bye to Anna, and headed south.

Joan had never been south of Calgary, and loved being able to look off into the distance and see the mountains. They appeared as purple triangles, against the bluest sky I've ever seen. I told Joan that she might be able to see some snow tucked into high gullies. It took her a long time before she spotted any, but just as we were passing Claresholm, she squealed, and pointed to a mountain, that shimmered in the morning light.

"Mummy, stop!"

I pulled to the side of the road, and we climbed on top of the van to see the newly fallen snow. The prairies can simultaneously make you feel serene, powerful and alone. Cars whizzed by, as I contemplated my daughter, lying back in my arms.

I think it is first time I have really looked at her in a long time; it must be because I can't remember her smiling like this, with her eyes sparkling in the morning sun. I peeked in the window and saw Suzy still sleeping peacefully; she always fell asleep in the car. Joan called for me, and as I looked up, we saw two coyotes running through the field. We watched them, and then slid off the van and continued down the highway to a new life.

It wasn't long before I was pulling off the highway into Lethbridge, and hopefully into a new life. Carol was expecting us at five o'clock, so I decided that we'd eat and then explore. As usual the girls were happy to go to McDonald's; the added attraction was the new playground.

Then we drove around, trying to see what the city was like. First we went into the river valley and saw Fort Whoop-up and Indian Battle Park. The park follows the path of the Old Man River.

Many paths meandered through the aged cotton-woods. We followed one and startled a doe with her two fawns. They froze for a second and then bounded off into the thick brush. Joan and Suzy laughed as they watched the doe shoo her fawns away from us. Our next wildlife encounter wasn't quite as positive. We all screeched to a halt and quietly backed down the path, to allow a tiny garter snake cross the path.

By the time we completed the circle trail, it was time to find Carol's house. Once we discovered how to get onto Whoop-up Drive, it was pretty easy. Carol lived in a new subdivision called Heritage Heights.

She was out front pulling a few weeds from her flower garden, when we all tumbled out. Joan and Suzy were shy only for a few seconds -- helped along by Carol's cat, Jinx. She gave us her ten-cent tour of the house and showed us where we'd stay.

Her home was just perfect for an invasion such as ours. There were two guestrooms downstairs, along with a family room (complete with TV, VCR and stereo), and a full bathroom. I decided the girls could share one bedroom and I'd take the other. I knew there were going to be some sleepless nights ahead, and I didn't want to disturb them. When I turned around, Carol was already bringing some of our things in. We left the girls playing with Jinx, and went up for another load. Only minutes later, we had our clothes unpacked, and our tooth brushes in the bathroom.

Even though Carol didn't have children, her house seemed prepared for them. The girls could take their pick of Disney videos, there were colouring books, Lego's, and lots of children's books. She always wanted to be ready when her brother, a father of 4, dropped by with his brood.

CHAPTER 3

Once the girls were settled with all the goodies, Carol and I went upstairs. We talked while cooking supper. Carol, although empathetic like her mother, chose a different tack. She straight forwardly asked me what had happened. At first it was difficult to admit that I had allowed myself to be so dominated and then abused physically and mentally.

Carol's comments were encouraging and non-judgmental, something she had learned from the abused wives she saw in her practice. There were too many, so she became an excellent recipient of their stories. It didn't matter if the women were from the Blood Reserve, from the blue-collar part of North Lethbridge, or from Ridgewood Pointe. Their stories reflected mine.

I couldn't decide if that was good or bad. I felt bolstered by the fact that I wasn't the only one who kept standing by her husband. It saddened me, though, to think how many of us there are.

I explained my plan for work, and suddenly stopped in mid-sentence. Robert was gone, but this baby was still coming. Carol's response to this sudden interruption of conversation was to steer me into the great room, sit me down and return with a cup of hot tea. She sat in perfect stillness, waiting for me. I just looked at her, until I blurted out the one fact I hadn't told her.

She told me she had guessed, but wanted me to tell her. That was when I started panicking; wondering how on earth I'd manage to have a baby, work and look after Joan and Suzy. I was already four months pregnant, but I could legally have a second trimester abortion. I just couldn't picture myself doing that.

Carol, as always very practical, helped me make a list of all the things I had to do before I could make an informed decision. When I added each step on the list, it was clear that I couldn't make any decisions until I had all the facts.

A couple of Carol's neighbors worked at the Research Station, and they volunteered to take me out there and show me around. The next morning, Carol's brother

John stopped by to take Joan and Suzy over to his place. His wife planned taking all the kids to Park Lake.

I thought it sounded like a big expedition, and laughed when I found it was only ten minutes away. That was about how long it took us to get to the station. I was given the grand tour of the grounds and the labs. The grounds were still brilliant with masses of fall perennials, and the last of the annuals. There was a one-hundred-year-old specimen maple tree that protected the flowers below under its umbrella of leaves. Masses of tuberous begonias marched along the front entrance path, taking us through the doors and into another garden.

I was hooked up with Dr. Hunt, who showed me the projects that his team was working on. Carol must have given him a call after I left, because he already was aware of my qualifications and that I hadn't worked for seven years. As we went from station to station he asked me to perform different tasks. I hoped it was his way of interviewing

Sure enough, after an hour of re-familiarizing myself with all the equipment and trying to figure out the new, I was told that he had an opening on his team. He seemed apologetic when he told me that it was as a lab tech, but he had to wait until I came up to speed before he could consider more. That offer would also have to wait until he was ready with an opening and I was ready with the necessary skills. In my eyes, his offer was an open door, and I walked through.

I had two weeks to find an apartment that I could afford; I was hoping to only spend four hundred dollars a month. I became discouraged by the end of the day. For some reason, I expected that it wouldn't be hard to rent in Lethbridge, but there weren't very many listings for apartments, let alone apartments that would accept children and were in my price range

I headed back to Carol's home, elated that I had found a job while simultaneously concerned about housing. There was no way that I would impose on Carol for more than a short time. She already knew that I had a job since Dr. Hunt had called her to thank her for sending me to see him.

When I began describing some of the places I'd seen, Carol's face fell. Apparently she had been through the same experience when she had moved to Lethbridge. The only difference was that she wasn't constrained by finances. I wasn't worried about the size so much, but rather the type of neighborhood, and closeness to school.

I had looked at a home that met the criteria for price, but failed horribly about the rest. When I walked in, there were three huge ashtrays mounded with cigarette butts. I felt an incline as I walked through the house to the kitchen. At the kitchen door, I looked back and saw why; the floor was sharply tilted. When I pulled my gaze from what I had just walked through, it took no more than a glance into the kitchen, to end the charade. The linoleum floor, most likely the original, was missing huge chunks.

I turned on my heel and thanked the tenant for allowing me to look, and left. Later that afternoon, I was hopeful that I had found the perfect place; a home on the north side that bordered on the school grounds. When I phoned back, the owners had decided to sign a long term lease with the city for use as a group home.

Over on the west side, just before Carol's, I checked on a duplex that had a "For Rent" sign in the window. It seemed perfect; the price was right and there was enough room to create a new home for the girls and me. There were a lot of children in the neighborhood, and it wasn't far from the university and on an easy route to my job. I told the lady that I'd love to take it, and was surprised when she said that she'd have to wait until that evening until she had talked to her husband. I told Carol my tale and she started smiling as I came to the end of my recital of woes. I couldn't figure out why.

"Did she tell you where her husband is?"

"Yes, he's already moved to Saskatoon; I think he is doing his Doctorate there. Why?"

"I know those people. We met at a fundraiser. At the time he had applied to the university and was waiting for an answer. They told me that they owned a duplex, and planned on renting it while they were away. I'm going to call her."

I kept my fingers crossed as I heard Carol praise my little family, and explain that we'd maintain the duplex as if it were our own. I heard Carol, ". . .um . . . hem," saw her nod, and then heard her name a date. Once she was off the phone, she let her smile beam at me.

"You have yourself a duplex, you move in next Saturday, and they have decided that they'll pay the city utilities." I hardly knew what to say! All I knew was for the first time in a long time; I allowed myself the luxury of looking into the future with hope.

That hope almost died when Carol told me there was one little catch.

"One of the reasons they decided to pay the utilities is that is still cheaper than having to store some of their things. They plan on filling half of the basement with furniture." I started breathing again and laughed; from my point of view they were doing me a huge favour, and they could put whatever, and however much they liked, in the basement.

Carol took me down to her storage area and told me that I could pick whatever furniture I'd like; both Carol and her husband Chris, had lived on their own before marriage, and came to the marriage with quite a collection of university era furniture. Everyone has those items, that are still functional, and have too many memories attached to just throw away.

I was in the process of digging out two twin beds that were perfect for the girls when I heard them arrive home with Chris; he had picked them up on the way home. The aroma told us that he had stopped at the Kentucky Fried Chicken down the street. By the time we were upstairs, bursting to share our news, the table had been laid and the food was ready for us.

Joan could hardly stop talking, "Mummy, we went to the lake, and we got to ride on those bikes in the water. We cooked wieners over a fire, and bought ice cream for dessert. The water isn't too cold." And on she went explaining her day; even Suzy tried to add her bit. It was wonderful to see them come alive, instead of shrink with fear

I told them that we had a house and that wasn't too far from Auntie Carol and Uncle Chris. Joan wanted to see it right away, and wasn't happy when I told her we couldn't see inside until we moved in. She insisted that we at least drive by, see our house and where her new school was.

After supper Carol and Chris drove us to the house. The girls and I walked around a bit where I could at least point out their bedroom window. We walked around the corner and down the alley so they could see the backyard.

The next week alternately dragged and sped by. Some days seemed as though they'd never end, we wanted to get settled into our new home now! The beginning of the week saw time go by faster as we walked over to Red Crow Elementary School and registered Joan for Grade One.

When I had left Westlock, I had copied everything I thought I'd need, so I had Joan's report card from ECS. Academically she did very well; the area that she needed to work on was social skills. I think she was afraid to bring friends home. What would happen if her dad came home early?

Although we didn't have an awful lot of things to move, I'm sure glad that Carol's brother and husband volunteered to help. They moved the heavy things into the house, while Carol and I unpacked the few things I brought with me. I only took what I felt was absolutely necessary: fry pans, a roaster, some cutlery and plates, bowls and glasses, blankets and a set of bedding for each of us and some towels.

Before long, our house was ready to become a home. Our clothes hung in our bedrooms, each of our beds were made up, and Joan and Suzy's toys were tucked into the corner of their room. Our toothbrushes hung in the bathroom, and our brushes sat ready, next to a basket full of hair elastics and scrunchies. Our towels hung from the rack. Their bright red gave colour to the stark white, creating warmth.

Our kitchen cupboards held our utensils, held our dishes and waited to be filled with groceries. For once, I had more than enough cupboards. I wouldn't have to worry about not bringing tablecloths with me; for the time being we'd be eating at the kitchen peninsula, most helpful since I didn't have a dining room table.

Our living room/dining room looked impressively large; two chairs, a coffee table and a floor lamp do not take a lot of room. Carol and Chris's old university bookshelves, made simply with bricks and board, were once again in use.

Some things I didn't scrimp on taking were my books. Robert certainly never read for pleasure, and I couldn't conceive of being without my books. They have been my companions throughout my life. They've helped me enjoy the good times. They helped me cope through awful times. There is something soothing about sitting down and rereading an old friend when your mind is whirling. As you give yourself up to the familiar story, you can focus once again on the characters you know so well. For awhile, your mind is given respite

Thankfully there were plenty of bricks and shelving, so I split my books between my living room, my bedroom and the girls' room. Joan shares my love of reading. In fact she taught herself to read when she was only three. I found her in front of the TV watching Sesame Street, with her book open. She found the word of the day, showed me and read it. Soon she was reading 3 words at a time. She began identifying words while I read to her.

Carol told me she had an errand to run, but that she'd be back shortly. I took the opportunity to settle the girls down for a nap. The last few days had been draining for all of us. Suzy eyes snapped shut as I laid her down. Joan didn't protest either; she hugged her blanket and Cabbage Patch doll, rolled over and was asleep.

I heard the door open, and there were Carol and Chris holding boxes overflowing with food. They had gone to Costco to provide us with all the necessities and stocked the kitchen with paper towels, juices, treats, cereal, milk, flour, sugar, and spices. When I opened the freezer to see if there were ice cube trays, I almost had to sit on the floor and cry. They had already filled it up with meat, frozen juice, ice cream and fries. When I tried to express my gratitude to them for picking the groceries up and tried to pay, they told me it was their house warming present. Carol knew how emotionally drained I was and that it was time to leave. Suzy, Joan and I all needed a rest.

I wanted to do something really different for supper; something more calm than the horror we had experienced each and every night. The perfect answer was found at the back of the yard: a fire pit and a stack of wood. I lit a fire and we roasted our wieners. The girls happily ate their hot dogs and watermelon without worrying that they'd be yelled at for having mustard around their mouths. Joan and I had fun seeing who could spit the seeds further.

My decision was right. I had made the right move. There wasn't any doubt in my mind as I saw the happiness in Joan and Suzy's faces.

CHAPTER 4

Carol and Chris showed up early Sunday afternoon with a huge sack of Taber corn; I loved it. We ate outside. Carol was smart enough to pack a picnic blanket that we could all sprawl on and not worry about the butter running off the ends of our chins.

Joan spent Sunday evening deciding what to wear to school for the all-important first day in a new school. She only missed the first week, so I didn't anticipate her having too much trouble fitting in. That worry disappeared completely while Joan was making one last ride around the block on her bike. A little girl who lived in the duplex next door asked if Joan wanted to ride bikes with her. Joan looked for my approval; I nodded a yes and shouted that it would be time to come in to get ready for bed in ten minutes.

Monday morning Suzy delayed the process by insisting that she dress herself totally, but eventually she was ready. I opened the door as the bell rang, and there stood Mandy, "Can I walk to school with you?"

"Have you checked with your mom, Mandy?" That was when I spied a woman waiting on the sidewalk.

She waved and introduced herself, "I'm Mandy's mom, Ann. Welcome to the neighborhood. I thought it might be nice for the girls to walk to school together."

"That's great, but I'll walk with them, too."

"Of course, I don't let her walk to school by herself yet. She is probably ready to, but I'm not."

Joan and Mandy were already skipping down the sidewalk, hand in hand, by the time I joined Ann to stroll after them. I felt comfortable instantly with her. I've always made my female friends quickly and trust my instincts. I felt that trust in myself come back, and realized how long it had been since I truly had a girlfriend. Robert didn't want me to spend any time with anyone not in the family.

Ann told me that they'd lived in Lethbridge for two years. They moved down so her husband, John, could go back to university. He was on a sabbatical from his job in Calgary so he could get his Master's degree in Education. I didn't realize that U of L's Educational Department had such an excellent reputation throughout the country.

Once at the school, we parted ways as Mandy had already been registered. Joan and I found the principal's office, and I began filling out a few more forms. I became hesitant when I came to the family information, and asked to see the principal. I was led into a woman's office, and I decided to be frank about my concerns.

"Don't worry about it. Just put his name down. You don't know his whereabouts, so just leave the phone numbers and address blank. I assume that you don't want anyone else picking Joan up from school?"

In my relief I just nodded. "I'm starting work next week, but I haven't made any arrangements yet." Her next words made my heart sink.

"One problem keeps coming up in Lethbridge. There are not enough day care spaces." My reaction made her quickly finish her train of thought.

"I do know of a lady whose daughter is in Grade One as well, and she wants to take in one or two children for after school care. Her name is Ann Morris."

"What is her address? I met a woman named Ann, this morning, and she lives next door. Her daughter's name is Mandy

I held my breath until she confirmed that we were talking about the same person. "Thank you so much. I'll talk to her as soon as I get home."

When Joan was introduced to her teacher, Miss Brown, she quickly sat down with Mandy. I kept telling myself that I shouldn't get my hopes up; Ann may already have the two children she planned on. As I turned the corner, I saw her car parked in the driveway, and I made a beeline for her door. She must have seen me coming, as the door opened before I had a chance to ring the bell.

"I was hoping you were coming home. Would you like to come in for tea?" Although her duplex was a replica of mine, it looked much cozier and inviting. I told myself that sooner or later mine would look better. The important thing was that we were safe. "I waited to walk home with you, but I didn't see you."

"I was speaking with the principal about some things. While I was there, she told me that she knew you were interested in taking a few children for afterschool care." I barely had the words out when she jumped in.

"You'll be working? What kind of shifts?"

I told her that I didn't have to start until 8:30, and I'd finish at 5:00. "You'd want to leave her here just after eight, she'd have lunch with us, and then you'd pick her up just after five?"

"That sounds right. I'm not sure how much something like this costs. I've always been at home with the girls." I dropped my eyes, and I'm sure she could see how tightly I held my body, waiting and hoping that this would work out.

"I'm not out to make a lot of money. It is just the three of us, but I like to make a little extra spending money. I did this last year, and I charged $250 a month." She looked at me as she continued. "I think this is different, since I'm sure the girls will be going back and forth all the time anyway. Why don't we say $175? When I worked I was an RN, so you don't have to worry about first aid or the kids being sick . . ." I sat sipping my tea, and I couldn't believe my luck.

"This has been an incredible day for Joan and me. I'll have to tell you that just last week I lived in Westlock with my husband. He announced one morning that he was leaving the girls and I. Circumstances made it impossible for us to stay there. I'm sure that he won't be any trouble. I mean, about showing up and trying to snatch Joan away. He was very clear that he was leaving us all. I've told them all this at school. Right now they have it down that no one is to pick up Joan other than myself. Tomorrow I'll tell them that starting next week she'll be with you."

"Great. I was wondering what plans you've made for Suzy? I can't take a little one, since I have back trouble. If you haven't found a spot, a friend of mine who lives just a couple blocks away takes in three toddlers. This morning she told me that one of the children she had lined up won't be with her. Do you want me to call her?"

"Yes, please. Do you know how much she charges?"

"Lora is different than me. She's a single mom, and this is how she makes her money, so I know that she's more expensive than I am, but no more than other daycares around town."

Sitting in the sunny living room, I could hear the murmur of Ann's voice, but not the words. Today had already gone so well, that I figured that my good fortune was used up.

"Lora said that she would like to meet you and Suzy, so let's walk over." We took our teacups to the sink and headed out. "Lora told me that she charges $350/month. How does that fit in with your budget? I just want to make sure that you realize that is what others pay."

"I think I'll be able to swing it. How is she with children?"

"We both went to Lethbridge Community College for our nursing, and she loved peds. She worked on the pediatric ward at the Regional Hospital. I know that she just couldn't face the thought of having her children away from her when they were little, so after her husband left her, she decided she put all that expertise to work. I've never heard a complaint."

By the time we finished talking about Lora, we were at her doorstep. She took awhile answering the door, but I was happy that it had. She had a freshly scrubbed little boy in her arms. That was very telling to me; she'd rather have someone wait, than risk the safety of a child. A lot of people will leave a two- year old in the tub by themselves, but I don't

Lora had a new, tiny house that she was very proud of. She told me that she had bought it herself. She had developed her basement, by herself, into a mini daycare. There was a spot for water play, a table held a deep sand pit that was full of digging tools, and a miniature house stood in the center of all the activity.

This was a confident, resourceful woman who, I discovered as we talked, shared my philosophy of child care. Ann must have already told her some of my story, because she already knew that Joan would be going to Ann's home. "If you feel comfortable with the situation here, would you like to bring Suzy over tomorrow? I know you don't start work until next week, but I like to have the mom's and children come over for short visits to start off. By the time she comes next week, she'll feel comfortable here." I knew I had made the right choice.

The next week seems like a blur. Each morning I walked Joan to school and then went on to Lora's. Suzy and a little boy named Matthew paired up almost right away. They both gravitated to the sand table and the crafts table. Lora's children were slightly older, and more active. Yet Lora was able to integrate their play easily. On Friday morning I still had numerous chores, so Lora suggested that I leave Suzy. She didn't create even the smallest fuss.

My most important appointment was with Dr. Rand, a colleague of Carol's. Dr. Rand was my type of doctor; he didn't rush me, let me ask questions, asked a lot of questions himself, and actually listened to my answers. Earlier, Carol had filled him in on the general situation. I gave the specifics.

When he asked me what my plans were, I told him that I just didn't know. It had only been two weeks since my life shattered. I had been concentrating on all the immediate decisions. I told him that I'd love a new baby, but with my newly awakened practical side, wondered if I'd be able to? His reaction was wonderful. He told me that I was healthy, that I didn't have any worries about the pregnancy. Why not give myself some time to figure out what was best for me and the girls? Some may have been judgmental or offered immediate solutions. I knew in my heart that I didn't have the strength to make any more decisions, not yet.

I started work the next Monday, and for the first time, I left Joan and Suzy with someone else for an entire day. At the lab, I kept checking and rechecking my work -- I didn't want to make any mistakes. I felt clumsy handling the Petri dishes and the test tubes; I was terrified that I'd drop them all. At first I was intimidated by all the young, knowledgeable staff.

Once I managed to get through the morning without dropping anything, I started to relax, and I noticed that my speed improved. Still I wasn't anywhere near as fast as when I first working

CHAPTER 5

I found my confidence build throughout that first month. I found myself looking forward to getting to work and once again using all the knowledge I had gained at university. It was due to that knowledge that I was able to admit to myself that I had a long way to go. I was doing excellent work as a lab tech, but I was a biologist. I longed for more involved work, research work. I listed my options: keep working in the same job, continue as a lab tech as well as taking courses at night, which would hopefully led to eventually working again as a biologist.

The university offered some of the courses I wanted in the evening, and I certainly didn't have to worry about pre-requisites. My worry was money. Tuition for one course almost equaled what I'd paid for a semester. However, I at least had a starting point for decision making.

Once I had completed this list I tackled my finances. I thought I had withdrawn quite a bit of cash from our joint account, but in the past month I had spent a lot. They weren't foolish purchases, rather necessities were bought. When we left Westlock, I could only bring the girls' summer clothes. Their winter clothes had already been given to a friend, since Joan and Suzy had grown so much in the past year.

I went to the Catholic Family Services for clothes. It is right on Third Avenue, and it didn't seem too bad a place. Certainly a lot of people went in and out. Never before had I shopped for second hand clothes; mortification reddened my face as I rushed head down, into the store.

One of the local radio stations had been asking for donations to a warm coats campaign, so I was lucky to have quite a choice. Ski jackets, ski pants, boots, leggings, cords, jeans, sweaters, flannel nighties, heavy socks, mitts and hats. I was loaded down as I wobbled to the car. I had a hard time believing that I had spent $150, since most items were less than $5. But Joan and Suzy needed everything.

I had to buy their shoes new, since their feet are so narrow. Before I took them shopping, I checked out the shoe stores myself; I didn't want to take them into a store that was too expensive. I had to laugh at myself: at the same time last year I had bought them not just one pair of shoes but three. This year the one pair would have to last a long time.

I had to buy some new sheets for Suzy's bed - her bladder still wasn't totally reliable, and I needed a second set for the middle of the night. I had the car winterized. I couldn't take the chance of a break down in the middle of the winter; one that I couldn't afford. I had to pay their school fees. I know they are a small amount compared to high school students, but $50 each was significant to me. I also had to pay for our duplex with the money I brought with me. I wouldn't be paid until the end of the month.

My tally astounded me: $1225 spent on necessities -- rent, daycare, clothes, shoes and school fees. I almost trembled as I again opened the university calendar to check out the fees. I just couldn't bring myself to commit to more than one course -- one alone cost $450. It was a classic Catch 22. If I didn't go to school, I would never be able to earn a higher salary, to support Joan, Suzy and myself, yet it strained us if I did. I tried to shut off the implications that my brain kept trying to churn up.

There came a day that another lab tech asked if I was pregnant: I wanted to answer no, but that was a lie that I couldn't even convince myself of. I guess my expression gave a clue to my emotions, because she just said "Oh" when I told her I was.

I kept my mind busy while I helped Joan with some of her homework and bathed Suzy while listening to her tales of the day. I would have loved to cuddle with them all night, but I forced myself to put them to bed on schedule.

I sat in front of the TV, but I couldn't tell you what was on. I just kept on thinking of the added expenses of having another child in daycare; another $350. That wasn't the only consideration. I didn't have any baby clothes or equipment, and since I'd have to go back to work right away, I'd need formula, and the list went on.

I finally forced myself to look at my emotional strength and whether I had enough left for another child. I was already exhausted each night. Once I left work, my other job started. I had to pick up Suzy, get her and I into the house, call Ann to send Joan home, and then make myself take time, before making supper, to listen to their stories and tell mine.

My chef's duties were next, and often they entailed the help of Joan. It was lovely to share that time with her, but I had to acknowledge that I could be testy because of the time that was slipping by.

Both girls are good eaters, so dinner was a happy time, a time I didn't want to lose. They would play together while I washed and cleaned up. By that time I was anxious to sit down, my feet up, and my mind off. Instead the evening chores dragged on.

Oh my God, I see bathing and reading to my children as chores! Those are the very things that I cherished. That was the mom I had planned on being. And I still had to work in time for a course as well as homework.

I knew where my thoughts were leading. I had to admit to myself that I had neither the energy nor the emotional strength to raise another child. I also admitted that I could not imagine aborting at this stage of the game. Adoption seemed to be the only right solution. Despite the late hour, I phoned Carol. I didn't have to say much before she said she'd be right over.

While I waited for her, I reflected on what a wonderful friend Carol had been. She hadn't pushed me to answer the obvious question. She knew that I had to concentrate on the essentials of the moment. She knew that I didn't have the energy to imagine the future. She, in a million ways, was there for me, being available for the time when a decision had to be made. Now was that time.

Amazingly, in the five minutes it took her to come over, I found a calmness descending, at least enough to be able to verbalize my thoughts. I guess Carol knew that it was going to be a long night. She came over with her nightie, and hot chocolate mix. I changed while she made the hot chocolate, and we snuggled into the couch. I needed a cocoon. I needed to formulate a plan that would allow me to grow away from these circumstances. I showed Carol my lists, and amazingly she laughed. I looked at her as if she were nuts.

"You were the only one I knew in residence who constantly had lists on the go. I remember lists about tests, lists about potential careers, lists of boys who were possibilities, and I think you had a list of what clothes you had."

As she finished I thought about how I depended on those lists to give me a certain amount of order in my life. Those lists helped me clarify my thinking. Yes, this is right, no, maybe this isn't true. Once again during a chaotic time, I reverted to my childhood habit of lists. I liked to first see everything in black and white, so I could then begin to shadow them with colour, layer upon layer. Carol didn't contradict anything I had put down; she only asked me one question, trying to help me clarify my vision of the future.

"Are you emotionally ready to say good-bye to this child?"

"I'll have to make myself do it. It is wondering about the future: is the child healthy, what does he look like, what is he like, what are his parents like, and what will he think of me? How do I know how I will be able to handle this in the future? I'm trying to make myself see the future, but I can't, all I can see is the next few years. I know that down the road, with 20/20 hindsight, I'll spend a lot of time questioning this decision, but I can't see any other path right now. I have to figure out what to say to the girls, and soon.   Joan announced the other day that I was getting fat, and Suzy was squirming in my lap, trying to get comfortable. I'll have to say something."

Carol came to the rescue with the offer to talk with a friend of hers, who is a psychologist. I looked past her, out into the yard, and with a start realized that another glorious prairie sunrise was beginning. Once more, a new life rose before me.

CHAPTER 6

One crisp fall night, I went for a walk and when I came home, I was drawn to my computer. The quiet in the house was profound. I began to write to my child. I had to tell him what my life was like when I made the decision to place him for adoption. I struggled for the words to explain it was because of my love, not because of a lack of it, that I offered him a new life. I wanted him to experience the great joy of a new parent who can't get enough of their baby's soft skin. I wanted his parents to hold him for the longest time, just to admire him and coo. I wanted him to experience those years of total commitment from his parents. I didn't want to deprive him of that.

I tried to tell him of the vision I saw if I didn't let him go. I saw him propped on my hip, as an irritable me was trying to squeeze in time for his sisters, for cooking, for cleaning, and for studying. I tried to tell him, that I would have failed him, and that wasn't fair to him.

I was lucky. Among my friends, three couples had fertility troubles. I could become pregnant almost instantly. I had been saddened as my friends struggled to hide their grief when they heard my pregnancy news. I told him that I knew there were wonderful women and men who would give anything to be parents. That is the commitment, the love that should be his birthright. I wrote to my child that when he is ready to look me up, I will welcome him. I won't have to welcome him into the family, for he always will be a part of our family.

The next morning Carol, Chris and the girls came to the house around brunch. They had a wonderful time with Auntie and Uncle. It was such a glorious day that we packed a picnic basket, and went down to Indian Battle Park, ate and raced through the crackling leaves. Once again we all flopped down on our blanket, Joan and Suzy curled like puppies around Chris. They had migrated to him since day one; an antidote to their father's absence. This seemed as good a time as any.

I took a deep breath and started, "Joan and Suzy, mummy wants to talk to you." I think my tone of voice hinted to them that it was a time to really listen. They turned their faces from the sun and looked at me. "I'd like to know if you are happier, now that we live in Lethbridge."

Joan looked thoughtful, and Suzy smiled. "Happy mummy." she came over and wrapped her small arms around my neck, and then went to sit in Carol's lap.

"Joan, honey, you look a little uncertain."

"I really like my new school. I like not always having to guess what daddy wanted. I love going to Auntie Carol's house." Her voice trailed off, I could hear the bitten off, but.

"You can tell me whatever you are thinking."

"I don't like it when you come home from work and get mad sometimes when you are tired." I almost melted as I looked into her face, and saw the fear in her face.

"Joan, you know what? I really hate it when I am like that. You are right, that when I get tired, I sometimes yell at you. I don't want to do that anymore. I want to spend more time with you and Suzy. That is why I've had to make a really hard decision. Do you remember when you told me that I looked fat, last week? You were right that I've changed, but not because I'm fat. I'm going to have a baby. I only found out about it the day before daddy left. Mommy's had to make a lot of decisions to make, remember?" Joan solemnly nodded. "I don't think I can take care of this baby the way that I took care of you and Suzy. I was with you all the time so we could play and learn together. You know that I can't spend as much time with you now. I know I wouldn't have enough time and energy for this baby. I love this baby too much not to give him what he deserves. You know that your cousin Stephen was adopted. That is what I am going to do with this baby. After I have him, new parents who have been waiting a long time for a baby, will take him home."

"Is the baby a boy, mummy?"

"I don't know, but I think it is. That isn't why I'm not bringing him home though." I thought I was done, but then I suddenly remembered the advice of the psychologist. "Joan, Suzy, I never want to be parted from you. You're a part of my life, and we will always be together, at least until you are old enough to live on your own."

Joan left the warmth of Chris' embrace and sat down in my lap. "How will you say good-bye to him?" The most innocent question can wound most deeply. I could only be honest with her, and admit that I really wasn't sure, but that I knew it would make us all sad. "Will he remember us?" We sat in the fading autumn light, amid the reminders of the cycles of nature, each with our own thoughts.

"I think it would be really nice if you could draw him some pictures, and maybe we can make a tape of stories for him. His new mummy and daddy could show them to him when he is older. I think we should find some pictures of us too."

Joan wanted to leave almost immediately; she told us that she wanted to get started making a picture for the new baby. On the way home, she asked what his name would be. I told her that his new mom and dad would give him a name that they liked, but we would choose one for him until then. I don't think that Suzy really understood, but she lay on the living room floor, scribbling a picture, alongside Joan.

I put them to bed early; I felt totally worn out. As I tucked Joan into bed, she told me that she was sad not to have the baby to look after. All I could say was that I was too. She was worried that we hadn't decided on a name yet. "The baby isn't due until April, right around Easter. We have lots of time. We want to take time and make sure that he has a very special name." With a kiss on her forehead, I slipped out of the room.

After I had my tea cup and cookies beside my chair, I pulled out all the forms that Carol had given me. The government forms really asked for a lot of information. Our statistics were easy enough. I knew both our health histories. What I didn't know was where he was. I was worried that he'd stand in the way; either by not signing the papers or by staying in hiding. No one I knew could tell me where he was. Then I had to write down why I was surrendering the baby.

By the time I finished, I was exhausted and crawled into bed early. Tomorrow, during lunch hour, I had to meet with a social worker. I can only imagine what she'll think of me. I'm not a teenager; what was so wrong that I was giving up my child?

I sat on a hard, wooden chair, facing Lila Stone; at least that was what her name plaque said. She didn't introduce herself; she just started asking rapid-fire questions. She asked me if I was being forced by someone to do this, if I really understood what was happening, and when I was due. I think I was there all of five minutes. She hadn't even given me time to respond to her questions, speaking over them. In the next instant I was standing outside, on the sidewalk, across from Woodward's. I tried to imagine what a frightened teenager would think of that whole process. How could that woman know what anyone's feelings were?

I don't think that was her prime motive, rather she wanted to have many babies available to her as possible. In the extremely short time I spent with her, I felt two conflicting emotions radiating from her. She was almost bristling at the thought that a mature woman would even consider this decision. Simultaneously, she was gleeful that she had a "prime baby" for adoption. The emotions that I most expected her to have, compassion and empathy, were totally absent. The anger I felt toward this woman, propelled me through the rest of the day. Only when I went to bed, did I stop and think again about my decision. I had an appointment with Dr. Rand in the morning; I couldn't help but wonder what his reaction was going to be.

He reacted as I had hoped the social worker would. He was caring and compassionate as he listened to my reasoning; he let me know that he was well aware that I hadn't made the decision to be selfish. Dr. Rand approved of the way I had shared the decision with the girls. He told me of some books that are intended to help children deal with a death. Obviously we weren't in the same situation, but he felt that I could get some insight on how they were feeling, and how to deal with it.

I can always handle a crisis better if there is something concrete that I can do. Now I had two directions; one, to gather information on how best to help Joan and Suzy, and secondly, to stay as healthy as possible, for this new life I'm creating, the new life to which I'm already trying to say good-bye.

CHAPTER 7

I was surprised by how soothing I found work. By now I could do my job automatically. It almost became a form of meditation. Sometimes meditation helps me concentrate my energies; at other times it served to keep my mind from jumping from thought to thought. That was what I needed to have the energy necessary to cope with the upcoming months.

Joan and Mandy had a great time together during the day. They weren't in the same class anymore, so they had lots to catch up on by the end of the day. As I drove home each evening, I tried to figure out what to say to Ann and Lora.

I was sure that they must be wondering if I was pregnant. Although I don't gain too much with each pregnancy, I knew that it would be very obvious soon. They both had been wonderful to me; they had both baby-sat for me in the evenings so I could go to class. More importantly, they had been friends. I didn't think that it was fair not to be upfront with them. They both knew what my life had been like over the past months; they'd been supportive and non-judgmental.

While driving up through the valley toward home, the setting sun blazed the trees with colour, created gold from bushes and painted the mule deer as silhouettes. Nature was reminding me that the seasons of our life continue, no matter how much we wish to stop the process. As surely as the last leaves would fall off the trees onto crisp, sparkling, morning snow, this baby would come to be born. Nature gave me the push I needed.

"Ann, its Carol. I was wondering if you had time to come over for a cup of tea this evening, around nine. I need to talk to you about something. I'd rather wait until our evening chores are done."

"Sure, I'd love an excuse to get out of the house. If I don't, then I won't have an excuse not to do the laundry. See you around nine."

I phoned Lora and asked her the same question -- I was lucky that they could both come. I only wanted to do this once. I had the kids in bed in record time, and for some reason, I rushed through the house tidying it up. Maybe I was trying to make a good impression. I jumped when the doorbell rang. In the few steps it took to get to door, I felt my heart jump up into my throat. Both Ann and Lora arrived together, Ann laden down with a chocolate cake. At least most of a cake; her husband had snuck a piece for himself and Mandy. The cake gave me an excuse to stall for a bit, but with each swallow I knew I had better just go ahead.

"I wanted to let you both know that I'm pregnant." I paused for comment, but they acted instead. Ann came over and sat beside me and took my hand into hers. Lora, sat on the floor next to my feet, and placed her hand on my knee. Their facial expressions almost moved me to tears, but I fought them so I could get the rest out.

"I found out I was pregnant the day before Robert left me. I was going to tell him that day, but he beat me to the punch for the news of the day. When I first moved here I couldn't even think about it. I don't know what I'd have done without your friendship. Your support gave me the energy to realistically figure out what to do. You know how tired I am with two children. I just manage to make my salary stretch to the end of the month, and I haven't been able to save any money at all. The only way to get a better job is to continue my courses at the university. I didn't work outside the home with Joan and Suzy, and I gave them all of my attention. That is what I want for this baby. That is why I've decided that I'm going to place this baby for adoption."

The silent support was palpable, and allowed me to continue. "I was so worried that you would think I'm a terrible person for coming to this decision." They both tried to talk at the same time.

"We know that you've made the decision that is best for you. It isn't for us to judge you. I think you are very brave to come to this decision. Maybe to me it isn't as strange to me as it may be to others. My brother and I were both adopted. It hasn't been a problem for either of us." Ann handed me a Kleenex as she finished, and gave me a hug.

"I know what you are going through," said Lora. Her eyes filled with tears as she told us her tale. "When I was sixteen I started going out with a boy from high school. We went out all of grade eleven and most of grade twelve. We didn't make love until the summer between grades. I craved the warmth it gave me, and we made love as often as possible. I felt so safe in his arms. In my house there wasn't much hugging -- truthfully, none -- and my skin craved the feel of his hands.

"We used condoms, but he couldn't always get them. When you live in a small religious town like Cardston, you just don't walk down the hill to the drugstore and ask for condoms.   Grade twelve was great until just before Christmas. I realized that my period was late. I was so petrified I didn't even tell my boyfriend. I kept thinking that it was just because of Christmas coming, and I didn't want to worry him.

"Christmas morning brought more than just presents under the tree. My brother pounded on the door, yelling to get downstairs. I felt okay until I hit the middle of the stairs. Mom had obviously been up for awhile, and was getting the stuffing ready. The smell of the onions simmering in butter seemed to chase after me to the bathroom. That was the beginning of my morning sickness, and the point where I couldn't fool myself: I was pregnant.

"I hurried downstairs as fast as I could, waved off the questions and tried desperately to pretend that this was a normal Christmas morning. All day my mind raced from thought to thought. I was trying to figure out who should I tell first, what should I say, and I imagined my parents' reaction. I decided I'd put that off for as long as possible.

"Thankfully I had planned to meet my boyfriend for a skate in the afternoon. As soon as he saw me, he knew there was a problem. I only got part of the sentence out, when he understood and wrapped me in his arms. The cold wind that numbed our faces couldn't numb our hearts. I hoped he would have some answers, but two frightened teenagers weren't any better than one. The only consolation was that we at least had each other to talk too.

"Later, when I was helping mom get supper ready, I suddenly felt faint as she lifted the lid on the brussel sprouts. I spun and ran upstairs to the bathroom as fast as I could, just make it in time. My mom was hard on my heels, but she wasn't very sympathetic. I told her I must have the flu. If I was on the phone, it seemed as though my mom would suddenly pop up. She finally heard what she wanted, and the shit hit the fan."

Lora stopped her recital, had a sip of tea, and then continued. "They instantly phoned my boyfriend's parents and had them come over. We sat in the living room, looking at *The Book of Mormon*, in its place of honour on the coffee table. There was lots of conversation, none that involved us. We were told to sit there and shut up. We were told what was going to happen. Apparently I had some relatives who lived in Edmonton; I was being sent there. I would have the baby, give it up, and never talk about it. Each time either of us tried to say anything we were cut off by a parent.

"The worst was yet to come. I heard a loud knocking on the door, and next thing I knew, the bishop is glaring down at us. I swear he lectured us for at least an hour. He told us how evil we were, that no matter what else we did in our lives, we would stay evil. We would no longer be eligible to be married in the Temple, and we were told that the people that we had gone to church with would no longer have a relationship with us. The bishop then turned his attention on Alan, and told him he was being sent to South America; not to go on a mission, but rather to serve those who were. He was their moral inferior, and would be reminded of it every day. He tried to protest; his father hit him and then pushed him out of my house and into the car. That was the last I ever saw of him."

It was my turn to offer comfort. When I gave Lora a hug, she was shivering with tension. I went to the hall closet and brought out a cuddly throw and wrapped it around her. Ann and I pulled her onto the couch, between us. All we could offer was our bodies' warmth and kind words. I think it must have helped, because she continued her story.

"The next day my father gave me an envelope of money and then they put me on the bus. I didn't talk to them again until the end of August, when I was sent back to Cardston. They didn't hug me, they didn't ask how I was, they didn't ask if they had a granddaughter or a grandson, they silently put my suitcases in the car and drove me home.

"I had always loved our house; it was big and I had my own room. This time, when I went into my room, it wasn't a sanctuary; rather it seemed a prison. I didn't allow myself the luxury of lying down; instead I sat in the middle of the bed, clutched my knees to my chest, bowed my head and cried. I cried for the loss of my precious little girl, I cried for the loss of my boyfriend, and I cried for the loss of my parents' love. I couldn't stop.

"The next sound was my mother coming into my room and coldly telling me I should have thought of that earlier, and they never wanted to hear or speak of it again. I didn't realize how loud my door was when it was slammed. Their message was received, and when I did cry, I made sure that the sound was drowned by music. I tried to be happy and accept that their pretense was reality.

"It didn't take long for me to realize that I couldn't live there anymore, so I went to work with a purpose; to earn cash. I worked in a florist's shop during the day and at a restaurant at night. When the Christmas season began once again, I couldn't stand it. The first night that mom and dad were out acting in the Christmas Story, I took all the money I had hoarded, walked to the highway, and hitched a ride into Lethbridge." Defiantly she looked at Ann and me, "I've never talked to them or about them again. This is the very first time I've told anyone about Debbie; that's what I named her. They didn't even let me see her!" All three of our faces ran with tears.

Ann told Lora, "I'm so sorry that you had to go through that. I'm glad that you don't talk to your parents. If I had the chance, I'd blast them for you! I bet that everyone thinks that they are such good, religious people too! They are all hypocrites."

"I'm sorry that I told you this Clare, knowing what you just told us, but I think for the first time I have friends who can accept what happened."

"You didn't hurt me Lora. You needed to tell us, just like I needed to tell both of you. In some ways, knowing that other people have gone through the same pain makes it a little easier to bear."

What else was there to say? We each withdrew into our thoughts, finished our tea and said good-night. I was so relieved that I had finally told them. I wondered why I had waited so long to allow them to support me. I decided then and there to inform my supervisor that I was pregnant and would be taking time to deliver the baby sometime in February. The next morning I waited for condemnation in her face when I told her that I wouldn't need to take maternity leave, since the baby wasn't coming home with me. Once again I was lucky; compassion was the only thing I saw in her face.

CHAPTER 8

My mind was remarkably settled as we moved toward Christmas. Carol and Chris insisted that we join them for Christmas; not just Christmas dinner, but they wanted us to come over on Christmas Eve and stay with them for the week. Chris's office shut down over the holidays and he had lots of plans for Joan and Suzy. With that decision made, I relaxed and realized that the girls had never had a Christmas full of tranquility. Robert seemed to think that Christmas was an excuse to blow his top every day. I knew Joan would disappear into her room to play with a new toy, afraid that her dad would find some fault. This year they were both giddy with excitement when Chris helped them trim the tree, set a snack out for Santa and tucked them into bed. By the time we relaxed in front of the fire; it was already the best Christmas in ten years.

We didn't avoid talking about the baby. In fact when Chris took the girls skating, swimming or tobogganing at the Sugar Bowl, Carol and I talked of little else. But each discussion ended with my decision firm. I could not envision my life with another child. The realities that I foresaw if I kept this baby were not pleasant: absolutely no time to give to each child, time that is their birthright, my patience worn down even farther, and no chance of making the kind of life that I want for my children. When I say my children, I don't mean just Joan and Suzy, but this little one, too. New Year's Eve arrived quickly. We bought sparklers, and all had fun running with them through the snow in the back yard. Midnight rang in without Joan. She had been determined to stay up, but her excitement and the fresh night air conspired against her. I made a single wish. I wished for the strength to carry out my decision.

I worked easily through January. Early February brought fatigue, swelling feet and hands. I didn't say anything to my doctor. I needed to work as long as possible.

I had hoped to work until just a few days before birth. Unfortunately, my blood pressure told the story, and Dr. Rand told me that I'd have to stop working and spend most of the next two weeks in bed. Carol came to the rescue, and that night she and Chris arrived to pack up the clothes we'd all need for a couple of weeks. I didn't even have to take the girls to Lora and Ann's homes. I luxuriated in the silence during the day. I couldn't remember when I last had days that I could call my own. I indulged myself and didn't feel guilty in the least for valuing my solitude.

The whole troop would arrive home just after five, and the girls would pile into bed with me and tell me about their day. Suzy always brought a picture she had drawn, and Joan usually had some schoolwork with a star in the corner. Often they would lay their head on my belly and talk to the baby. I'd bite my lip as Joan told the baby that she would have been a good big sister, and that she loved him. Suzy just liked feeling him moving around.

February 15th is a day I'll never forget. I was in the kitchen cleaning up after lunch, when, with a gush, my water broke. I dragged some towels from the laundry closet to mop up the mess. On the way to bed, I grabbed an old shower curtain, stuck it on the bed and covered it with towels. I thought I'd probably stay at home until sometime late that evening, so I didn't bother phoning Carol.

I have vague memories of falling asleep. The next thing I recall was waking up in full, strong labor. I timed the contractions, and to my horror found that they were only 3 minutes apart! I was even beginning to feel an urge to push; definitely time to call Carol.

While I was waiting for the receptionist to put me through, another contraction came, and I had to resist the urge to push. When Carol came on the line, she heard what was going on. I remember her telling me that she already had called 911. While I was still on the phone, I heard the ambulance pull up. They just made it into the bedroom in time to catch Patrick. I had already decided that if it were a boy, I'd name him after my brother, one of the most kind-hearted men in the world.

Things continued moving swiftly, and soon we were at the hospital. Carol met us in the ER and took Patrick in her arms to nuzzle him. Then she popped him back into my arms and delivered us to post-partum. I went right into the delivery room to allow the placenta to be delivered. Dr. Rand helped me, while Carol did the honours for Patrick. She declared him gorgeous and healthy, and big. His weight of 8 lbs. 8 oz. was surprising to us all. Where had he been hiding? The Lethbridge Regional Hospital is compassionate, and puts new moms who are placing their babies for adoption in private rooms. This avoids all the inevitable questions from other moms.

I had already decided that I'd keep him in the room with me. I wanted to spend as much time with him as possible. I surprised people when I told them that I planned on nursing him, but I was determined that he get the benefits from at least a few days nursing.

I whispered to him as he nursed, telling him all about his two sisters, his mom and how much we loved him. How we wished that things were different and he could come home with us. I had some of the girl's little sleepers with me. Each time I changed his diaper, he was in a new outfit. I wonder if he was bothered by all the pictures. Carol and Chris brought Joan and Suzy to the hospital so they could see Patrick. Joan was beaming as she helped Suzy hold him, sitting in the easy chair. My heart sank as I saw the look on her face; I knew what was coming.

"Mummy, can't we bring him home? See, I could help you look after him." I know she wasn't aware that she was twisting a knife in my heart.

As tears ran down my cheeks I went over to my three babies and told them that I couldn't do that to Patrick. He deserved the same love that I was able to give them. I held my little guy almost constantly, the knowledge that I couldn't in a few days fought to deprive me of that brief happiness. Each hour the clock marked off took me further along the road that I myself had created. Each hour brought me closer to dying of heart pain. With each hour, I had shorter and shorter time left to change the route.

Pain as terrible as this is difficult enough to bear when it comes from an outside source. When you are the creator of the pain, it sharpens and tears even more.

Lila Stone made her appearance the following day. I must admit that she admired Patrick, as was only right, but then she was all business. Had I changed my mind? When was I leaving the hospital? She told me that she'd be back the next day, with all the forms that needed signing. Then she left, without a word of consolation or empathy.

For the next hour, I stood over the bassinet watching Patrick sleep, my mind creating a whirlwind trying to catch all my thoughts.

Finally I decided to give into the fatigue that hit in the form of Lila Stone. I managed to get myself comfortable, anticipated going to sleep, and then my grief shoved to the surface. The tears flowed and flowed. I couldn't have stopped them if I wished. I didn't want to -- it was my grief and I was entitled. I contrasted the births of my two girls; their dad was at least with me afterward and made a big production of being the proud Papa. Even though I'm sure it was all show, at least we were happy during that time. For the first time since Patrick was born I thought of his father. Patrick didn't look like him; he actually looked like his namesake. He deserved a Dad like his uncle. I could only pray that was what he got.

I arranged for Carol to be with me at ten in the morning. I didn't want to be alone with that woman when I had to sign all the legal forms. The first thing she said when she came in was, "Dr. Adams, I need to see her alone." Thank heaven that Carol knew that I wasn't up to dealing with this woman at that point in time.

"Ms. Stone, Clare has asked me to be here, and I plan on staying." It was obvious to me that Ms. Stone wasn't used to someone refusing her. Her mouth opened, closed and then she turned to me.

"I want you to read all these papers; they're the same as those you saw in my office. When you are done you will have to sign them." She thrust them at me, glared at Carol, and turned her back on us. I will admit that I looked at them, but I have to confess the words did not register in my brain. My only thoughts were of Patrick. I guess I took too long, "Haven't you finished reading them yet?"

"Yes, I'm finished." She handed me her pen, showed me where to sign, which I did, and she gathered them into her briefcase. As she left my hospital room, she turned to me and told me that I had ten days to change my mind. With that she left.

I turned to Carol to see if she was appalled as I was. Her answer was etched into her face as she came and hugged me. With that, the tears started and whatever strength I thought I had dissolved. I collapsed into her arms.

"I can't bear it. Am I doing the right thing? It isn't fair to Patrick to think of myself. But I am thinking of him. I'm thinking of the girls."

Carol gently lifted Patrick from his bassinet and held him as I showered and dressed. When I came out of the bathroom, I could see that Patrick's sleeper was wet from Carol's silent tears. All I could do was join them, hug them, and add my tears. Patrick stirred in Carol's arms as he looked up at us and started cooing.

Carol finished packing my suitcase, and took it and my flowers down to her car. The nurse came in with Patrick's bassinet card, a lock of his hair, and his hand and foot prints. She was kind to me. She told me that she was mad; she had been outside my room, ready to come in, when she heard Ms. Stone.

This young woman didn't condemn me or judge me; rather she asked what she could do to help. I asked her to watch for Carol, and tell her that I was saying good bye to Patrick. I don't know how long I sat there with him in my arms, trying to memorize every feature of his face, trying to retain his baby smell and trying to tell him how much I loved him.

I became aware of Carol trying to stifle her tears as she leaned against the door. Behind her was a wonderful nurse from the nursery, who came in and waited until I was ready. Carol gave him Patrick last kiss. I lay him in the bassinet and walked the longest hall in the world. I hesitated at the door of the nursery. Once I took Patrick in I'd have to leave without him. I closed my eyes and tried to breathe as I delivered Patrick to his life without me.

CHAPTER 9

Just then Patrick started to cry, and my breasts let down in response. I forced myself to turn and walk out the door, without looking back. We walked slowly to the elevator, and I wasn't really aware of anything until the car door slammed shut. I certainly couldn't speak. Just drawing each breath took amazing effort. I dreaded getting back to her house; I wanted to feel and hug my daughters, yet I knew that their warmth would flood my memory of their births and how happy and different it was from this.

The silence in the house was profound; I looked to Carol for an explanation.

"Joan and Suzy are at the park for a little while, with Chris' mom. We thought it would be better to give you a little time to yourself before having to answer their questions." Then she bustled around, getting me comfortable in the big lounge chair, putting the kettle on, and bringing me a bouquet of red roses. "I want you to have these. Maybe when you are feeling really awful, you can focus on the beauty of the roses. Perhaps they'll help."

What could I say to Carol? She, her husband and her mother had done more for me in the past months than my husband over the years. My mother used to know when I needed her support, and instinctively knew what would work. This day I missed her more than the day she died six years ago. I was wounded deeply, and I wanted my mom.

The impossibility of this situation alternately set my mind awhirl, or I'd focus on Patrick exclusively. How could I face Joan and Suzy? What would they think of me? The psychologist had explained that I might see some regressive behavior. They didn't really comprehend the events surrounding Patrick's birth. She told me that they may be frightened when they misbehave; they may think that I'll send them off, like I did Patrick. It would be my job to constantly reassure them that they'll always be with me. Even if they did something bad, I wouldn't stop loving them.

I could hear their excited chatter as they walked up the street. Moments later, Joan ran to me and gave me a big hug and kiss. Suzy wanted nothing more than to sit on my lap and suck her thumb, something she hadn't done for almost a year. Joan went with "Grandma Louise" into the kitchen to help with tea. Joan carefully negotiated the distance with a plate of Peek Freen Jam Thumbprints. Just as she handed me the cookies, she noticed that my blouse was wet on both sides.

"Mummy, did you spill something?"

"Sweetie, remember when you came to see me and Patrick in the hospital, and I was feeding him?" She just nodded, and I went on. "I wanted to nurse Patrick, just like I did you and Suzy, and I made milk for him. Now that I'm not nursing him, my breasts are getting rid of the milk. It will take a while to stop, but don't worry, I'm okay."

Looking at Joan, I could tell she wanted to ask me something, but wasn't sure if she should.

"Honey, what is it?"

Whispering, her head bowed, she asked, "Did you dress Patrick in the sleeper I picked out for him? Did you give him my favourite little teddy bear?" Her voice was breaking as I motioned for her to come and sit with us.

"Honey, just before we left the hospital Auntie Carol and I dressed him in the teddy bear sleeper and put your teddy in with him. We gave him lots and lots of kisses from you and Suzy. It is all right to feel sad, and when you do, come and tell me, and we'll be sad together. Sharing makes it easier for all of us; don't be afraid to cry, Honey. We've been doing it all day."

With that the sobs came, and her choking voice told me, "I really would have helped you look after him, mummy."

"I know, Honey, and know you would have been a great big sister to Patrick, just like you are with Suzy."

Silence descended as if everyone had run out of words. Carol came to me and took Suzy and Joan to their room for a nap. They fell asleep instantly. Fatigue suddenly and totally took me, and I fell asleep right where I was. I awoke dazed and confused; I couldn't see Patrick's bassinet. Reality hit an instant later, and again I thought and I thought.

Every day that went by was counted off. I would tell myself that I had nine days, then eight days to change my mind. My whole body was crying out for Patrick. My milk supply, far from decreasing, was drenching me regularly, a constant reminder of that severance from my body

The first afternoon that I was by myself, I actually went as far as finding Ms. Stone's card. Her number was there, all I had to do was dial. A few times I dialed a couple of numbers, only to hang up.

I argued with myself, I knew that circumstances hadn't changed, but lots of younger, poorer girls than I have managed to raise their children. Many times, both sides of that argument were won and lost. The only argument that I couldn't win against myself was the thought of Patrick's new parents. I remember so well, when my friend Vicki adopted her first little girl, the anticipation that coloured their lives, the preparation that had gone into the new arrival, and the utter joy when they were told that they were the proud parents of a little girl.

I had seen her that first night in her new home, and she was a gorgeous little thing. The most special sight was that of her parents bending over her crib, their faces beaming love to their precious baby. My trouble is that I can vividly picture things that I haven't seen. I could picture the devastation of their lives if they received another phone call; this one telling them that the birthmother changed her mind. I swear before God that I couldn't do that to Patrick's parents. That was the only thing that kept my hand from completing the phone call to Lila Stone's office.

The last night to change my mind finally arrived. I both welcomed it and cringed at the thought of it. Carol was wonderful. She too, had been counting, and she asked me what I needed from her. I know she would have come and waited the night out with me; however, I felt that this was something I needed to do on my own. She told me that she'd pick up the girls from daycare, and take them home for an overnight stay.

The silence that enfolded me seemed to throb in its intensity. My heart leapt into my throat, and I could feel each and every one of its beats. My intense emotions acted as a stimulus for my breasts. I was almost constantly drenching myself. My body was physically saying its good-bye.

Sometime later, I don't know how long, I felt as if I couldn't breathe in the oppressive silence. I turned the TV on, hoping that something would catch my mind's attention. Nothing did, but the time did seem to pass slightly quicker.

As the February darkness fell, the lack of a moon was even more noticeable. I walked through the darkened house, not knowing where I was going. I went through the girl's clothes, held them to me and hugged them. That led me to the one little physical piece I had of Patrick. I had brought home one of the sleepers he wore in the hospital and tucked it under my pillow.

I didn't bother turning lights on, I could find it easily by touch, just as I had been doing since I came home. I allowed myself to cry. I cried for myself, I cried for the pain that I was inflicting on myself, and I cried for Joan and Suzy, who would feel the absence of Patrick as well. I knew that they couldn't verbalize it, as I was able to, but I knew that their lives' were irrevocably changed. I would no longer be the same mother. I would have another layer added to what they were used too.

Pain would become part of me, and shape the rest of my days. Patrick's absence would forever hover over my little family. No matter how hard I tried, I couldn't fall asleep. I knew that the worst thing to do when you have trouble sleeping is to lie in bed, tossing and turning. I swung my legs over the edge of the bed, and immediately stripped off my nightie, which was soaking wet. I couldn't find a clean one, so resorted to an overlarge tee-shirt.

Without thinking where I was going I found myself sitting at the computer. In the past, a few games of solitaire would make me drowsy; that night it helped me focus my thoughts. I decided to write to Patrick, in the hopes that he'd be able to understand why I made the decision to place him for adoption. As I wrote I could see his little face, as clearly as if he were in the room with me. I was strengthened, and continued the story.

Dear Patrick,

Tonight will be the longest ever in my life. I must decide before the morning if I am going to change my mind and bring you home to your sisters, Joan and Suzy. When they were newborn babies, I was so happy bringing them home with me because I knew that I had the time and energy to spend my days with them, trying to shape what type of people I'd not only love, but be proud of. That is the commitment that I want to give to you. I know that I can't. I know that you deserve it.

When you were born, it was your birthright to be loved by a mother who had the patience, the time and the opportunity to give you, what Joan and Suzy had. I know that at this point in my life, I do not have those things. The one thing I have the most of, I give you freely. My love is yours to hold next to your heart throughout your life. I will send that love to you each day. My heart is bursting with the love I have for you; that is what makes it possible for me to consider not just my needs, but yours, Joan's and Suzy's.

Never feel that you weren't loved, and that is why you were given up for adoption. The exact opposite is true. As your new mother and father's love for you grows, remember that our love, too, grows daily. I hope and pray that a day arrives in the future when we will once again be able to touch with our bodies, not just our souls.

I pray that your mom and dad will always know how much they mean to me, even though we have never met. When you are old enough to think about finding me, tell them that I know who parents are. They are the people who pace the floor with a sleepless baby. They are the ones who delight in each new thing that you do. They are the ones who sit in a hot and stuffy doctor's waiting room, holding you, worrying about what is wrong. They will be the ones who take a deep breath and allow you to head off on your first day of kindergarten.

Your dad will be one who sits up waiting the first time you have the car for the night. Your mom and dad will be the one's helping you study, helping you pull from the maze of your talents what your career may be. I celebrate the parenthood that they will provide for you. I will never share in those things, physically. Never believe for a moment that you aren't cuddled in my heart. I await the day when I can meet your mom and dad and thank them.

I can already picture you with your new family. With all their love, and all of our prayers, I am sure that you will always be loved. Good-bye Patrick.

All my love,

Your birth mom, Clare

With that good-bye, I knew I had the strength to stay firm, and follow through with my decision. I printed the letter, folded it, slid it into the envelope that was already waiting, full of pictures of his birth family, and a watch that once belonged to my grandfather. I sealed the envelope and went to bed. I must have been asleep before my head hit the pillow. The next thing that I remembered was the sound of the school bell. I showered, dressed and left the house. I drove to Ms. Stone's office and was relieved to hear that she wasn't in. I left the envelope with her assistant, turned on my heel, and walked out into the blinding light of the sun, bouncing over the new fallen snow. My new life beckoned.

CHAPTER 10

All the firsts bring fresh pangs of pain. Over a period of six years there are a surprising number of firsts in a little one's life. Today is Patrick's first day of Grade One.

I surrender to the memories I have of Joan and Suzy's first days of school. I remember shopping for Joan's new school clothes. I took Joan into Edmonton, since there are so many more clothing stores. We had a wonderful time as she tried on different outfits. I didn't worry about the cost; Robert insisted that his girl's were dressed in the best. So I spent more money just because the little tee shirts, the corduroy pants and the sweaters had Strawberry Shortcake on them.

Of course we had to buy matching hair barrettes, lunch kits and pencil boxes. Joan always wanted to her outfits to be fully coordinated; that was what she got. We were loaded down with parcels when we finally reached the car. As soon as we got home she tried each and every outfit on for her dad. She already knew that was what he wanted.

The Tuesday after Labour Day arrived quickly. The night before Susan asked me to see what she had put out on her bed. She had laid her Strawberry Shortcake tee shirt, her matching sweat pants and her pink sweater out, in the shape of a person. After her bath, she jumped into her new Strawberry Shortcake nightie and snuggled under her blankets. She was excited, not nervous, about going into grade one. Westlock didn't have nursery schools, but Joan had already spent a year in the school in ECS. She loved everything about ECS; her teacher, her new friends, and the work she did.

I was up early the next morning because I promised Joan that I would make her favorite breakfast. The bacon simmered on the fry pan, and the French toast had just landed on the griddle when Joan came downstairs, and into the kitchen. She had a surprise for me; usually she waited for me to help her with her hair. This morning, she was not only dressed, but she had combed her hair and she already had her new barrettes in. She was so proud of herself, and then she helped me set the table. By the time Robert showed up, breakfast was on the table, the girls were seated and everything was calm. I silently prayed that he'd remember how special a day it was for Joan and keep his temper in control.

He surprised us and joked with Joan about what a big girl she was. He had another surprise up his sleeve. He wasn't going into work until he had walked Joan to her school. I checked her knapsack to make sure she had all the necessary supplies. Robert helped her get it on her back, I snuck in a kiss on her cheek, and off they went, hand in hand. That was the man I fell in love with. Where did he hide?

Suzy's first day of Grade One was totally different than Joan's. Her first day was not even in Canada. After three years of upgrading my education in Lethbridge, I was back doing the work I loved. I was once again researching plant biology. I had developed an interest in cereal grains and how they can be grown in extremely windy, dry climates that also experience great fluctuations in temperature. I was making progress with my work in Lethbridge and began corresponding with a biologist affiliated with the University of New Mexico.

Kele Martinez was actively investigating which cereal crops could grow in an almost arid land. The Colorado River brought whatever water was left after the people of Wyoming, Utah, Colorado, California and Arizona fulfilled their needs. A trickle would be the word that best described what was left of Colorado River once it reached New Mexico. The Palliser Triangle of the Canadian Prairies wouldn't be able to support farming if it weren't for irrigation. Lethbridge sits within a steppe climate that is warm and dry, with an average rain fall of 325 mm per year. New Mexico is classified as a desert climate: that is, very hot and very dry. Albuquerque sits at an elevation of 1620 m and receives just 207 mm of precipitation.

Part of my research was devoted to producing cereal grains that were more drought tolerant and lost less moisture through wind evaporation. Both Kele and I had worked independently and ended up at the same point. I was surprised to receive a letter from the University of New Mexico, more specifically from the Dean of Biological Sciences. Kele had been successful with his application to the American Federal government, and was awarded a large grant to further his research. There was an urgency behind the government's grant. The population in the area was growing very quickly; more land had to come under production without excess water usage. He wanted me to join him in New Mexico for at least a year.

His letter produced numerous feelings: pride, excitement, fear, and wonder. I had to let those feelings percolate for awhile, and didn't say anything to Joan and Suzy. I asked Carol to come over once the girls were in bed. I hardly let her sit down before I thrust the letter into her hand. Again she helped me by listening to my list. Again I had produced a list; it is still a useful way of clarifying things

My biggest concern had nothing to do with the job; I knew that I could contribute a lot, and that it would be both challenging and satisfying. My concern was for Joan and Suzy. There had been so many changes in their lives: their dad's leaving, Patrick's adoption, my working full time and going to school. Could they handle another move? By the time I loaded Carol down with all the reasons I shouldn't, I already decided that I would seriously investigate accepting the job.

The next morning I sent a letter off to Kele, explaining my personal situation, and that I would love the change to meet with him there. He phoned the following week with an invitation from both himself and the dean. Kele told me that a ticket would be waiting for me at the United Airlines Desk in the Calgary Airport. It would be up to me to choose the dates.

When I sat down with Joan and Suzy that night, I told them about the job and that I was going to fly to Albuquerque the next week. Children want details; both wanted to know what kind of school they would go to, where we would live, and what the city was like. I was relieved that they didn't seem to be upset, just curious. Carol came to the rescue once again and volunteered to take the girls to her home. They both had fun going over to her house, especially since baby Shannon was born two months ago.

As the plane lifted and flew over Lethbridge, I realized how much I had grown in the time that I lived there. I was confident of my professional abilities, I felt free to make decisions for my little family, and most of all I was content. I spent much of the four hour flight reworking my list of questions I needed to answer in order to make a decision.

I was able to pick out Kele at the arrival area because once before we had enjoyed a brief visit at another airport when we were both heading for different conferences. My bags arrived quickly; Kele swung them into the back of his truck. We were soon heading out of town to his test plots.

Our conversation quickly turned technical. I was only reminded of the elapsed time when the sun began to set and the temperature dipped. Kele drove me back into town, and we made plans for the next day's itinerary. Kele and his wife, Mansi, have a boy and a girl the same age as Joan and Suzy, so they knew that I'd want a tour of the schools and the neighborhood. Kele needed to go to his office, so Mansi was my tour guide. First she took me to her son Neil's school.

I would call it a Catholic school; in the States they are called Parochial schools. My first sight of the students made me very happy: school uniforms! It sure makes back to school shopping easier and cheaper. All the students seemed interested in their classes, and there was very little misbehavior. After my tour, I spoke with the Sister who was the Principal. I showed her Joan's latest report card and Suzy's progress report from ECS. She was amazed how much Joan had already studied, and commented that schools in Canada seemed to demand more of their students. Sister asked me what I thought of Joan skipping a grade. We discussed the pros and cons, and decided to see how she'd settle in after the move.

Mansi took me for a "local meal" and then on to see housing. I was amazed at how cheap the rent was. Most of the houses I saw had a pool; a great attraction for us. I loved an adobe house just down the block from Kele and Mansi. There was more than enough room for my little family, and the visitors that we were sure to have.

The next morning I went to the university with Kele and met with the dean. He asked for my general impressions, and then we got down to the specifics of the job: salary and health care. I would not move my family somewhere that didn't have as good of health care as at home. I was satisfied on all counts; this would be a year that I wouldn't have to pinch every penny, and the doctor's office was just a few blocks away.

After I signed all the paperwork at the university, I went back to what I already thought of as my house. I signed my name again. With that, I committed not only myself but Joan and Suzy to a totally new experience. I was so excited on the flight home that I couldn't concentrate on Kele's newest paper.

I gave up and dragged out the information about Albuquerque. I was able to identify where the house was, and as I gradually scanned the map, Albuquerque's lay out became clearer in my mind. I found the route that I would take to work. I would have only a fifteen minute commute. Gazing out the window, I realized that the city felt very comfortable to me, probably, although much bigger, it felt very much like Lethbridge.

It was very strange that I didn't worry about Joan and Suzy's reactions to the news. I felt that they wouldn't raise a fuss. Chris brought Joan, Suzy, and little Shannon to meet me at the airport. Before we left the terminal, I had dug out the girls' presents. I managed to find a doll very much like the one my dad had brought me from Texas years before. You put it together by laying out the back piece, overlaying it with batting, and then adding the front cloth, which was imprinted with the doll's face and dress. It had little holes spaced entirely around it. They were big enough for little fingers to thread the wool through. Since I didn't have much spare time to shop, their other presents were tee shirts from the university.

While Chris was driving us home, I told them what the neighborhood was like, who our neighbors were, what their school was like; but I refused to answer their questions about the house. I wanted to wait until we were home and I could show them all the pictures of the house. I shooed them upstairs so I could lay the pictures out on the kitchen table. When I was ready I called them down. Both of them liked the cinnamon colour of the house and wondered about the small windows. This certainly wasn't the type of house they were used to. That let me explain about the climate and why you want to keep the heat out in the summer, and why you needed to keep the warm air in during the winter. I turned to Chris and answered his question, and when I turned back, both girls were squealing over the swimming pool.

"How far away is this swimming pool, Mom?" asked Joan.

"It's in our backyard. See there is even a diving board!" I knew that was a seller, since last year Joan joined the Diving Club at U of L. I couldn't keep my big surprise any longer, and pulled out more pictures. "Suzy, look at your room."

"Where is Joan's bed, Mom?"

"This house has a bedroom for each of us, and one for visitors!"

With that I handed Joan the pictures of her bedroom, and she joined in Suzy's excitement. Chris already decided that the guestroom had more than enough room for Carol, Shannon and himself.

"When are you starting to take reservations?"

"Whenever you are ready to make them, I want you to be our first visitors."

"Well, I'd better head home. I want to be there when Carol gets home, so I can tell her where we're going on our next holiday!" With that he scooped up Shannon, and headed out the door.

I didn't feel like making supper, so we hoped into the car, drove to the south side, for burritos. It seemed to be the right choice.

CHAPTER 11

The next day was the start of an incredibly hectic two weeks. The first task I had was telling our landlords that we were moving. That was hard to do, since they had been absolutely terrific to us. They had been back in Lethbridge for two years and had become good friends. I couldn't believe that they hadn't ever raised our rent; I was so lucky. They didn't have to worry about renting the duplex, considering the short supply of quality rental units. Now they could earn a little more from their investment

I went through all of our clothes. Thankfully both Joan and Suzy had lots of summer play clothes which would be perfect for after school and on weekends. The principal of their new school, Sister Maria, told me not to worry about uniforms until I got there. Apparently, during the first week of school, everyone brings uniforms that have been outgrown to sell them.

The hardest decisions to make were about winter clothing. At first I thought it was ludicrous to take along cold weather clothes, but it does cool off during the winter nights. Most of what they had was going to be small by the time they'd need them, so we donated them to the Catholic Charities Clothing store. I didn't have to think twice about that; all I had to do was remember how much I needed them, when we first moved to Lethbridge.

I decided to put most of my winter clothing in storage boxes down in Carol and Chris's basement. I was pretty sure that they would be much too heavy, and I was tired of wearing the same clothing. I hadn't bought myself anything new for such a long time; I thought I'd be crazy not to take advantage of my new salary and new stores. In many ways it was embarrassing when the movers the university had hired came to pack us up for the move because of the small amount of furniture they had to pack. I hadn't spent very much money on furniture since our new life had begun. I decided that we could live with what we had so we could spend our "extra money" on fun activities for the three of us.

We all had city passes to the pools and skating rinks. During the weekends, the three of us had gone swimming at Nicholas Sheridan pool. For me, one of the best features was the hot tub. If we went on Friday nights, the hot water would ease my muscles after a long week at work. An added plus was that it made the girls sleepy, and I ended up with a quiet evening to myself. Joan and Mandy were in the same swimming class after school and Ann took them. I was able to get Suzy in an early evening class during the week.

I had made the decision that we wouldn't just sit at home on the weekends, and we had spent a lot of our time traveling around southern Alberta. There was a lot to see

We had driven down to Waterton National Park a couple times a year. The girls loved watching the deer and sheep wander around through the town. We hiked up the path so we could see Redrock Canyon.

The redness of the rock is brightened by the contrast with the deep forest green and the bluest of skies. I'm sure that every shade of green must be visible on that hike. On the shady side of the canyon, mosses have taken over to create a patterned carpet, draped over the worn rocks. Part of the path looks as if a wave has just splashed over the sand. The sign ahead confirms the impression. We were standing on the rocks that millennium ago were at the bottom of a great inland sea.

The mountain sheep apparently enjoyed their photo opportunities, since they meandered through the parking lot providing easy shots for the tourists. In the opposite direction from the canyon, there are many paths. I was always a tad nervous walking on them because of the grizzly bears. Waterton National Park, as well as Glacier National Park on the American side, probably has the largest concentration of grizzlies in the world.

I would find sticks for Joan, Suzy and I; during our hikes we'd rattle them along behind us, knock at trees and try to make as much noise as possible. We weren't crazy, just prudent. Most grizzly bears prefer not to be around humans, and if they are given plenty of warning will leave the area.

Our other favorite activity in the park was driving through the buffalo paddock. I always pondered what it must have been like before Europeans arrived. Reports from elders of the Blackfoot Confederacy told of waiting two days before a herd of buffalo finally passed by. The immensity of such size was almost impossible to comprehend. Once comprehended, it became shameful to realize that Europeans virtually eliminated the buffalo.

I felt it important that the girls understood the history of the area. I explained what had happened in terms that hopefully they would comprehend. I told them to imagine that all the grocery stores, and all the furniture stores, and all the clothing stores closed without warning. Then I asked them to tell me how they would eat, how they would get furniture, and where they would buy their clothes. During the drive home, I explained to them that was basically what the Blackfoot and all the other Plains Indians had gotten from the buffalo. I told them how a tipi was made from the hide of the buffalo, how their bones were used to fashion furnishings for their homes, weapons and toys. I told them that most of the food that the natives used came from the buffalo. Their survival was dependent on the preserves that were made in times of plenty, and that the pemmican could be easily taken for travel.

We didn't have to go out of town for adventure. The Oldman River winds through Lethbridge and the river valley has been very thoughtfully developed. Developed probably isn't the right word, since most of the area has been left in its natural state. An interpretive center explains how the strange, haunting hoodoos were formed, shows examples of the wildlife that can be found, and offers guided walks. Joan and Suzy loved going.

"Mom, shush, look!" Suzy whispered. We stopped in the gathering dusk and I followed her gaze. A doe was gracefully watching over her three fawns. We stood as statues, for how long I don't know. Perhaps a rabbit was fighting through the brambles. Whatever the noise; the doe quickly nudged her fawns through the thick bush. In an instant they were gone.

We walked along the path, and just as it approached the river bank, we were startled by a red blur rushing past us. At first I didn't realize what it was, since I had never seen one in the wild. The red fox dashed in front of us and then scuttled into the thick brush. Our last sight of him was the white tip of his tail. The three of us kept rooted to the spot. Joan was really excited, and immediately wanted to get home.

"Mom, that's just like The Fox and the Hound, isn't it. I want to go home and read my book and Suzy can look at the pictures."

We stopped dawdling, and headed to the end of the trail, but the wild life conspired that night to slow us down. Around one corner, fellow hikers had come to a halt. There were two fawns on one side of the path, and its mother on the other. I thought it was pretty apparent that she didn't want to move until we were gone, but she didn't want to leave her fawn. I persuaded the others to quietly back down the path so she could collect her fawn and disappear into the gathering darkness.

Another highlight of the river valley was Fort Whoop-up. I think it is a highlight only if people understand the message. The fort tells the history of the Lethbridge area, when Europeans first showed up. American profiteers from Fort Benton drove huge oxen trains up to the Lethbridge area. There they would fill the wagons full of buffalo skins. These people didn't do their own hunting; rather they depended on the Blackfoot to sell the hides to them. However, the traders weren't honorable. They used rot gut whiskey and shoddy trade goods to quickly place the natives in a situation in which they became dependent on the traders. When their rifles and their horses were gone, so were the means to get food for their families.

Once hooked on the whiskey, they would sell anything of value. That included their horses, and their rifles. Without those, it was almost impossible for them to provide for their families. Most no longer had the skills to hunt with bow and arrow. They had been trading with other tribes for rifles for quite a period.

I felt that it was critical that Joan and Suzy know about the native people of the area. Joan had a couple of friends at school who were native. They had come to play at our house and Joan had been to theirs. I was happy that race was not an issue for her; I had tried to raise the girls that way. Shortly after a visit at Halona's house, Halona's mom called me and asked if Joan could spend the weekend with them at their house on the Blood Reserve.

"Halona talks about Joan all the time. She is a really shy girl, and hasn't made too many friends in the city, until Joan became her friend. Now she not only has Joan as a friend, but Mandy too. Halona really wants to have her come with her so they can pick Saskatoon berries."

"I've really enjoyed having Halona over here. She is a very polite little girl. Joan talks about her all the time. She told me that Halona danced at the school during Native Awareness Week. Joan talked about her dress and feathers for a long time. One day I was upstairs doing some homework and suddenly became aware of some music. When I went downstairs, Halona was showing Joan some steps. I know Joan would love to go with you and she certainly can."

After we hung up, I went to tell Joan that she was going to spend the weekend on the reserve. She was so excited that the rest of the week dragged until it finally Friday afternoon. I left work early so that I'd be home when Joan was picked up. Halona's mom, Lena and I chatted for a bit, and she gave me her sister's phone number, as they were going to stay with her. I watched the truck disappear around the corner, and looked forward to Joan telling me about her weekend.

"Mom, look at all the berries I picked today!" were the first words out of her mouth when she slid out of the truck Sunday evening. I could tell that they had been picked that day -- her shirt was almost purple instead of yellow. It was getting late, so Lena just said good-bye, and I sent Joan off to strip and get into the bathtub. She was so full of news that she wanted me to sit in the bathroom with her.

"Her auntie's house isn't very big, but a lot of people live there. Her auntie has six kids. She's a grandma, too. A baby lives with her, too. There were puppies and kittens all over the place. We chased them all over the fields. I forgot to take the bread out of my knapsack, Mom." She stopped long enough to get a breath and me to get a word in.

"What bread?"

Joan grinned and told me, "Halona's grandmother visited and made it. It sort of looks like a lumpy donut. We shook cinnamon sugar on it and it's really good. I brought some home for you and Suzy." She stopped talking long enough for me to give her hair a good shampoo.

Eventually I learned that Joan had been talking about fry bread. She was right about it being really good. Lena told me that if I wanted, the next time she made some, she'd call and I could come over and learn how to make it. Fry bread tastes best right out of the pan. I started making it regularly.

Joan and Halona were playing quietly in her room one evening and I thought I'd check on what they were doing. Both were bent over Joan's desk, and when I peeked over their shoulders, I saw that Halona was trying to show Joan how to do some bead work. Both were beginners, but they were producing pretty patterns. How precious is the openness of children?

All these things had been more important to us than spending money on a new couch or a new table. We had fun, we were together and we all learned together. Those were the thoughts in my head while I supervised the movers in their careful packing of our small household. I had to walk through the house with the foreman of the packing crew to make sure that nothing had been left behind. Although empty and hollow, the rooms resonated with memory. Here, in this house, in this city, I managed to provide a better life for my children. Here in the living room, I came to the conclusion that I could take a chance. This is one more step toward that change.

We used Carol's as a base for the next two days. Joan and Halona had a sleepover at Mandy's. Suzy went to the park for one last swing and slide with her friends. Carol invited Ann and Lora for a girls-only lunch. We had wine with lunch, but that wasn't why my eyes were tearing.

These women had given me the very things I needed. I needed support, I needed people to give me practical advice, I needed to have my self-esteem bolstered, and I needed their friendship. I couldn't begin to thank them enough. If it hadn't been for them, how would I have managed to go back to school, and back to work? Who sat with me as I decided to divorce Robert, and who sat with me when I signed the divorce papers. No matter the paths our lives take, Carol, Ann and Lora will always be a part of mine. Even if we can't be together physically, they are part of the new me, so I always will hold them close to my heart.

Finally it was Friday morning, time to drive to Calgary. Chris drove us up. Shannon was still nursing frequently, and it would have been a strain on both her and Carol if she had come. The last hug turned into last hugs. What was there left to say?

Before the escaping tears ran down my cheeks, I turned and got into the car. It is only a short drive from West Lethbridge out to the highway. I didn't see it clearly through the mist of my tears. By Coalhurst, my eyes were dry. I didn't want to get the girls upset; after all we were starting an adventure.

We didn't have to wait long at the airport; the boarding call came twenty minutes after we checked in. Chris was a doll and talked the agent into letting him help with our carry-on luggage until we found a cart in the international departure area. A quick kiss on the cheek and he was gone. I decided to take advantage of the pre-boarding, as we had to maneuver two teddy bear backpacks, and my briefcase.

I had to clear American customs before we boarded. All the paperwork had been completed by my new employers. All I had to wait for was my A4 visa to be issued. Joan and Suzy were really excited about their first flight. They weren't afraid at all, had fun pushing the light for a flight attendant, and ordering a pop. We changed planes in Denver, and then we were off for the remainder of our flight. Both Joan and Suzy were asleep for most of that portion; it had been a hectic two weeks, the past two days in particular. I woke them shortly before we landed so they could see New Mexico from the air. It was pretty brown, and they saw the mountains to the west, and they both thought it looked like Lethbridge. They noticed all the swimming pools. We landed, collected our baggage, and were met by Kele and Mansi.

CHAPTER 12

Joan's first words were, "They both look like Halona. Are they Blood too?" She said it very matter of factly, and when I glanced at Kele and Mansi they didn't seem perturbed, so I answered her.

"No honey, I think they are from the tribe around here." I explained to them, "One of Joan's best friends in Lethbridge is a Blood Indian."

Mansi sat down beside Joan, smiled at her, and told her, "I think it is great that you have Halona as a friend. You are right that I'm native. My tribe is the Hopi. That is why my name is different. My mom and dad gave my brothers and sisters traditional names. Mansi means picked flower."

As we walked outside Joan told Mansi, "I really like your name. When does it change?"

Mansi looked at me, so I explained that the Blackfoot Indians were given new names at different stages of their lives.

"This is my only name. Ours don't change." This satisfied Joan's curiosity.

It wasn't long before we were on the highway into town. The girls were reassured by the familiar sights of cattle, growing corn, and waving barley fields. Once I recognized the area, I tried to remember the exact turns, and made only one mistake.

Kele pulled the car into the carport and started to unload our bags. I pulled the key from my briefcase, opened the door and we piled in. Suzy snuck under Joan's arm and beat her into the house. They ran around the house, not knowing where to look first, their bedrooms or the pool. They compromised and quickly went between the two, my warning to them trailing behind. I reminded them of the safety instructions I gave them about the pool. They had to stay outside the locked gate unless I was with them -- always.

I went back to the carport and grabbed the one bag left, and trailed Kele and Mansi into the house. I showed them whose bedrooms were whose. I was busy hanging the clothes up -- there were hangers in the closet, courtesy I later found out, of Mansi. Mansi called to me from the dining room, and I joined her there. At the doorway, all I could do was stop and stare. A card table had been covered with a beautiful cloth, and set with dishes. When I thanked her, Mansi told me the rest of her surprise,

"I knew that you'd want to stay here, so I made supper already, and it is in the oven. I hope I bought the right kind of cereal for the kids. We brought over our guest mattresses, some towels and blankets. If I forgot anything, I can run home and get it."

I must have stared at her, her cheeks showed a blush. I stopped staring and gave her a hug.

"I can't believe how lucky I am. This is just wonderful. I really appreciate it. You are right. I know the girls want to explore their new house, rather than spend the night in a hotel, thank-you so much."

Kele rejoined us to let me know that the luggage had been taken out of the car, and that he checked to make sure the swimming pool door was locked.

He put his arm around Mansi and said, "Let's go home now and let them settle in. Clare, I'm going to be out in the field tomorrow, so Mansi volunteered to take you over to the school, the grocery store and any other place you need to go. Tomorrow night I'll bring your new car home. Buenos Noches."

Joan came and stood next to me quietly. "I like them mom." Suzy joined us and told us that she already had seen a girl her age, in the yard next door. With that, we sat down to Mansi's dinner and then pretended that we were having a sleepover as we lay side by side on the living room floor. A new adventure had truly begun.

It is the little things that announce a new culture. Mansi picked us up and took us to the school. The girls were shocked to see the playground. It was totally opposite what we think of when picturing a schoolyard in Canada. The open, green fields were replaced by an asphalt courtyard. Once we met the principal, she took Joan and Susan for a tour. Suzy had made the announcement in the morning that now she was a big girl going to school, she wanted to be called Susan. Once the tour was finished Joan asked me where the gym was; she looked as if she didn't believe Sister Angelina's answer.

"Where do you have gym?" she asked.

"We use the courtyard for a gym, unless it is raining. Then we use the church meeting hall. See?", as Joan looked to where Sister Angelina pointed. "I'm going to take you to your classrooms now. Shall we show Susan her room first?" We all nodded in response.

Susan struggled with Suzy while we crossed the courtyard; Susan won and she didn't cry or act shy when her teacher came to introduce herself. Miss Frank was a tiny young woman, who looked as if she had just finished school. She squatted down, so she was at Susan's level.

"The whole class has been waiting for you to come. We haven't had a student from Canada before, and they have lots of questions for you." With that she showed Susan her seat, and turned to her class. "Children, this is Susan; please remember she is new to not only this school, but to this country. If you are playing with her, try not to start talking Spanish to one another. She won't understand. Thank you. Everyone turn over the piece of paper on your desk, and take your crayons out."

By this time, we had withdrawn from the classroom, ready to take Joan to her class. I was able to look through the Jalousie windows, and when Susan saw me, she held up a map of Canada.

The Grade Four classrooms were on the same side of the school, but at the very end. Joan's self-confidence had blossomed with our move to Lethbridge, and she didn't hesitate to enter her classroom. Mrs. Alvarez almost bumped into her as she tried to hurry out the door to meet Joan. "Joan, we've been waiting for you to come. All the children have lots of questions. I hope you don't mind if they ask?"

"I don't mind Mrs. Alvarez." She followed her teacher to her table and was shown her supplies. I caught her eye to remind her to give the teacher the gift we had brought from Canada. Her hand went up and when Mrs. Alvarez nodded, "Mrs. Alvarez, I brought something from Canada for the classroom. It is a jigsaw puzzle of Canada." When Mrs. Alvarez came to her table to accept the gift, she gently turned Joan around to see their surprise for her.

In the corner of the classroom, alongside the American flag, was a Canadian flag. I grinned and waved from the courtyard, and then trailed Sister Angelina back to her office. We once again talked about Joan's wider knowledge base, and again came to the same conclusion; we'd observe for the first while. I told the Sister that I was teaching both children their Social Studies, from the Alberta curriculum, through Distance Learning. I didn't want them falling behind in that, as preparation for our return to Canada.

Mansi had been a doll, trailing along with us to provide any needed support. When we finished our business at the school, Mansi drove me the local grocery store, a Safeway. While many of the familiar brands and foods were stocked, there were many that, while I had a vague idea what they were, I didn't know how to cook with them. At home, I always bought crushed chilies, because I didn't have any idea how to cook with whole chilies.

As we wandered the aisles, Mansi told me that she did a lot of her shopping here, but if she didn't have time to make tortillas, the closest and best was at the grocery store attached to the gas station. We went there after Safeway; Mansi not only didn't have to get out to fill her car; the attendant brought out the tortillas and milk she ordered. That would sure be great after a long day at work!

After a few more stops at neighborhood specialty shops, we were finally back to the house. The carports took the place of garages at home. They sheltered cars from rain and heat. There were a few garages to be seen, but generally they were avoided because of the heat build-up during the day.

We carried the grocery bags in through the door that led into the family room, and the kitchen. One thing I particularly liked was the lack of stairs going into the house, and in the house. After we had put all the groceries away, I noticed Mansi putting small, round, black plastic disks in the cupboards.

"What are those, Mansi?" From the look on her face, she must have thought I was crazy, but answered me anyway.

"Combat roach bait. Don't you put them in your cupboards in Lethbridge?" My facial expression told that story. I obviously knew that warmer climates had to deal with roaches, but hadn't even thought about it in regards to my own kitchen!

We went back to the mall and found some nightlights for the whole house. Any books that I'd read always emphasized that cockroaches didn't like the light. If I had to get up to go to the bathroom during the night I refused to be met by them. Mansi was fascinated that roaches weren't a problem in Alberta, and neither were rats. I'm afraid that for the first couple of months in our new house, I'd open a cupboard door quickly and jump back, while at the same time trying to peer in to see if it was 'safe'.

We grabbed tacos for lunch, and finished our chores in time to pick the girls up from school. They finished school at ten minutes after two, which was very surprising to me. In Lethbridge, the elementary school children weren't home until after three o'clock. Obviously this was a concern as far as childcare. I would not be home at that time. That must have been a common problem, because Mansi brought it up. She didn't work outside the home, but had a lot of friends who did, and they used the after school care that the school offered. I would be able to pick Joan and Suzy, oops, Susan up on my way home from school.

Once we had all the children in the van, she took us to the closest J.C. Penny store. Both children needed new clothes, as their hot weather clothing had taken a beating during the summer, and they both had grown. Joan and Susan tried on a lot of clothes that afternoon. We ended up with a good selection of clothing that was not only reasonably priced, but "in

I already had their uniforms hung up in their closets. Each had a blue plaid kilt, white blouses, navy blue walking shorts, and white polo shirts. Also hanging in their closets, since we didn't have our furniture yet, were their gym uniforms; blue shorts and a light blue t-shirt with the school emblem on it.

Mansi and I collapsed into the poolside chairs left behind by the previous renters while the kids found a new reserve of energy when they threw themselves into the pool. Mansi's children, Neil and Emily were water babies like mine. Neither of us would allow them on their own in the pool. Mansi told me that there were usually a few drownings every year, within our own community. The cause, most commonly, was a lack of supervision.

Mansi and I chatted quietly until she hauled her kids out of the pool. She had to get home, and get to work on her own chores. The girls and I walked around to the front of the house, to their car, with them. Obviously we didn't even come close to being mistaken as locals. Mansi, Neil and Emily casually strolled barefoot through the grass. The three of us hadn't moved off the pool deck before we had our thongs on. We weren't ready yet to step barefoot on cockroaches, on hairy spiders, or some other weird bug.

We stood watching our new friends drive off, marveled at the reddening sky, turned and went into our house. I decided to cook familiar things at first, since Joan and Susan, reported that their school lunch was "local food." That was the best they could describe it, because they didn't know the names. Both of them found it very different to have everybody in the school stay for lunch. They weren't allowed to bring their own lunches, and no one was allowed off the school property until the end of the day. They could bring their own snacks for afterschool, so they'd have some familiar food during the day.

I lit up the barbeque and cooked our pork chops and the funny rice I bought at the Safeway. Mansi told me that was what everyone ate here. She told me how to cook it. Apparently the key is once you've added your water and brought it back to a boil, you do not look under the lid for nineteen minutes. I think the rice was Japanese; very sticky with a slight nutty flavor. We all liked the flavor, and from that time on, that rice is what we eat.

Joan and Susan chattered away, telling me all about their first day at school. Both of them liked their teachers and had already made friends in their classrooms. It really helped that they knew Neil and Emily to make the day easier. Neil and Emily had brought the girls with them during recess and lunch break, and broke them into their circle of friends.

Susan laughingly told us that the little boy who sat in front of her asked if she lived an igloo. I'm glad I had briefed them on some of the questions Americans, especially those in the South, ask of Canadians. I had sent them both to school with a supply of postcards showing pictures of the Lethbridge area, cattle, the mountains, Blackfoot women, children and men in their dancing outfits, elk, bear, deer, rodeo bull riders, and the city of Calgary. Susan answered him by showing him a picture of Lethbridge. He realized that we lived in houses like those in this area. He asked to see the rest of the postcards; he must have liked what he saw, he put his hand up for the teacher.

"Miss Frank, Susan has some pictures. They don't live in igloos!"

Miss Frank came down the aisle and asked Susan if she could show them to the whole class. Susan nodded, and followed Miss Frank to the front of the room. The other children sat in a quiet semicircle around Miss Frank and looked intently at the pictures, especially when it was their turn to hold them. Miss Frank started asking questions, but the students quickly picked up the ball.

They all were excited seeing the bull riding, because it was something they were familiar with. One little girl remembered that her uncle drove four days and four nights, in order to bull ride at the Calgary Stampede. Susan showed her postcard of the Stampede parade, and that time it was the horses and the natives that enthralled the kids. Susan couldn't answer all of their questions, but she proudly told me that she knew most of the answers. I told her that any time Miss Frank would like, that I could come to the school with more pictures and more answers. While Susan was winding up her tale, Joan could hardly sit still.

"It was almost the same in my classroom. Mrs. Alvarez told me that the class had a surprise for me. Each of them, after looking at books about Canada, drew a picture for me." Joan ran to the door to collect her knapsack, and by the time she returned, was pulling out the pictures that were hers to bring home.

"They did a really good job, Honey. I can tell that they learned something about the Lethbridge area. Look at the deer that someone drew. I really like this drawing of a jingle dress. Do you have the picture that Neil drew?"

"Here it is mom. His picture is the biggest."

"He can draw very well, can't he?" Both Joan and Susan nodded. "He seems to really like our mountains. I like the way he drew some cows, and put an oil pumper in the middle of the pasture."

We sat quietly commenting on the rest of the pictures, until it was time to get ready for bed. I had to chuckle when Susan told me that she didn't have to have a bath because she had already been in the pool. Rather than fight over it, I thought a demonstration would work better, so I asked to bring me her comb. I only combed her hair for a second or two before she complained about the knots. She took her comb back and without a word marched into the bathroom and jumped into the tub with Joan.

They must have been tired; usually they spend a long time in the bath. This bath lasted just long enough for both of them to wash their hair. Their hair blew dry in the warm evening breeze as we sat on the patio for our bedtime story. Once they were tucked into their beds, I hauled out my research notes and spread them on the table so I could review them before my first day in a new office. I allowed myself the luxury of a cup of Twinning's tea.

I dragged the phone over and called Carol and Chris. They must have been waiting by the phone; it was answered before there was a full ring. I quickly filled them in on what we had been doing during the past two days. They were amazed that we had done so much. They were very happy that Susan and Joan liked their new school. They both laughed when I told them about the nightlights, but then told me that they would have done the same thing.

I heard Shannon gurgling in the background. That was all the prompting my eyes needed. They filled with tears, but I held them back. It wouldn't be long until we were together again. I said good night, hung up the phone and got to work on my latest data

Time flew until suddenly I was aware of how deep and still the night had become. The darkness told me that it must be late. Instead, to my astonishment, it was just ten-thirty. I had been so absorbed in my work, the lack of a twilight had gone unnoticed. That darkness announced to me that I was living with a different rhyme. It was time for bed

At dawn, the sun came streaming through the windows. It wasn't the cool, watery light that I was used to. This morning sun glared from the eastern horizon, painting my walls with the colours of the earth. The red dust shone on the wall; the colour of the dried grasses mixed with the red.

I didn't get up right away; I had lots of time. Instead, I lay in bed and watched as the dawn showed its ever changing art. The sun must have woken Joan and Susan up shortly after; they both trooped in and jumped into bed with me. Together we observed and came to know the new colours of our world.

I think breakfast is breakfast everywhere. I think all kids must love cereal; the only difference, which we would learn, is that a tortilla often replaces toast. Our orange juice was spectacular. Oranges were so cheap that I brought out my new juicer, and the girls learned just what orange juice is supposed to taste like.

Both of them were wide awake once they were out of bed, so we didn't have to rush. We all went about our morning routine, and were ready, with time to spare. I drove them down the block so they could walk to school with Neil and Emily and of course Mansi. I was surprised that the children didn't walk to school, because it was only a few blocks. Mansi told me that the concern wasn't that it was too far, or that they had to cross the street. Kidnapping, drugs, and violence were what motivated parents to either drive their children or walk with them to school. With a quick kiss to each of them, I left them in Mansi's care, and headed off to my new job.

CHAPTER 13

One of the exceptional traits of Americans is they identify a desire and they throw all of their energies toward achieving that goal. We usually see it manifested by an almost obsessive drive to be number one, especially when it comes to sports. Many high schools here have antiquated labs, few supplies, and few teachers with specialized knowledge in the subjects that they teach; they do, however, have first class, modern athletic facilities. They'll hire football coaches and not even consider the irony that their teaching staff struggles to teach in less than ideal circumstances. Most coaches are paid more than teachers!

I passed the local football field as I drove toward the freeway. The young men practicing on the field appeared to have the same equipment as professionals. Their gym was a brand new, soaring structure. Once past the field, I drove by a building that must have been a lab, considering the number of ventilation vents on the roof. I would have to guess that the building was at least fifty years old. When I had come for the interview I had the opportunity to visit the Biological Sciences Building, and was most appreciative of the equipment. I am sure that I saw every conceivable piece of equipment that we could possibly imagine. Some, I'm sure had no relation to our work. These pieces were there because they were new, they were high tech and rich alumni paid for them. I would reap the benefits of their generosity.

Unfortunately, those students who lacked athletic skill, and instead excelled in academics, had to struggle with equipment that no longer worked properly, or hadn't been used by the scientific community for a decade.

I tried to push these thoughts to the back of my head so I could fully enjoy the first day of my new challenge. Kele met me at the door and escorted me to our office in case I had forgotten. As we walked, Kele introduced me to the men and women who would be my colleagues for the next year.

I was pleasantly surprised to see that Kele's office had been renovated since my visit. A wall had been knocked down and the new larger office was arranged to easily facilitate our joint work. Our desks faced one another, so it was easier to communicate as we worked. We wouldn't have to get up and go out to another office each time we had a thought. We each had plenty of work space. My computer terminal was at the far end of my desk on a specialized unit. I had plenty of cupboard space; I can't work if I have piles of paper all over the place.

Both Kele and I were anxious to get started; soon we were comparing our research notes. The time flew by, and before I knew it, Kele asked me to join him for lunch. We headed upstairs to an area I hadn't seen before; a wonderful dining room. A group of fellow researchers were waiting for us at the far end. Kele went around the table introducing them all to me. I turned to nod and smile at each person; the last person I expected to see was one of my professors from U of A. He greeted me with a big smile and hug of welcome. It was obvious to me that he knew I was coming.

Dr. James taught me each of my years on campus, and our relationship changed from me being a terrified student to our respecting one another. He had been very disappointed that I didn't go on and get my master's degree. I felt his disappointment in two ways: he obviously thought I'd do well, and he knew that I wanted to continue. He had been a dear when I told him that I wasn't coming back. Dr. James had met Robert a couple of times at various events on campus, and knew why I changed my mind.

After a few brief words, we ate our lunch and brought the other scientist up to speed on where our research was taking us and what we hoped would be the outcome. The conversation was very lively as each gave us different slants on the research, depending on their specialties. Too soon, it was time to head back to our office. Dr. James, Trent, stopped until he had a chance to ask me to join him for dinner sometime in the near future. I told him I'd be thrilled.

Over the afternoon's work, it came to me that one of the initial ideas that I had for this project came from some experiments I did at U of A. I planted some test crops, each of which had different cell structure and varying degrees of osmosis and evaporation. My results at that time were very positive, and suggested that we could improve cereal crops through cross breeding. The important, practical aspects seemed quite evident to me. If these new crops could be developed, farmers in drier areas did not have to be so dependent on crops such as wheat and canola.

Eleven years later I was actually involved in work that could see my theories verified. The presence of Dr. James was an added bonus. I had someone whom I both admired and trusted to consult with.

Time must fly faster in New Mexico, because next thing I knew, it was time to head home. Some people may not enjoy this part of their day, but I always did. I let my eyes explore my surroundings and let myself appreciate the physical beauty. New Mexico provided new vistas to appreciate. The mountains loomed so that you would swear that they were only a few miles away. The mesas stood proud against the sky; their solidity comforting. They told me that they had withstood time: the ice, the rain, and the wind each had shaped them. Their shape had changed, but their strength remained.

Almost too soon, I was at the school. I went in and collected Joan and Susan. The short drive home was crowded with questions. Mine to the girls, Susan's and Joan's to me. Our ride wasn't long enough to finish all of our news, so we quickly decided we'd finish in the pool. What a luxury; drive home from work through beautiful scenery and then jump into our pool. Between the dunkings and the squeals, we caught each other up on the day.

"Time to get out of the pool, guys." I called to the girls.

Almost immediately I heard, "Can't we stay in longer, Mom?"

"No, I'm sorry. Remember the rules we all agreed upon? I have to make supper and can't supervise you right now. After supper you can come back out if you like." Thankfully there wasn't any arguing. Maybe they did remember that I told them if they didn't follow the safety rules, they'd lose pool privileges for a week. I hated setting down rules before we had even flown to New Mexico, but I was determined that we'd enjoy our pool safely.

CHAPTER 14

I sat at the counter in the kitchen and peeled and sliced our carrots, deboned the chicken and checked the instructions for the rice. I heard the girls in the family room giggling over shows that were new to them. After a bit I heard *Sesame Street*, and Big Bird was speaking Spanish. Just as supper was ready, Big Bird said good-bye to all his friends. To some he said, "Adios," and to others he said, "Buenos noches." Both Joan and Susan rushed in to tell me they knew Big Bird was saying good-bye and good night. Joan set the table with the plates and glasses and Susan put out the cutlery and the serviettes. Both of them wanted to show off their new words, and they used our supper for their vocabulary.

"Mom, do you know what the word for carrot is?" Joan asked. I had to confess that I didn't.

"It is la zanahoria -- I think that is how you say it."

Susan didn't want to be left out of my lesson. "Mom, I know what rice is. It's el arroz. We are drinking el agua. My friends tried to tell me everything we had for lunch, but I can't remember what chicken is."

"That's okay honey, you learned more Spanish today than I did. But I had fun at work today. I met lots of new people and found someone I knew. Do you remember when we lived in Westlock, and sometimes we'd go into Edmonton, to the university?" They both nodded. "Do you remember that sometimes we'd go out to the university farm, and I would talk with Dr. James? He was my teacher. Anyway, he has already been here a year and will be here until next year. It made me really happy to see a face that I know. It is sort of like you guys right now. When you're alone at school I bet you look for Neil and Emily, right?"

"Sometimes I get scared if I can't find Emily quickly." told Susan.

"I'm glad you have a friend you can sit with at lunch time."

It was almost dark by the time we finished clearing up. Joan and Susan decided against another swim; they just wanted a cuddle and a story before climbing into bed. We piled into the huge recliner made for two. I had seen it in the store when I was out shopping with Mansi, and decided right then and there to buy it. Not only did I buy it, I paid extra to have it delivered that night. Sometimes you have to be wild and crazy. It had been a long time since I had made such a major purchase

As the story wound up, we sat entwined, listening to unfamiliar birdsong. A barking dog down the street broke the mood, and we headed off for the bedrooms. Susan was tucked in first, Joan gave her a kiss and then I gave her one on the other cheek. Joan gave me a hug and kiss, and slipped into her bed. "I really like it here Mom."

"So do I, honey. I think it will be a fun year. I can already imagine all the trips we will make. You'll have lots of things to tell Mandy and Halona, when you write them. Are you going to start the letter for your class in Lethbridge?"

"I started it at lunch. I thought I'd put something down each day for a little while before I send it."

"That's a good way to do it. You don't have to remember so far back. Goodnight, Sweetie."

"Night, Mom" was the last I heard from Joan. She must have fallen asleep almost instantaneously.

That first week of work flew by. I felt great fulfillment as Kele and I created the framework needed to test our theories. We didn't have to concern ourselves about designing the experiments around what equipment that was on hand. If we needed anything else, all we had to do was request it. I was intrigued to see the group dynamics at work over lunch. All of the scientists ate together and discussed their work. People who worked on other projects often asked questions that arose from their particular niche. Those questions often led to side experiments that would help clarify others' work. Of course, Trent's questions and comments had particular importance to me, since he had helped me so with the experiments that were the genesis of this project.

My reaction when I first saw Trent was exactly the same as when I ran into a boy from my high school during my first week in residence. It was such a relief to see someone who knew your name, where you were from and what you were taking. I remember that time so vividly; all I did was repeat that information endlessly.

During those early days in residence, Dean and I had spent a lot of our time together. It was certainly easier to be adventuresome while in the company of a friend. In my mind's eye I substituted Trent for Dean. When Trent was my professor, he was living with a very nice woman. He was wearing a wedding ring now, so perhaps they married. Trent and I hadn't yet caught up with all the news of the past decade.

On Friday afternoon, everyone working on our floor gathered for an hour to bring the week to a close. This time allowed everyone the opportunity to interact in a more personal manner. Trent and I found ourselves a corner and promptly started a decade in review. Trent had married Nina, and within the year they were expecting a baby. As he related his story, emotions fought for control of his face. Clearly he loved Nina and was thrilled that they were having a baby.

I clenched my hands while I listened and watched; something awful was coming. Trent took a deep breath and continued. He and Nina became the proud parents of a little girl, Julia. He talked of her black, curly hair and blue eyes that gazed intently on everything. With that his head bowed and he gazed unseeingly at the floor. He continued his voice hoarse with control.

His car hadn't started one winter day. Nina volunteered to drive him to the university, since she was planning on going to the shopping center. She dropped him off at the main entrance of the Biological Sciences building. He kissed her. He opened the back door and kissed Julia on her cheek while she played with her car seat toys.

The next time he had seen them was in the morgue. A car couldn't stop at an icy intersection and crashed into Nina and Julia. Nina was pronounced dead at the scene. Julia lived for a short time in the University Hospital emergency room, but her injuries were so severe that she died almost immediately.

During this time Trent was busy supervising his students as they went from microscope to microscope, taking their lab exam. Normally he was never disturbed, particularly during examinations. He opened the lab door to see a white faced colleague who asked him to go to the Dean's office. He told Trent that he would take over in the lab.

Trent hadn't any idea what was going on, but quickly went to see the dean. On one side of that office door his life was happy and fulfilled, on the other he was devastated to learn that he was no longer a husband or a father.

Trent was whispering by the time he finished his story and his head hung even lower. I fought to control my tears, but my control was gone. What do you say? I couldn't think of words; instead I acted. I pulled my chair closer, leaned in and took his hands in mine, and murmured what I hoped were comforts. I wanted to shield him from curious glances in our direction.

Once we both had reasonable control, we left for the weekend. I didn't want to leave him. He needed a comforting presence. I used my car phone and called

Mansi. After I quickly explained the situation, she beat me to the punch and told me she'd take the kids home with her, and they'd have a sleepover. With that I turned to Trent and told him that we were going out for supper.

I wasn't a very good host, I had to ask him where to go. I didn't know any restaurants yet. At first Trent insisted that he'd drive his car so I could follow him. I insisted that he wasn't in a fit state to drive. I opened my passenger door; he got in, and gave me directions.

When I pulled into the restaurant parking lot, I realized that we were not at a Mexican restaurant, but rather one that focused on beef. I must admit curiosity about American beef; living in Lethbridge I heard a lot of discussion comparing our meat to that south of the border. The consensus was that our beef was far superior.

I used that as a neutral topic of discussion while we selected our dinner choices, and then waited for them. I thought back to Carol's mom and the comfortable evening she created for me when I needed not to think. Our steaks arrived, and just from their appearance, I decided which side of the argument that I was on. I was amazed at the marbling throughout the meat. The beef not only tasted different, but its' texture was different. Over the course of that meal, I decided that while in the US, I'd mostly stick to poultry, pork and fish.

When our tea and dessert arrived, Trent took a deep breath and began talking about Nina and Julia. His eyes sparkled when he told me of their excitement when they learned that she was expecting. Together they shared the experience of pregnancy. They prepared the nursery together, they shopped for baby furniture together, but couldn't find the crib they had in mind. Each evening Trent went to work down in the basement. While he cut, nailed and sanded the wood for their baby's crib, Nina would sit in an old comfy chair beside his work bench, and read through baby name books. One evening they were sure of a name they both liked, and by the next night they'd change their name.

One evening they were both very tired and went upstairs without putting everything away. When they next descended to their workshop, Nina realized that the name book had fallen between the side of the chair and the cushion. When she pulled it out, she glanced down to where the book fell open. The first name she saw was Julia. She knew, and once she told Trent, he too knew that was the perfect name if they had a little girl.

Something told them that they were going to have a daughter. They weren't as concerned about picking out boys names that they liked. Together they went to Lamaze classes at the hospital, and each evening faithfully practiced the breathing exercises, the relaxation strategies, and the stretching and flexibility exercises. Nina continued teaching her ECS class. She told Trent that her work was more like practicing to be a mom. She pulled out all her child development and child psychology texts from her university days.

Trent's voice held a tremor of tears, but also of love. It was clear that he loved his wife and that they both had been thrilled with idea of parenthood. He pulled out his wallet and showed me a picture of Nina, her belly and radiant smile ample proof of her happiness.

"Nina said there was a great advantage being pregnant during the summer. It's the only time that you can go around in a bathing suit with a big belly and feel comfortable about it. Toward the end of August, Nina went swimming almost every day, and sometimes twice a day. When Julia was really active making her mother more uncomfortable, she'd settle down when Nina went swimming. It worked great just before bedtime."

I remembered only too well.

"I was pregnant during the summer too and I had one great excuse to cool off. Joan wasn't quite three, and we had a two foot deep plastic swimming pool that was probably ten feet across. It sat smack dab in the middle of the backyard. We didn't have the fence up, we'd just moved from our other house, but I had Joan as a reason to explain to any passerby's why a woman was sitting in a kiddies' pool. That pool was a Godsend. It was so hot that year."

Trent laughed and said he could just picture me, sitting in the little pool, and watching my new neighbors go by. He switched gears and again started his story. "Nina only missed her due date by two days. I was really anxious hoping the baby would arrive before classes began. I ran out of time, and sure enough I was back on campus for registration when Nina called the department.

They found my T.A. and sent him over to sit in the classroom. Remember that horrid system of going from Prof to Prof getting registration cards? I quickly went over what I need him to do and flew over to the U of A hospital. I didn't have to go home for Nina, her sister drove her to the hospital. I think I made the walk from Biological Sciences to the hospital in record time.

"We had gone on a tour of the hospital as part of pre-natal classes, so I at least I knew where I was going. The nurses had just finished her prep, and she looked both excited and serene. She told me that she'd felt something during the night, but thought it was just the baby being very active; it wasn't until I left for work that she started having regular contractions, that were slowly gaining in their intensity.

"The nurses interrupted Nina so they could check the progress of her labour. Nina's nurse was from the pre-natal classes and it was comforting to have her there. She told us that Nina was almost 7 cm. Soon the contractions strengthened and came closer and closer. A hard contraction hit, and the nurse reminded us of the techniques we had been practicing. I felt better knowing that I could be of some help. It hurt to watch Nina go through so much pain, even when you've planned for it and know the outcome."

I nodded, my mouth full of baked apple. "I know what Nina went through. My first delivery moved pretty quickly. I knew the breathing and meditation exercises, from my Lamaze classes. I'm sure it would have been easier if Robert had been with me."

Trent couldn't believe his ears, "You mean that Robert didn't stay with you for the labour and delivery? I can't believe a man doing that, especially now that we're allowed, no -- encouraged."

"Robert told me that if he saw me during labour and delivery that he'd wouldn't be sexually turned on by me."

If possible Trent jaw dropped further. "You mean to say that no one was with you?"

"The nurses were very good. One of them, Jan, even stayed until I had Joan even though her shift had ended. I know exactly what they thought of Robert, even though no one said anything. My hardest time was transferring from my bed onto the stretcher for the trip to the delivery room, and then shifting to the delivery table. I was barely in position when Joan decided it was time for her entrance. She was a darling baby. She didn't cry, she calmly gazed at me, and when Jan helped me start nursing, Joan immediately latched on and started nursing. Jan gave me encouraging words as she tidied me up before I was transferred to post-partum. I saw her lips tighten when Robert stood up from the chair in the lobby to see his first child. The way he carried on you would have thought he had done the hard work. Jan noticed that he forgot to ask how I was. I thought for sure that the next morning Robert would bring me flowers. He didn't even show up; told me later that he was too busy."

Trent and I lapsed into a companionable silence, gazing into our tea, as if there were answers to be found there. I couldn't help thinking about Patrick. At least when he was born Carol was there to help me. I felt guilty about the pain I was feeling. Patrick was alive. Trent lost both his wife and his daughter. I almost told him, but decided that I just couldn't heap my pain on top of his; maybe later, but not now. He needed to talk about his life with Nina and Julia.

"I was so proud, so happy when I brought them home from the hospital. My mom and dad, my sister, and Nina's parents came to see her that night. She was the first grandchild. Both sets of grandparents had waited a long time to have a grandchild to spoil. It started that night, when they came laden down with gifts for Julia. Nina certainly didn't have to worry about washing clothes everyday; Julia had enough clothes that she could be changed at least four times a day and still would have clean clothes for a whole week. I don't know if our parents got together and came up with the idea of investments for Julia, but that night they gave us Canada Savings Bonds for her." Trent suddenly straightened up, and put his hand to his forehead. "I forgot all about those. I don't know what I have to do about them."

Here was something I could do that was concrete. "Trent, I have a friend who works for Revenue Canada, in Lethbridge. I'll give her a call tomorrow and see what she says. Don't worry about it right now."

Looking across to Trent, I suddenly realized that he was exhausted. I knew I felt that way. I slipped out to the washroom, paid the bill, and then collected Trent.

"Are you becoming a thief?" Trent asked, as we walked by the cashier.

"Don't worry; I've already looked after it. I think we both need a good night's sleep. I'll drive you home and then tomorrow I'll come over and we can go to the University for your car."

The drive to Trent's was silent; both of us enmeshed in our own memories and in each other's pain. He lived about fifteen minutes away from me, in a luxurious apartment tower. As I pulled into the porte cochere, Trent let me know how much he appreciated my companionship and support. We agreed on what time I'd pick him up the next morning.

CHAPTER 15

Before I left to pick him up, Trent phoned and asked me to bring the girls with me so we could go exploring. That sounded great to me. I pulled in front of his door accompanied by Joan and Susan's giggles of anticipation. They thought it funny that I, who usually had everything planned, didn't know where we were going.

It was a quick drive over to the university. Trent transferred all our belongings into his Explorer. He told us that since we were going out into the country, he'd rather have it just in case we decided to go off road. It didn't take too long before we felt like visitors venturing into a new land. The importance of our civilization faded before the grandeur of the mesas.

Their morning colour was burnished gold. Walking around the base of these monuments to time shakes one's preconceived notions of what time is. The very sun was a constant reminder that time passes inexorably; the sun was very insistently bringing us this message through our eyes. The golden mass that loomed over us changed colour quickly. The shadows thrown by the sun constantly changed. I remember looking up to a deep shadow halfway up the mesa. At first it was a black, sinister opening. Just fifteen minutes later the darkness developed hues of blue, stricken through with gold. It was mesmerizing. My other senses translated the timelessness of the mesa. Under my feet were tiny pebbles that crunched. The wind was their mother; their mother who sang around the mesa over centuries of time until they were born. How long had these pebbles been scattered around the mesa? They must have been there long before anyone from Europe even conceived that there were parts of the world unknown to them. I can only imagine the Anasazi when they came to this land. It would have been impossible not to be awed by this land. Their identification with the substance of their space had to have brought spiritual awe. This was mother earth. Individuals were dominated entirely in this part of mother earth; they were at her mercy and she demanded tribute from them.

Other than a constant lookout for snakes and scorpions, I too felt that awe. How quiet that space was. It demanded inward reflection. Just as when we lived in Lethbridge, and I'd walk the river valley, I let my thoughts drift to Patrick. He too is part of mother earth. His birth belonged to nature; he would not be denied. I am always comforted with such thoughts; I somehow feel that nature is protecting him, and allowing him the cycle of life. Almost inevitably that cycle intersects with mine.

At these times I try to send my love to Patrick. I always picture Patrick, or his mom and dad, thinking or talking about us. I want them to know that I'm doing well, that my cycle continues, as does theirs. I want Patrick to know in his bones that I await him; I await him when it is his time to seek me out. Time is again challenged in this magnificent setting. While thinking of Patrick I heard Trent laughing as he chased Joan and Susan around the mesa. I heard his warnings that they shouldn't run too fast or the pebbles might trip them up. The next remark I heard from them was Trent telling them that we were going to climb part way up the mesa.

"There you are. Didn't you hear me calling?" asked Trent.

"I have to admit that I didn't." I said as I drew up beside them.

"Mom, Mr. James is going take us to see some painting on the walls." Susan told me.

Trent leaned over and asked softly, "Doesn't it seem too formal for Joan and Susan to call me that?"

"What do you suggest?", I asked him.

"Since I hope to see them often, would it bother you if they called me Uncle Trent?"

"They have a special uncle in Lethbridge and I think that is a good idea." We soon sat down in the shade of a lone tree, and I told the girls that Trent would like them to call him Uncle Trent. They reacted like I thought, throwing their arms around him and kissing his cheeks. He hugged both of them and then cracked the whip and moved us onward and upward. Joan got to the pictographs first, and by the time we rounded the corner, was intently peering at them.

"Uncle Trent, these are like the ones at Writing–On-- Stone Park. The only thing different are the animals."

Trent asked me where that park was, and I explained that it was south of Lethbridge, almost on the border. It is another one of those spots that encircle the earth and demand introspection. You approach the park across the flat prairie, and just as you drop down into the river valley, you are teased by a glimpse of the past. The hoodoos begin to stand guard as you wind your way down the hill. They grow in number and size until you reach the treed riverbanks. There they stand as row upon row of sentinels. If they only they could tell us what they've witnessed.

The Blackfoot Confederation told their story in the pictures that they left in place. This was their sacred area in which to pray for a vision. The praying was accompanied by fasting and communion with the land. Those blessed by the Great Spirit and granted a vision left pictures sketched into the soft stone. Animals and people are portrayed.

Over one hundred years ago, the pictures began to change. Pictures showed men with beards and rifles. Those pictures showed the beginning of the end. Within a short time, the RCMP built a fort across the river. Their job was to keep profiteers, the so-called traders, from crossing into Canada. Presumably they weren't very busy, since there are numerous names of those posted there, scratched into the rock. The significance of the place was lost to them, as they added their graffiti. I could have gone on forever, but suddenly I saw movement on my right side. I jumped up, grabbing the girls as I did. I backed up until my back was pressed against the warmth of the mesa. Trent laughed, jumped up and shooed a scorpion up the path.

"They generally don't bite people, unless they crawl into someone's shoe. They really don't like being stepped on." We all stared at Trent through his explanation, and then informed him we were ready to head back down the trail. The sun was painting the mesa from a different angle, using shades of umber and ochre. The sky seemed to echo the stone, and we were treated to a radiant sunset. We walked around the base to make sure that we hadn't left any garbage behind us.

Joan and Susan didn't fall asleep the minute they hit the highway, like when they were little, but they both sat quietly, rewinding the images of the day. Once we were all back at our house, Trent and the girls revived themselves with rowdy play in the pool. Our supper was almost ready. Before we left I had everything organized; all that was left to do was throw the Hawaiian ribs on the barbeque. That is what we call them anyway. A friend went to Maui for a holiday and obeyed the order given to her by her friend/travel agent. There is a market called Azeka's, and they are famous for their ribs. These ribs are marinated in a secret sauce and the taste is unbelievable, after you throw them on the barbeque for a couple of minutes per side.

My friend approximated the sauce, and complains that it still isn't quite right, but to me they are delicious. All that was left for me to do was put the rice on, and toss the salad. When I turned to set the table I was surprised to see

Joan, Susan and Trent finishing the job. "Mom, Uncle Trent told us that we should set the table, because you've been busy cooking since we got back.", said Joan.

"Thanks honey. Here are the glasses. Can you fill them with water please?"

"Sure, Mom. Do you want water or juice?", Joan asked.

"I'll stick with ice water, thank you."

"Uncle Trent, what do you like to have for a drink with supper?"

"Joan, I think I'll have the same as your mom. I always have water with dinner. I'll run and change out of this bathing suit. Come on Susan, I'll race you for the bathroom."

Trent chased Susan out of the kitchen and I could hear her squealing as they rounded the corners. I smiled to myself as I reflected on how lucky Joan and Susan were to have two wonderful male role models in their lives. First they had Uncle Chris, and now Uncle Trent.

While I poked through the fridge to see what salad dressing we had, I realized that Trent was more animated, closer to the man I knew in Edmonton. I decided that Susan and Joan were as good for him as he was for them. I knew that at times he looked at them and saw what should have been in his life; despite that pain, their energy allowed him to move past that pain.

After Trent and the girls did the dishes, we piled into his 4 x 4 and drove over to the university to pick up my car. We opened the windows and waited until the heat dissipated before we got in. Joan and Susan gave Uncle Trent a good night kiss, and hopped back into the car. Trent and I stood leaning against his car as he told me that for the first time since Nina and Julia died, he had a wonderful day. I told him how much we had all enjoyed it, and said good-night. The girls waved good-bye as I backed up and headed home.

CHAPTER 16

"What are we going to do tomorrow, mom?", they both wanted to know. I was very tired at that point and suggested that we play it by ear. They looked at each other and started giggling.

"What's so funny, guys?", I demanded.

Joan volunteered the answer, "Mom, you always have our days planned. You are starting to sound like Mansi."

"You're right. Maybe now that I've finished school, and this move has happened, I can relax a little." We pulled into the carport, and I told the kids to get ready for bed. I didn't get any argument. Both were exhausted from the busy day. I could hear the water running as they brushed their teeth, and by the time I went into one room and then the other, they were struggling to keep their eyes open.

Both murmured the same thing to me. "I really like Uncle Trent, mom. When is he coming over again?"

"Soon, I'm sure. Goodnight, Honey."

I wandered through the house restlessly; finally I poured a cold glass of juice and sat on the edge of the pool. My mind was doing its jumping trick again; no one thought held my attention. I was very aware of my body, however. I kept shifting, trying to get comfortable. I failed. I felt sweat trickle down between my breasts, and that made up my mind. I always wanted to swim as God intended us to be.

I stood up, went to the patio door to see if the girls were still sleeping. They were, so I pulled my tank top off. I pulled my bra off. Then I bent over and pulled my shorts and panties off. I felt marvelous as the wind dried the sweat from my body, unbelievably giving me goose bumps. I walked through the darkness of the backyard and stood with my toes in the water. The water slipped over my body, caressing me. I felt a freedom that I had never felt before.

I lost track of time as I lazily swam back and forth, and floated. Floating provided a new sensation. My breasts were above the water and cooled by the breeze. It was as if they were separate from me, and for the first time, I truly was aware of their sensations. Almost simultaneously a thought leapt into my mind. I fantasized that Trent was with me in the pool. The fantasy ended as soon as it had begun. I was shocked that I was thinking of him in a sexual way. I truly can say that since Robert left me, I hadn't thought of any man in that way. I tried to rationalize those feelings by telling myself that I was merely reacting to what had once been a taboo relationship. My conscious mind may have bought that explanation, but my mind, during sleep embellished the possibilities.

I slept in the next morning, and woke to Susan and Joan arguing about which cereal to bring me in bed. "I'll take a small bowl of each - I can't make up my mind." Soon they both joined me in bed, and we crunched on our cereal while watching *Tiny Toons* adventures. "Do you guys want to do anything special today?"

"Emily wants us to go over to their house this afternoon. She said they have a surprise." Joan told me.

"What time do they want you to go over?", I asked them.

"I'm not sure, Mom," said Susan. I reached over their head and phoned Mansi to see if she did want the girls over, and if so, what time?

"I was just going to call you. Can you come over with the girls at two o'clock?"

"Sure we can. What's the surprise?" I asked her. I thought it was just for the girls.

"You'll have to wait until you get here." Mansi laughed. "See you then."

The day became hot quickly, so we changed right from our nighties into our bathing suits. We spent most of the time in the water, just getting out to grab a bite for lunch. The time must have sped up, for suddenly it was 1:30. We hurried into the house, and each had a shower, washed our hair, combed it, dressed and then we walked down the street. We noticed a few extra cars parked in front of their house, and rang the bell.

Just as the door opened I heard a baby's gurgle. Mansi quickly drew us into their living room. A beautiful teenager sat in the recliner, holding a newborn. I quickly looked at Mansi, and confirmed my guess that the teenager was related to her. Joan and Susan rushed directly to see the baby. Already they knew the baby's name, Martha Anne.

"Mom, look at Martha. Look at all her black hair; she looks like Halona's baby cousin." demanded Joan.

"Clare, this is my niece Maria, and her little girl.", was the introduction made by Mansi.

"Maria, you have a beautiful baby. I think she looks just like you."

Maria was very shy, and just glanced up long enough to say thank-you. She held onto Martha tightly, as Joan and Susan looked at her. "Would you like something to drink?" Mansi asked us. She looked at me and nodded toward the kitchen.

"I'll give you a hand." I told Mansi after almost everyone responded to the offer of a drink. Just in the short distance to the kitchen I noticed the change in Mansi and Kele's home. There was a lot of baby furniture and clothes. I brought the glasses to the table while Mansi mixed up the lemonade. She got to the point very quickly.

"Maria just had her baby two days ago in Santa Fe. She is only fifteen and doesn't feel that she is ready to look after Martha, so we'll take her until Maria finishes high school." Mansi looked at me, and seemed surprised at my reaction.

"Do you mean you are adopting her?"

"Oh no, we'll just look after her until Maria is ready for her. Don't you do that in Canada?"

"No, if you don't take your baby home from the hospital, that means you've decided to put the baby up for adoption." I explained.

"Does your family bring the baby home?" asked Mansi. I realized that she didn't understand adoption as it is practiced in Canada. So I told her that strangers picked who was going to adopt the baby, and that you never again saw your baby.

She looked at me as though I were nuts. "How can mothers do that? Why don't the relatives look after the baby so the mom can visit the baby until she brings him home?" she asked me. I had to turn away. I grabbed some napkins from the drawer, and tried to regain my composure.

In all truthfulness I could only reply, "I don't know. That is the law. I'm adopted and I don't know who my parents were, or even what my cultural heritage is. My adoptive family is Irish, and so I call myself Irish, but I'm not sure."

With mutual astonishment on our parts we took the drinks and cookies into the living room. Once everyone was finished, Maria gave Martha a bottle, took her into a bedroom to change the baby, and then came out, red eyed but composed. "I think dad wants to leave for home now." she said. She placed Martha in her Auntie's arms. The silent man in the corner, whom I was introduced to earlier, as Mansi's brother, stood and nodded. Juan told us that the other three children at home would be expecting them home for supper. He held his granddaughter, spoke to her in Spanish, blessed her and kissed her. He then handed Martha back to his sister.

"We'll try and come down next weekend." he told Mansi. I could see that Maria was trying to control the tears that were forming in her eyes. She wasn't successful, and ducked her head as she turned and left. Susan and Joan sat in stunned silence and looked from Martha to me to Mansi; not understanding.

I thought I'd better explain the different custom here. I prayed they wouldn't say anything about Patrick. Somehow they picked up on my silent prayer, and they concentrated on Martha. Mansi took them down to the hall to the room that would be Martha's. Her crib was all set up, and her clothes were in the dresser. Joan and Susan looked at them all, and showed me all the little frilly dresses they found hanging in the closet. "These are too big for Martha, aren't they Mom?" asked Joan.

"It won't take her long to grow into them. Aren't these the cutest little things you saw?" I asked them both. Susan and Joan both agreed. Mansi bundled Martha up, in a very light blanket, and laid her on her side. We all quietly tip toed out of the bedroom.

"Auntie Mansi, how come you didn't tell us that you were getting a baby?" Joan wanted to know.

"I didn't know until yesterday. Maria's oldest sister was going to take Martha, until Angelina's baby ended up in the hospital. They thought she'd be home in a day or two, but yesterday they found out that she has a more serious heart problem than they thought. Their little girl will have to spend quite a bit of time in the hospital, so we all decided that it is best this way. Maria will be able to come from Santa Fe every week. Martha's abuelo is in Albuquerque a couple times a week because of his job, so he'll see her a lot. Besides, I haven't had any little ones since Emily was four. That time, we had the cutest little guy; my cousin is his abuela -- his grandma. That is how we do it down here. Alexandro was four days old when he came to live with us, and then when he was almost two he went home to his momma and abuela. They live on the other side of the river. His momma finished high school and finished her first year at the university, before she knew that she was ready to look after him."

"I'm so glad that you shared your surprise with us, Mansi. You are very lucky to have Martha with you. I'm sure you'll be seeing more of the girls now. They just love little babies. I think we'll head home now though. I still don't know what we're going to have for supper. I still have to do some grocery shopping for this coming week. See you later." I called as we walked down the sidewalk.

The girls talked to one another on the short walk home; they sensed my need for some time. When we were home they decided to watch TV and see some of the shows that were new to them. I methodically looked through the cupboards, making a list of those things I'd need to buy for the next week. I wasn't up to cooking anything new for supper, so I added pasta to my list.

A lot of other people must have been low on groceries as well since Safeway was packed. By the time we were home, had the groceries unpacked and dinner on the table, it was almost 7:00. We were a quiet threesome as we tidied the kitchen up and had our showers. Both girls surprised me when they told me that they were sleepy and wanted to go to bed early.

I think their emotions were roiling around inside them, but they weren't ready to talk about them. I tucked them in, and then restlessly wandered through the house. I finally gave in and went into the bedroom and knelt on the floor in front of my dresser. I pulled the bottom shelf open and dug under the clothes for the memory box I kept. I pulled it out and over to the bed. I sat with my back supported by the bed, and opened the box

His scent still lingered on his sleeper; when I rubbed it against my face I might as well have been kissing the softness of his cheeks. The tears that had been burning within since this afternoon finally flooded over my eyelids. Why couldn't someone have looked after Patrick for me? Maria may be separated from Martha, but not permanently, and whenever the need is there, she can visit Martha or call and see how she is. Martha will always know who her mother is; she'll probably be living with her mom in a couple of years from now. It won't be hard on her, because she'll have a relationship with Maria from the start.

Patrick won't know me. The government will try and pretend that his adoptive parents are his biological parents. I know that they are his parents; they look after him day after day, month after month and year after year. But that does not change the fact that they are not his biological parents.

What will he be told about me? Will they picture me as someone who didn't care about him and threw him away? Will they gently explain that I wasn't able to look after him? What will he believe deep in his heart? Will he be mad at me for not bringing him home with me? Will he understand that I did what I thought was best for him?

Why do we demand that mothers in our culture who cannot look after their children at a particular time, be punished the rest of their lives? What other mothers are not allowed to know what their child looks like, what their child is like, and even at the most basic level, if our children are alive and healthy? We are condemned to a life of wondering; we are condemned to a life centered around a void. Isn't this solution kinder, more humane? Part of the problem is that for society to show such compassion it must first offer forgiveness. Our society isn't yet ready to forgive. By the time my mind reached these conclusions I was exhausted and crawled up onto my bed. Sleep was merciful and came almost immediately.

CHAPTER 17

"Mom, it's time to get up!" That bit of news started my day off. I managed to open my eyes to see Joan standing in the doorway, already dressed. "I gave Susan her cereal and juice. She is getting dressed now. We have to leave in fifteen minutes!"

"Oh, Joan! Thank you for waking me up. I guess I forgot to set the alarm. Will you make me a couple pieces of toast for me, while I jump into the shower?" I'm so lucky to have such a wonderful daughter. She nodded and disappeared. It is certainly handy to be able to shower quickly. My thick hair is a blessing. I don't have to wash it every morning, and if it looks awful, I can just put it up and out of the way.

By the time we were backing down the driveway, we were only two minutes behind schedule. The girls hopped out at Mansi and Kele's house and rushed in to see Martha. Kele's car wasn't there, so he obviously wasn't running behind schedule.

When I walked into our lab, he was just sitting down with a fresh cup of coffee and was studying our latest data. I hate being late or feeling late, so I rushed around to get organized. I could feel Kele's black eyes on me; wondering and worrying. He didn't say anything about it to me, thankfully. I wasn't ready to share that part of me yet. By the end of the day we had both come to the conclusion that we wanted to travel to our test sites and run some in-field studies. We chose Wednesday for our escape from the city.

The next morning Kele told me that Mansi asked the girls to stay for supper with her on Wednesday so we wouldn't have to rush back. Tuesday evening was busy as both girls needed some help to complete their homework. They went for a quick swim in the pool, showered and then were more than ready for bed. I noticed that they were going to bed earlier than when in Canada. I think that the quick sunset is the answer. In Alberta, we're used to a long twilight, most especially in the spring, and kids play outside a lot longer.

I organized everything for the morning so we wouldn't have to rush. I packed each girl's knapsack not only with their school things, but bathing suits, towels and thongs. I dug out my work boots, my hat, sunscreen, and my field kit. By the time I was done, I was sticky with sweat and decided a dip in the pool would be wonderful. I went into my bedroom, undressed and grabbed a towel. After the freedom of my swim the other night I planned on not wearing a bathing suit, unless I had to; that is during the day, and with the girls.

The slight breeze dried my body before I reached the pool, and diving in gave me goose bumps. What a wonderful way to relax in the evening! As I floated, the stars glittered above me, appearing close enough to touch. My mind drifted along with my body, and I suddenly realized that my thoughts were again straying to Trent; wishing that he was in the pool with me. My fantasy rolled along and supplied all the details.

I stopped floating at the end of my fantasy and tried to think rationally about Trent. He was a work colleague, but someone whose research efforts were following another path. He and I were definitely able to talk to one another about our feelings, and yet we were already comfortable with our silences. We respected each other's work, and we both knew that we were heading back to Canada within a set period of time.

My mental list gave me enough information to decide two things. If Trent initiated a deeper relationship, I would happily respond. I knew I'd have to tell him about Patrick. Even in the short period of time we had, I felt the constraint of watching what I said, and felt the tension of should I tell him now or wait until later. I decided to ask Trent for supper on Friday evening.

With the decision made, I went back to floating, apparently my most open position for fantasy. The wind picked up, rattling the drapes. I got out of the pool, dried off and padded through the house, closing some windows, tying some curtains back. I wasn't sleepy when I climbed into bed, but I knew the next day would be very busy. I started reading and the next thing I knew, the alarm was going off. I was anxious to get going, and as soon as the girls were ready I dropped them off with Mansi. Kele and I went out in his 4x4, since it was more suited to the terrain.

We drove further than I had yet been from Albuquerque. The air was refreshingly cooler as we climbed in altitude. Once at our test sites, we quickly checked the crops, and were pleased with their growth. Our control crops suffered in comparison. We started collections for the tests that we planned on doing.

The morning sped by; suddenly it was lunch time. I packed a lunch for both of us, and it turned out that Mansi had the same thought. We had a multicultural lunch. Potato salad, bread, ham and fruit combined with tamales for a taste treat. I brought salt as seasoning, Kele brought chilies. He brought a variety of peppers with him in deference to my Canadian tongue; they ranged from mild to hot, to four alarm. I hadn't been brave enough yet to try the top of the line, but I was becoming adjusted to hot peppers.

The time rolled around to one o'clock and I began to see the wisdom in taking an afternoon siesta. My eyes fought the urge to close and surrender to the heat. Kele noticed and decided that it was best that I rest; it was apparent that my body wasn't acclimated yet. I dozed in the shade of the car for an hour or so, and then felt able to get back to work.

The rest of the afternoon was busy with more testing and discussion about the new test plots that we were going to start the following month. We left the site around five o'clock and drove back to Albuquerque. Once again the vistas that surrounded us filled me with peace. Kele began telling me how much he enjoyed having Martha with them. He told me that she was a happy baby, who slept well, and already gurgled at them. She took her bottle well, and tolerated the attention given to her constantly by Emily and Neil.

I told him that I, too, had been lucky with Joan and Susan. I went into their house for a few minutes and, upon the insistence of the girls, sat with Martha in my arms. I had loved it when my girls were that age, and cuddled Martha while memories of my babies flooded through me. I pulled myself away to gather the girls; I was exhausted and still had chores to get done that evening.

When I awoke the next morning, I was reminded of muscles that hadn't been used for awhile. Rolling over was in itself a chore, getting out of bed was agony. It served me right for allowing myself to get out of shape. I didn't have any excuses not to exercise now, since I had a pool in the backyard. I decided then and there that I was going to use it for more than relaxing and fantasizing

I wish I could say I jumped into my bathing suit and ran out to the pool; instead I eased into my suit, and slowly made my way to the pool. Almost immediately I felt the soothing effects of stretching in the water. I was actually able to swim a few lengths before it was time to get out.

CHAPTER 18

We were busy that day since we had to correlate all data from our field tests the day before. During lunch there was great excitement among our colleagues about our preliminary findings. Some of their questions led us to new trains of thought. The afternoon was spent answering some of those questions, and in turn, we modified some our plans for our new test plot. At the end of the day, Trent and I walked to our cars together, and I confirmed with him that he was still able to come to dinner

"I wouldn't miss it. I want to see Joan and Susan again. I really enjoyed taking the three of you to the mesa last weekend. We'll have to take another trip soon," he told me.

"I know the kids would love to. They really enjoyed your company and are very happy that you are coming over tomorrow. I'll see you in the morning. Goodnight, Trent."

I made sure that I had all the necessary ingredients for the next day's supper. Earlier in the week, I had gone to many different grocery stores looking for canned plums. I finally found them in a tiny grocery that I just happened to walk by. One thing I did need was the white wine; it felt odd just to walk to our local Safeway and pick it up. I've always enjoyed setting an interesting table when I have guests.

When I was running around looking for the plums, I had come across a house wares store. I couldn't believe the prices; they were incredibly low. I will admit that I indulged myself; of course rationalized by the low price. I picked up new serving dishes and accessories that complemented the dishes I already had. I don't think everything has to match exactly.

I loved candles when I was in university, and I couldn't resist their allure in the store. The candles I bought must have been five inches across, and I found wonderful, deep holders. I wanted such holders so I could place them on the patio, as well as inside, without worrying about them being blown out. Joan and Susan were pyromaniacs like their mother and loved having them flicker throughout the house. I made it a strict rule that someone had to be in the room at all times, and definitely, candles weren't allowed in their bedrooms.

I set the dining room table that evening, and fussed with it until I was satisfied that it was pleasing to the eye. Every time I set a table or plan a meal, I can see my Grade 9 home ec teacher, Mrs. Wolfe. She not only taught us how to cook, she taught us that presentation and visual interest were an integral part of the meal. I can still see her informing us that your meal plan should not only be nutritious, but should offer a variety of texture and colour. I'm sure she'd be appalled if someone served chicken breast, mashed potatoes, and cauliflower. I can still evoke a mental picture of Mrs. Wolfe as she described that particular sin. She taught us that we showed our love, our respect or our friendship, when we took the time to create a welcoming table, whether for guests or for family.

I judged the table to measure up to her standards, and went into the kitchen to bake a cake. I found that the only time to bake in this climate was early in the morning or later in the evening. Joan and Susan stayed up long enough to help with the chocolate covered beaters and bowl. The house smelled wonderful as the cake baked. I watched TV until it was time to take the cake out. When I turned the cake out of the Bundt pan, the cake came out just as it should. I dusted it with icing sugar and set it in the fridge to cool. You can't leave baking out on the counter to cool; you'd attract bugs.

I could feel my body getting stiff once again, and headed out to the pool. My towel was already there, so all I had to do strip off. Just the cooling air against my skin revived me; the water enveloped and cushioned my muscles. My mind definitely had made a connection between the pool and thoughts of Trent. When I pulled myself from the pool, I was more than a little aware of the question flitting through my brain. Will Trent and I develop a closer, a more physical relationship? I knew what my vote was; however, I also knew that Trent would have to come to the same answer in his own time. I did know that I was going to tell him about Patrick. He had told me all about the tragedy in his life, and it didn't seem fair to hold back what had gone on in my life.

I could hardly wait for the day to end, and when I picked up Joan and Susan, they shared my mood. Susan was first, "When is Uncle Trent coming over Mom?"

"He's coming over at six o'clock. I didn't want him to come until supper was almost ready. Once I'm cooking, will you and Joan help me out, and wash up all the dirty dishes, please?"

Joan quickly told me they'd help out. They weren't just looking forward to seeing Uncle Trent; they could hardly wait for supper, one of their favorites. By five minutes to six, the food was ready, the kitchen was cleaned, and the three of us had changed into summer dresses. I helped Joan light the candles on the table, and then I went outside to the patio with Susan and helped her light the candles there. We heard the bell, and by the time we were back in the house Trent was on his way to us. He was very thoughtful: he presented flowers to me, and mini-bouquets to each of the girls. We all gave him our thanks as we headed indoors to find vases. Both Joan and Susan immediately took theirs into their rooms. I gave him a quick thank-you kiss, on his cheek. I placed my bouquet on the window seat, next to the dining table.

When the rice was ready I served up dinner. I carefully placed the chicken breasts down the middle of my new platter. Then I spooned the sauce over them. The burgundy sauce spilled over them and onto the platter, glistening against the cobalt blue. The Plum Chicken created a masterpiece not only for the eye, but for the nose. The fragrances of cinnamon, sherry and lemon combined in a heavenly scent and wafted throughout the house.

Trent was seated at the opposite end of the table, and helped both Joan and Susan with the platter. He helped them pass the rice, and then laughed with them as a mandarin orange segment slid from the salad spoon, and plopped on top of his rice. Watching Trent with the girls, I could picture him in different circumstances; having supper with his wife and family. If anyone was a family man, Trent was.

He thoroughly enjoyed his meal and asked me where I found the recipe. He liked my story of how I arrived with it. I told him that a friend's sister lived in Paris for awhile, and was given the recipe by a neighbor. It passed from that neighbor, to my friend's sister, to my friend, and to me. "I've only shared it with two people." I told him. "It is one of those recipes that is great when you have company; it tastes great, is easy to make before your company arrives, and there is an interesting story attached."

"I hope I can persuade you to part with it. I love it, and you said it was easy to make. Those are the kind of recipes that I need." he replied.

Joan and Susan tried to drag him off to the pool, but he protested that he was going to help me with the dishes. I shooed them all off; I really didn't have many to do, and it gave me a bit of time to compose my thoughts. I was just putting the dishes away when Mansi and Kele arrived to pick the girls up. Joan and Susan had been invited to go with them to the drive-in. They came out of their bedrooms, struggling to pull their nighties over still damp bodies. Off they went, waving good-bye until the next morning.

Trent and I sat out on the patio, relaxing in the soft, night air. He told me that this night had been what he pictured all the time he was a father and a husband. That seemed to be the opening that I had been waiting for.

"My life hasn't been the one I imagined, Trent. I want to tell you something; I've wanted to since you told me about Nina and Julia, but I couldn't find a right time." Trent sat quietly, giving me an encouraging smile. "The morning that Robert announced he was leaving me, I planned to tell him that I was pregnant. I'm glad I didn't blurt it out before he told me he was leaving. Without him, I at least could make my own decisions

I then proceeded to tell him of our move to Lethbridge, the support I had from my friends, and then of dawning realization that I couldn't raise Patrick. Trent's response was to bring his chair in front of mine, and hold my hand. From somewhere he produced a Kleenex, which I needed by then.

"Oh, Clare, I'm so sorry that you had to go through that. I wish I had been there to help."

I gulped a refreshing breath and started my tale once again. "He was a beautiful baby, Trent. When he lay on my stomach, he looked at me with these wise eyes. It was if he knew that our journey in life wouldn't be together. I almost melted then. My whole being cried out to shout No, I've changed my mind. I wanted to take my son home with me. As always, the practical side of me insinuated itself and asked what kind of home.

"I can to this day feel his body lying in my arms, as I fed him, as I bathed him and as I dressed him. When the social worker came to the hospital to have the papers signed, I felt like I was signing my own death sentence. I held my son in my arms and tried to tell him why I had to make this decision. I lay him in his bassinet, and pushed him down to the nursery. I forced myself to turn away. I had to force my legs to carry me away from him; I was walking to my voluntary death.

I couldn't continue, my tears were streaming down my cheeks as in my mind's eye I saw that scene once again. I will never lose that until the day that I die. Trent pulled me to my feet and enveloped me in a bear hug. He allowed me the sobs that racked my body; he held me as my body shuddered with the memories. When I finally was able to look at his face I was shaken to see tears streaming down his cheeks.

"My God, I don't know how you had the courage to go through with it. I can only imagine what it must have cost you. When I was told about the accident I was absolutely numb with sorrow; but it wasn't a choice I made. My hand wasn't the cause of the pain. I know how much you must love Patrick, in order to put yourself through all the grief that you've had to carry with you." He said just the right thing, and what he said next made him even dearer to my heart. "Do you have any pictures of Patrick? I'd love to see your son."

We went into my bedroom, and sat on the floor as I pulled my memory box out. The pictures were in an envelope. I pulled each out and showed him Patrick with his sisters, with me, and with Carol. He saw pictures of Patrick awake and asleep, and in each outfit we had for him. He intently examined each photograph, and pronounced Patrick to be in my image. He marveled that Joan and Susan had been able to spend time with their little brother.

He asked how I explained it to them. I told him about the invaluable help I was given by friends and professionals. We sat in silence, leaning against the bed, holding Patrick's sleepers; thinking. It was my muscles that made me move. I had to stand up or I might have been stuck on the floor for the night.

"Thank you Trent. Thank you for listening. I hope you understand why I didn't tell you earlier."

"Of course I do. It isn't fair, is it? Why should we both have had such terrible things happen to us? I know you're a good person, and I'm pretty sure that I am, at least most of the time. Do you know what one of the men I worked with, one of those born again Christian types, told me? He said that God must be punishing me for something that I did, or that he had a plan for me to learn something through Nina and Julia's death. In my darkest times I kept going over and over that morning wondering if only I had said something about the weather, that Nina wouldn't have been driving, and the accident would never have happened. Do you think this sanctimonious fool really thought he was being helpful?"

My Irish temper flared on his behalf, "I can't believe that anyone would even consider saying that to you, particularly a so-called religious person."

Trent continued, "I was lucky that someone with more empathy gave my mother-in-law a book called, "When Bad Things Happen to Good People". A Rabbi whose son died wrote it, and he too was bombarded with the platitudes that are spewed around at such times. He seems to equate platitudes as poorly thought out, stock sayings delivered during times of tragedy. He wasn't able to accept that God would kill his son because he hadn't prayed hard enough, or he hadn't followed a rule one time. It is a thin book, but I've read it over many times, and have found it to be the most comforting thing I've come across yet. If you'd like, I'll bring it to you."

"Thank you, Trent, I'd like that." By this time we were in the kitchen, and decided that another piece of cake would go perfectly with our tea. I piled strawberries over the whipped cream, and as I ate, a couple of the berries dribbled down my chin and onto my blouse. "Darn, now I feel sticky all over." My hands were as red as my chin, while I tried to repair the damage. "I know, let's go into the pool." I think I knew what I was suggesting at the time, but it wasn't consciously thought out. Trent walked over to his suit, picked it up, and grimaced.

"My suit is still wet, and it's cold. I hate putting on a wet bathing suit."

Before I could stop myself, I hurriedly told him, "That really isn't a problem. When it is dark, I like to swim in the nude.

I'm sure he read the invitation in my eyes, and we both headed out to the pool. We each went to a chair and laid our clothes across it. I dove into the pool, and the water replenished me; body and soul. We played like children; we played tag, we stood on our hands and we splashed one another. I don't know how long we did that before all of a sudden we met in the middle of the pool.

Trent could stand, I couldn't and I held onto his shoulders. Our eyes met in consent, and we moved toward one another until our lips joined in a kiss, a kiss soft as a feather. We looked at one another and kissed again; this time our passions that had been buried so deeply, were reawakened. We moved to the shallow end, and I stood in the waist deep water, facing him. Gently he followed the outline of my body, with his fingertip.

This time it wasn't the air giving me goose bumps. We were both seized with an urgency that led us to the chaise lounge. For the first time since I was married, I gave myself to another man; for the first time to a man who cared for me. Trent gave himself fully to me, and in doing so, allowed me to give in fully to my passions.

At some point in time, we moved into the house and to my bedroom. We lay there and talked about our feelings, not just emotionally, but physically. Trent and I both agreed that for the time being, we'd keep this new aspect of our relationship private. Unfortunately, that decision forced Trent to get up, dress and go home early in the morning. We made plans to meet on Sunday and take an outing to one of the missions. We kissed at the door, and I felt awful closing it. I really wanted to run out and drag him back inside, but I knew we had made the right decision. We had to be sure about our relationship; we had to find out if there was something more than shared tragedy that bound us. I'd have to be satisfied with our available private time, and the time Joan, Susan and I shared with him.

While I lay in bed waiting for sleep to claim me I compared making love with Trent and having sex with Robert. I only just now knew that Robert hadn't being making love to me. I remember feeling anxious throughout our sex life; would he criticize my body, he would complain that I was too boring, or if I tried something new, he would almost accuse me of having an affair. He'd get mad if I tried to justify myself when I'd tell him that I had read a book, for ideas, since he last complained that I was boring. Then he'd criticize me for being so stupid that I had to read how to have sex. Apparently he thought himself an exceptional lover. I now knew that he highly overrated himself. In reality, he was a selfish lover who cared only for his needs, and nothing of mine.

CHAPTER 19

Joan and Susan were ready when I picked them up at Kele and Mansi's. They insisted that I go in to see little Martha; just as they promised she looked absolutely adorable. She wasn't sleeping, just looking about, from her crib at all the excitement. She looked very much like some of the Blackfoot babies that I'd seen at the school when the moms all descended on the school to pick the children up

Both girls wanted to know, in order of importance; were we going to spend the day with Uncle Trent, and where we were going. By the end of the block they knew we were going to visit San Miguel Socorro Mission, which was only seventy-seven miles south of town. We arrived early enough in the day to avoid the crowds; necessary if you want children to enjoy the experience. We didn't stop for lunch until siesta time, and then found a lovely picnic spot. Once again the girls found reasons to be close to Trent; it was a good thing he had two hands.

My suggestion that we head home for a swim was agreed upon, and it felt wonderful. I felt my cheeks flaming when Trent and I arrived poolside simultaneously. We felt so conspicuous in our bathing suits; we knew what the other was thinking. While swimming I tried to get enthusiastic about dinner, but couldn't even come up with an idea. Trent came to the rescue. He asked me if I had a sitter nearby, and his eyes lit up. "Why don't you phone and see if she can baby-sit tonight? We can go over to my place for supper and we can order pizza for the kids."

It was sort of embarrassing how quickly I accepted the idea. We were lucky, the university student who lived down the block wasn't going out and was happy to baby-sit. While we were waiting for her to arrive, I popped into my bedroom and changed. I chose my dress to match my mood; it was a royal blue, with red and yellow flowers; its bias cut skirt twirled around my legs. Ten minutes later we were on the road, enjoying the evening breeze, driving to my first date in years.

Trent's apartment building was as luxurious inside as it was on the exterior. Crystal chandeliers hung over the lobby, casting romantic light over the love seats hidden among the plants. I certainly anticipated seeing his apartment. What I didn't expect was seeing Trent insert a key into a slot in the elevator control panel.

My quizzical look must have prompted an explanation. Trent grinned shyly and then looked to the floor, "You have to use a key to stop on the penthouse floor." Before I could say anything, he hurried on. "I decided that if I was going to temporarily change my life, with this move, that I'd do it in style. I really hadn't planned on a penthouse, but when I saw it, I couldn't resist it." We stepped out of the elevator and walked a short hallway to his penthouse. Trent opened the door, I entered and felt pulled forward to the balcony. He hadn't even turned the lights on, which would have spoiled the magnificent view

The city spread out, as if a magical carpet, reflecting the stars. I don't know how long I stood there breathing in the view, before I felt Trent's presence behind me. Trent wrapped his arms around me and we stood in companionable silence. After some time, Trent showed me the apartment, and I was totally amazed that the city lights could be seen even from there. I had to laugh when I saw the fireplace in the living room,

"Why would someone put a fireplace in? Would they ever be able to use it?"

"I actually used a fair number of times last winter. Remember that at this altitude there is quite a difference between summer and winter. Joan and Susan will be able to roast marshmallows here, during the winter." Trent told me. "To me the most beautiful thing about the fireplace is this marble surround." I came over and stood next to him, and ran my hands over the green marble, and told Trent that I too loved that type of marble.

"Come on upstairs and I'll show you the rest of the apartment. When my mother came down for a visit, she thought I was nuts to have such a large place, but I love having all this room. My bedroom stays a sanctuary, and my office work remains separate in the office. I can't stand to have the two mix." I walked up behind him, quite happy that the stairs weren't steep, and my knees didn't hurt. He showed me the guest bedroom and bathroom, his office, and finally he ushered me into his bedroom. I had to gasp.

"I can't believe this Trent. This is the furniture I've always wanted; Gibbard, right?"

"Yes, it is. Nina and I started buying it shortly after we were married. It took a little while before we agreed on a style of furniture. I kept dragging her into Scandinavian shops, and when I'd get enthusiastic about something, Nina, rather than saying outright that she didn't like it, would always murmur a rather non-committal response. That was my signal that we weren't finished looking yet. One summer Nina and I were down in Calgary visiting my mom, and were with her when she had to buy some furniture polish. I didn't realize that she went to McArthur's Furniture for it instead of just picking some up at the grocery store

"We went in with her, and she introduced us to one of the owners. Mom and Ken were busy discussing a chair she was considering, so Nina and I wandered through the store. The store was in a wonderful, old, brick building, long and narrow; we climbed to the top floor and worked our way down. On the third floor we rounded a corner and came to a halt. We stood still, and I think we were both holding our breath. The furniture was displayed in a room, and we knew. We both knew. This was the furniture that we would put in our home. We were attracted not only to the style, but to the deep mahogany finish. We entered the room, and followed the lines of furniture with our hands. The four-poster bed was magnificent. The dining room table was elegant; the clean Queen Anne styling gave it the understated beauty that we both responded to."

While Trent talked, I wandered about the bedroom, following the lines of the furniture with my hands. I thought about the heavy oak furniture I lived with during my marriage. Robert came home one evening and told me that he ordered furniture and it would arrive the next day. We had talked about the Gibbard furniture, and I thought that maybe he was going to surprise me with it.

The next morning I raced around the house cleaning, in anticipation of the arrival of the furniture. I just finished when a truck parked in front of the house. When the men started to bring the furniture in, I realized that Robert hadn't considered if I'd like it or not. It was heavy, oak furniture, with hideous, overblown carving. I stood holding my arms across my chest, trying to hide my disappointment while directing where each piece should be placed. My only hope was that he'd only bought dining room pieces, but my hopes were dashed as the men brought in piece after piece.

When they finally left, I slowly walked through the house, trying to come to grips with what I had to live with. I knew there wasn't any point in arguing with Robert; I would have to adapt. It took me awhile to realize that Trent had stop speaking, and I banished all thoughts of Robert from my mind.

"It is absolutely wonderful. All the time I lived with what I had, I could picture what my house would look like if only I could decorate it." I wandered into the ensuite and was thrilled to see something I'd hadn't had for a long time. "This is the only thing I missed when I left our house in Westlock. I loved soaking in the Jacuzzi and reading while I relaxed."

Trent chuckled behind me, "Would you like to try it out tonight?" His hands were already lifting my hair from my shoulders, looking for a zipper.

My voice dropped to a whisper. "It just pulls off." I lifted my arms so he could ease it off my body. When I changed before we left my house, I also changed into silky underwear. I felt Trent's lips run along my shoulder while he undid my bra, and then his hands slipped down my body, hooked my panties, and pulled them from me.

My back felt a chill as Trent moved from me, "Just let me run downstairs for a moment. Do you want to run the tub?" I nodded as he disappeared. I was already laying back in the tub, luxuriating in the deep, hot water. I waited until it was high enough to turn on the jets. The lights were turned off, and the warm flicker of candlelight took over.

Trent must have stopped in the bedroom, he brought a candle in. He stood there, comfortable with himself, and turned the Jacuzzi on. He lay behind me, and we didn't say a word. His hands explored me, and then I turned around and became more familiar with him. Time seemed to stop, only beginning again when the water cooled. Out of the tub, we wrapped ourselves in huge, velvety bath sheets. I padded over the luxurious carpet, and gazed out at the lights. Again we were able to give each other complete fulfillment. We lay curled into one another, until our stomachs reminded us that we really had to eat.

I poked around in Trent's fridge, but he came in and said, "I promised I'd take you to supper. I'll call this restaurant I know, and they'll deliver." It sounded good to me. We sat out on the patio, and shortly the food arrived. I didn't know what he'd ordered, but it certainly smelled good. "This is one of the benefits of living in Albuquerque: barbeque ribs, corn and Spanish rice." Trent told me.

The proof was on our faces, and on our hands. The ribs were heavenly. I make great ribs, but I wouldn't compare the two styles. I leaned back, stuffed. I would have been much happier if I didn't have to get up, dress and leave. The clock wouldn't allow me; I told the sitter to expect me home around eleven. While Trent drove me home he asked, "Do you find this as fantastic as I do? You and I seem so right." He glanced at me, waiting for my reaction.

"Yes, I feel the same way. In some ways it is very scary. We have a history, but we've only had a relationship since I moved here. It is hard to believe the past two days. Time seems to have sped up. I think we need to continue what we are doing and give ourselves time. If this is as right as it feels, I don't want to do something wrong." When I finished, he let out a breath, and then smiled. We drove the rest of the way in silence, holding hands. Soon we kissed goodnight and Trent walked the baby-sitter home.

CHAPTER 20

The weeks went by, spent in the same way. Trent, the girls and I would go on an outing each weekend. Joan and Susan became even fonder of Trent, if that was possible. Joan was old enough to pick up subtle clues in behavior.

One day when we stood at the sink peeling carrots she asked, "Mom, Uncle Trent is your boyfriend, isn't he?"

I refuse to lie to my kids, so I told her, "Yes, honey, Trent is my boyfriend. We didn't want to tell you until we knew how we really felt about each other. Sometimes two people can be drawn together because they share a common history. You've seen pictures of Nina and Julia, and know that they died. We've gone through a lot too; dad leaving us, the move to Lethbridge, and the most important thing, Patrick. Time is what we need to see if we really love one another. Do you understand, Honey?"

"I think so, mom. When will you know?" she asked. Kids sure cut through situations and arrive directly in the middle.

"I wish I knew honey. All I know is that neither of us wants to go too fast. If I marry again, it will be the last time, and I don't want to make any mistakes. I don't want anyone or any situation to hurt you again." That was the best answer I could give her at that point. "Can I ask you do something for me, Joan?"

"Sure Mom."

"I'd like you to keep this a secret between us older girls, just for now. I don't want to get Susan excited about this until we know if this is a serious relationship." Joan came over to me, and gave me a hug, telling me that she would try not to say anything to Susan.

"What if she asks me if Trent is your boyfriend? Should I lie?"

"No honey, don't lie. If Susan asks you questions like that, you could say things like, I think so, and then let me know. I'll talk to Trent this week. Grab the lid of the pot, please." We cooked together, and Joan told me all her adventures of the day.

I wrenched myself back into reality. When I think of our year in New Mexico, I can picture things so clearly. Yes, today is Patrick's first day of Grade One. I still think of him as Patrick. I don't know if they kept that name for him or if he has a new name. I am sure that his mom is sitting at their house, wondering and worrying about his first long day. I wonder if she is thinking about me at all. It must be easier for her to picture what I'm like, rather than vice versa. She has all the information that I provided about myself: health history, the circumstances regarding Patrick's birth and how I arrived at my decision.

All I know is that there is a couple somewhere in the province that couldn't have children, and dearly wanted them. I have to continue putting my faith in an unseen, unknown person; the person who gave Patrick to them. I admit that when I think of Ms. Stone, my faith is shaken. I pray that she isn't typical of all social workers. When I look at the clock it is just after 12 o'clock and Patrick is probably sitting down with his new friends to have lunch. I must have known that this would be a day to wander through my memories, because I took the day off work. Joan and Susan wouldn't be back from school until five-thirty so I give in to my urges to dwell in the past.

The Christmas we spent in Albuquerque is one I'll never forget. Trent, the girls and I went tree hunting wearing shorts. That was quite a change from freezing to death back in Canada.

I was overruled and we came home with a huge tree. Trent set it up for us, and strung the lights. He reminded me of my dad when he flat on his back placing them. The big difference was the lights; they were shaped like red chilies!

We had a Ponderosa Pine, very different than our previous trees, so the new lights didn't look odd. We decorated throughout the house, in anticipation of our visitors. Carol, Chris, and Shannon were coming for a two-week visit, and we were all excited. Joan and Susan could hardly wait to see how much Shannon had grown, and they wanted to take her to see Martha. I planned on a lot of girl talk with Carol; I hadn't told her much about Trent, I wanted her honest opinion of him, not clouded by mine

The day finally came, and we piled into the car for the trip to the airport. We were there early and walked up and down the concourse, trying to pass the time. Suddenly a stream of people flowed through the International arrival area: Men in suits, business women carrying their briefcases, students, but for what seemed the longest time, no friends. Finally, I saw buggy wheels and then the faces. Joan and Susan spotted them at the same time and rushed forward, flinging themselves into Carol and Chris's arms. Next, little Shannon was covered in kisses. It is amazing how good a dear friend's hug feels after such a long time.

We tried to catch up on the past months while they did the paperwork for their rental car. After shifting all of their luggage into their car, I gave them quick directions to the house just in case we got separated. We arrived home without losing them, and then they were given the grand tour.

"The house is wonderful, Clare. It's just like you described it in your letters - I pictured it almost exactly like this. Oh, look at the pool. I can hardly wait to use it." Carol told me.

"Not too many people here swim at this time of the year -- they think it is too cold. We still do on the warmer days. We're lucky that for some reason, we have a heated pool. Want to go for a swim tonight?" I asked her knowing what her answer would be.

We went back into the house and found that Chris and the girls had all of the luggage put away, and the rented playpen was occupied. I prepared the supper earlier in the day so it didn't take long to have it ready. I served tamales for supper. Joan and Susan loved being able to show their uncle and auntie how to unwrap the cornhusk.

All my lessons with Mansi finally paid off -- she had me throw out a lot of tamales before she was satisfied. I did better with the sopaipilla that I served for desert. Chris and Carol drooled when they saw the billowy shapes, drizzled in honey. We gathered in the kitchen and cleaned up, talking the entire time. Before supper, Chris had promised the girls he'd go swimming with them, so we eventually shooed them off to the pool. Carol and I enjoyed each other's company, as we sat over our tea. I held Shannon in my arms, and delighted in her softness, and how she was now gurgling, trying to join in. I passed her to Carol so she could have her supper. The sounds from the pool quieted, and soon they trooped in. By this time Shannon had finished her supper and was asleep in my arms.

"Night, Mom." called both girls. "Uncle Chris told us that he brought us a new book, so he's going to read it to us before we go to sleep." I blew them kisses.

Chris told us, "I'll put Shannon to bed, read to the girls and then I'm going to relax in front of the TV. Why don't you two go for a swim?" We didn't need a second invitation. Carol headed off to their bedroom and returned with her swimsuit.

When she saw me heading to the pool without mine, Carol asked, "Do you keep your suit out at the pool?"

I beckoned her forward, and told her of my discovery. Soon Carol was enjoying it as well. We talked as we swam, we talked as we exercised and we talked as we lounged in the spa. I told her more about Trent, just enough that she would get the idea that we spent a lot of time together. The next day, we were invited over to Trent's apartment for a BARBEQUE. He expected us whenever we had finished our sightseeing for the day.

I took them out into the desert. I wanted them to experience it as we had. Carol and Chris immediately sensed the peace and the power that was given by the desert to those people open to the experience. I took them to the same mesa that Trent had first shown us. Unfortunately the colours weren't as vivid since the sun was so much lower now that it had been in December.

We were hungry by the time we were finished, so we stopped at the first restaurant we came to across on the highway. We were going to go to Santa Fe, but decided to wait until we had a whole day. Instead, we spent the afternoon visiting a few of missions that surrounded Albuquerque. Carol and Chris's particular favourite was the Mission of San Agustin de la Isleta. Its age is what I think appealed to them; apparently it was established in 1613.

We spent our time walking on top of the walls and threading our way through the walls that still stood. We headed back to the house in the late afternoon. We were all tired and warm. Shannon had been such a happy baby all day that she startled us when she started to fuss. Once home, Carol took Shannon into the cool living room, and nursed her. I sat with her and talked while Chris, Joan and Susan dove into the pool. I could tell their energy had returned from all the water being splashed.

"I always enjoyed the closeness when I nursed Joan and Susan. I wish I could have nursed Patrick for longer than a few days. I don't even have to close my eyes to picture him nursing. He was just like Joan and managed to hold onto my hair."

Carol peered at me through the gathering darkness, "Does it bother you to be with Shannon?"

"No, please, I didn't mean it like that. I love to see you, Chris and Shannon together. I've known since we moved to Lethbridge that someday you'd be great parents. You were both great with the girls when they really needed you. And you are the same with your nieces and nephews. I will tell you what was hard. You've heard me talk of Kele and Mansi; well this past fall, their family grew temporarily."

I saw Carol look at me questioningly, so I continued. "They took in their niece's baby for a few years until she is ready to look after little Martha. She's still in high school, and just can't be a mom right now. Mansi thought I was odd, for thinking that this arrangement was unusual. She asked me what happens in Canada. When I told her that a mother never sees her child again, she was horrified. She couldn't believe that we'd do that. I can tell you that I bit my lip hard that afternoon. I haven't told them about Patrick. I don't want to take away from their pleasure. Sometimes it is hard to look at Shannon and think that I'd still have Patrick with me right now, if we had the same sort of choice. Children here are thought of just like they are on the reserves at home. Each life is to be treasured, and kept within the family of the tribe."

Shannon fell asleep with her mouth still attached to Carol's breast. There is such closeness between mother and child at that time. We sat in stillness, sharing the time, each with our own thoughts. The solitude was broken with the arrival of three wet, dripping bodies. I shooed them off for showers or baths.

"My baby-sitter will be here in about half an hour, so we'll have enough time to freshen up." Chris appeared and took Shannon and put her in her playpen. Half an hour later the doorbell rang and Angie was ready to take over the kids.

"You'll be at Trent's?" she asked. I told her she was correct, and that I really didn't know how late we'd be. "Don't worry. I have a lot of studying to do, and it doesn't matter to me where I do it."

CHAPTER 21

If I do say so myself, Carol and I looked smashing. We both wore dresses; in my time here I'd learned that they really were the coolest thing to wear. I always felt wonderful wearing my royal blue dress. I felt very feminine in it from the way it draped over me, and swirled around my legs. I pulled up in front of Trent's apartment, and the doorman opened the door for Carol.

"Now this is what I call service." Carol said as she accepted the doorman's help.

Chris was impressed that the doorman knew my name and teasingly said, "Well, we know where you spend quite a bit of your time." I blushed a little when I pulled my penthouse elevator key from my purse. Carol and Chris looked at me, so I thought I'd better tell them, "You need a special key to get to the penthouse." The doors opened and Trent was waiting for us in the lobby. I made the introductions while we turned the corner to Trent's apartment. Chris and Carol were drawn to the patio, as I had been. They talked easily with Trent as we stood in the dining room while Trent served drinks. Trent offered mini burritos as appetizers and salsas that ranged from mild to burning.

Chris started with the hot. After his eyes stopped watering, he decided to downgrade to medium. We all went onto the balcony with Trent so we could talk while he barbecued the pork roast. The aroma was tantalizing, and became more so once he started brushing plum marinade over it. Just as it was coming time to take the meat off the barbeque, I slipped inside to make sure the table was laid like I planned. The chandelier glistened when I turned off the rest of the lights and lit the candles. I saw their silhouettes. Carol had her head thrown back, laughing at something Trent said. Chris was busy helping with the marinade. A definite comfort level had already been established and I could picture the two couples together in the future. It was at that moment that I knew, without any doubt I wanted Trent as my husband, for the rest of time.

Before my mind had a chance to worry over the details; different cities, not in our own country, etc.; they came in. Trent delivered the roast pork to the table and carved at the table. I didn't know people did that anymore, although that is what I remember from growing up; my father always carved at the table. He'd ask what part of the turkey, or how much roast, we'd like, and then cut to order. I had thought everyone did it that way.

The evening passed fluidly. After our meal we sat on the balcony and talked. We all were able to share how our professional lives were going without boring the others not in that field. The moon finally emerged from the shadow of a cloud, and when I glanced at my watch, I saw that is was well after midnight. "I hate to break things up, but I'm really tired, and we'll be up early when Shannon wakes up in the morning."

Trent walked us down to the car, and after glancing hesitantly at Chris and Carol, kissed me good-night. We were silent as we drove through the soft evening breezes, each lost in our own thoughts. Finally Carol broke the silence.

"He's the one isn't he?"

I could only reply truthfully. "I was pretty sure before tonight, now I'm really sure. When I saw him out on the balcony with you two, and I saw that everyone was so comfortable with each other, something came over me, and I knew. Trent and I have talked about this relationship, and we've been trying not to rush so we'd know if really cared about one another, or if we were only drawn to each other through tragedy. I know now, I wonder if he does?"

I had trouble falling asleep that night, despite being tired. I wanted Trent beside me in my bed. I wanted him there to hold me, to comfort me, and to make love to me, I wanted him there every morning, and I wanted him to sit with me as we read the paper, and as we did the grocery shopping. The last thing I remember before falling asleep was asking myself, "What next? What do I say, or should I say anything?"

The morning came very early, when Shannon woke to be fed. I got up and joined Carol while Shannon nursed. I brought her a cup of coffee, and shocked myself. I clearly remember putting her coffee cup down beside her, and watching Shannon's little hands hold onto her mother's breast.

"I want to have Trent's baby!" It was a good thing Carol wasn't drinking her coffee; it would have burned Shannon.

"I didn't think I'd ever hear that after Patrick was born," she replied, and continued as I opened my mouth. "I'd be shocked if we hadn't met Trent and spent last night with him. You know he loves you?"

"I can only hope! To be perfectly honest, while I was trying to fall asleep last night, I kept arguing with myself. I told myself to get up and go to him. Then I'd decide that wasn't the sensible thing to do; that I should let him have time."

"Stop being so sensible for once in your life! Give in to your impulses. He loves you and you love him, and he loves Joan and Susan. That's what is important. Go get dressed, right now, and go to him." Carol told me. I looked at my watch and saw that it was only 6:30.

"He'll be in bed still."

Carol interrupted my silent excuses. "That's even better; you'll be the only one who has to get undressed!"

CHAPTER 22

For once in my life I gave into what I wanted. I hurried into my bedroom, stripped, and slipped a sun dress over my naked body. I touched my body with my perfume wand, grabbed my purse and left, without another word. I didn't want to talk myself out of it.

It is amazing that one car trip can at once seem the longest and the shortest of your life. I parked my car in the porte couchere, knowing the doorman would park it for me when his day started. The elevator stood empty. I fumbled for the elevator key. In sixty seconds I was there. The door opened and the lobby stood empty. I could still change my mind and go home; I ordered myself down the hall. I unlocked the door, locked it behind me, and stood leaning against it, quietly seeing last night. The certainty that this was right and good calmed me.

Trent was asleep on his back. I knelt beside the bed and kissed him awake. His eyes opened, two startlingly blue eyes fixed quizzically on me. "I love you Trent. I don't want to live apart." I couldn't say anymore than that; I had to wait for his response.

"I've been waiting for you to say that. I was afraid to tell you, in case by saying it I would push you away." Then Trent spoke through his actions. His hands slipped down the silky dress, caressing me. In silence Trent slipped the straps off my shoulders, found the zipper, lowered it and pulled the dress over my head. I knelt in silence beside him, and offered him my body in silence. He pulled me into bed with him. There wasn't any rush -- we had a lifetime stretching in front of us. We laid in bed enjoying the warmth of the sun over us, when Trent propped himself up on a elbow, and looked down at me.

"Will you marry me? Can I marry into your family? Will you let me be a father to Joan and Susan?"

"That is what I want most in the world, and I know that Susan and Joan love you, and want you in their lives." I hesitated for a minute, looking at the wall opposite the bed, biting my lip.

"I've known you long enough to know that when you bite your lip like that you have more to say. What is it?" Trent asked me, as he reached to turn my gaze on him.

I took a deep breath, and told him my feelings earlier that morning, watching Shannon nurse. He took me in his arms, "I'm so happy you feel that way. I wasn't sure that you'd want another child, now that Susan is in school. After Nina and Julia died, I was sure that I'd never have another child, but almost from the time we met, I could picture our baby." We cuddled and talked, and decided that we wouldn't say anything until Christmas morning.

The next week was hectic while we finished our Christmas shopping and drove all over the place sightseeing. Christmas Eve finally arrived, and we all went to Midnight Mass. Midnight Mass embodies a particular dignity, no matter where it is celebrated. The church was decorated as no other Christmas church we were ever in. Behind the alter, a wall hanging of brilliant colours depicted the Nativity story.

The women of the parish had woven the wall hanging in their traditional manner, and it reflected the heritage of those who made it. A Hispanic Mary rode the donkey, and Joseph, in a sombrero walked beside her. They walked a path bordered by cactus. The weavers created a brilliant star, the star that was to bring a message of hope and love to all. What else is there to say?

Joan was very proud to be a member of the school choir, which sat in the sacristy. Christmas carols were sung to the accompaniment of the birds that flitted through the open windows.

We walked the few blocks home, and tucked in two sleepy girls with reminders that morning came much quicker when you slept. Once they were asleep, "Santa" began his work. It was a lot more fun because I was not alone. We filled the stockings with all the traditional items, except one. We had looked and looked for Japanese oranges in the stores; No one knew what we were talking about. In a pinch we settled for tangerines, which are to be said to bring good luck if they come with a single leaf. We made sure each was topped with just one leaf, but I didn't think we needed it. I had everything I wanted.

Soon the floor beneath the tree was piled high with presents, and we could head to bed. By that time, "Santa," had eaten the milk and cookies set out by the girls. I embraced Carol and Chris as they crossed the room on their way to bed.

"I hope you both know how special and important it is that you are here for me; my first Christmas away from

Canada. I love you both." With kisses exchanged, we all went to bed.

Morning came very early. Joan and Susan yelled at us from the door to get up because Santa had left presents. I heard them rushing to wake Carol and Chris, they wanted to show Shannon her first Christmas. By the time we were all in the living room, Trent had the tree lights on and candles lit, creating special lighting for a special morning. He and I kept exchanging glances, and I wondered if I should say something or not. Finally we were no longer sitting surrounded by a pile of presents; rather, we were almost buried under wrapping paper. I hadn't been able to do that for the girls for a long time. This Christmas, I think they got every present that they wanted, and then some.

Joan spotted something, "Mom, there are three little boxes still under the tree." Trent, who was still sitting on the floor, beat her to them. He slid over to me, and came up onto his knees.

"Clare, will you marry me. Will you let me love you, Joan and Susan? Will you let me be a part of your lives?"

I could only nod yes to each answer before I finally threw my arms around him. I had unwrapped the box, but had not yet opened it. Trent sat me down beside him on the floor and told me to open it. Inside the box was a beautiful ruby and diamond ring. He slipped it onto my finger with Joan and Susan pressing around him to see.

"Joan and Susan, these boxes are for you. I thought it was only right that if I asked your mom to marry me that I should ask each of you. Will you both let me share your lives, and allow me to love you and protect you, to be your dad?"

They each hugged him, knocking him over in the process. Then they opened their presents and held their breath. Trent slipped a miniature ring onto each of their ring fingers. The four of us sat on the floor, huddled together, and I couldn't ask for more. My best friends were with me to witness the beginning of our new family.

CHAPTER 23

Joan and Susan were determined to show Shannon how all of her toys worked, as well as theirs. Finally we all realized that we were starving. Carol and I went into the kitchen and I got her started on the French toast and bacon. I prepared our special treat, papaya with lemon, a heavenly way to start the day. Carol kidded me that she had an idea something like that might happen.

"How come you didn't tell me more about Trent before we came down?"

"You know how much I value your opinion, and I didn't want to influence you in anyway. I was holding my breath hoping that you'd see all of his good qualities. Neither of us wanted to go too fast; it had to be love and not sadness that created what we have. If it wasn't, then we'd be inventing a new tragedy. Now we know that it is love. We love one another for who we are. We know and respect each other's past lives. We can talk about it openly and naturally. I didn't think I'd ever feel like this. I can't say again, because now I know what is like to be truly in love. I can't even describe what I felt toward Robert, but I know now that it wasn't love."

Carol stood in her nightie turning bacon and flipping French toast. "I am so happy this has happened. You deserve it. Do you have any idea about when you'll get married?" I must have looked silly, standing there, mouth open, but nothing coming out. Finally I called out and asked Trent to come into the kitchen.

"Carol just asked me when we're getting married and I realized that was just one of the questions. Where are we going to live? Our jobs are in different cities."

Trent laughed and pulled me into his arms. "Let's eat first and then figure it all out."

With that we took all the food out and sat down to breakfast. Afterwards, the guys washed the dishes, and Carol and I sat with our girls. We enjoyed watching them go from first one toy and then to another. Carol roused herself as Chris came in, and they headed off to give Shannon a bath. She had tried some of the French toast herself, and managed to get syrup in her hair and any other place she could reach. Joan and Susan got dressed, and went outside to ride their new bikes. I doubt they'd be doing that if we were in Lethbridge. Even if there weren't any snow, it would be too cold. Trent and I took advantage of the quiet and had a shower. We lathered one another with the shower gel, my ring sparkled even more than before, if that was possible.

While I washed his back I said, "I bet I know how you decided what kind of ring to get me. You remembered me telling you about that ring I didn't buy when I a chance at that auction. I think it was fantastic that you thought to ask the girls and give them rings, too."

I began to show him my pleasure more directly. Once we were both competing for space on the bathmat, I brought up our future plans, or rather, the lack of them. "I've been thinking since breakfast. Are you really set on living in Edmonton? I'm willing to move from Lethbridge. The reason I'm thinking this way, is that both cities hold bad memories for us. Maybe we should start our lives in a new city. What do you think?"

"I really didn't plan on staying in Edmonton, it just worked out that way. I was offered a professorship after I finished my doctorate, and just never really thought about leaving. After Nina and Julia, I just didn't have the energy to contemplate it. What do you think about meeting at the halfway point, and settling in Calgary?"

I told Trent, "That was what was going through my head. It would be easy enough to visit friends and relatives in either Lethbridge or Edmonton, but what about our jobs? What if we can't both get jobs in Calgary?"

Dried off, we moved into the bedroom and lay in the sunbeams. Trent told me it wasn't a problem for him.

"You probably don't know, and I've never had any reason to mention it, but I don't have to work. I plan on continuing, because I enjoy my work, and my research is just starting to be translated into practical applications." Trent ducked his head and continued. "My mother's family was very wealthy; they were very shrewd investors in land in both Calgary and Edmonton from the end of the 1890's. They also invested in the oil industry early on. The end result was a family foundation for the past sixty years. When the university couldn't fund my project, I presented the foundation with a proposal. The result was that I could hire the associates that I needed for my team, and I built and equipped a new lab. I've been thinking about this over the last few weeks, and I think I could set something up at U of C. The Heritage Trust Fund has attracted a lot of scientists to U of C." Trent looked at me expectantly. I didn't know which news to react to first.

"You're right; I didn't know why you were at U of A. I had no idea that you are rich. Do you really mean you don't have to work?" Trent's cheeks were getting red and it wasn't from the sunbeams.

"It surprises a lot of people. Most people don't know because the foundation is named after my great-grandmother, and uses her maiden name. But yes, I could quit work today if I wanted to. You have to look at this as one very major advantage that we have. We can plan our wedding, we can buy a new house in Calgary, and we don't have to worry about anything else. I think that the formation of our new family should take precedence over everything else. Not too many people are as lucky. Most have to squeeze their family in at the end of a busy work and school day, when everyone is tired. What do you think?"

For the past four years I watched every penny, so that I'd be able to make sure the bills were paid. Now, Trent was handing me the opportunity for all of us to start a new life together, tranquilly. I couldn't foresee anything wrong with that plan. I pinned him under me, and straddled him.

"Okay, if we have to, we'll let life be wonderful." We dressed and called Susan and Joan in.

"Joan and Susan, can you come in here please? Uncle Trent and I are making plans. We thought that Calgary would be a good place to live. We'd be closer to the ski hills, but it is not too far, so if you want to visit your friends in Lethbridge, they could come up or you could go down. What do you think?"

Susan jumped in with her question right away. "Can we go to the zoo?" She had a wonderful time when her ECS class took the bus to Calgary for a trip to the zoo, but when she came home, she complained that they didn't have enough time and didn't see all the animals. She was thrilled with an affirmative answer.

Joan, practical as always, asked if they would have their own rooms if we moved to Calgary. "I just don't think I can share a room with Susan again. I like having my own room, and I'll be in Junior High next year."

"Honey, you'll have your own room, and I think maybe your own telephone in your room. Would you like that?" She almost knocked me over with her hug.

CHAPTER 24

I'll admit that never before have I had a Christmas like that in Albuquerque. Carol and I spent time together getting the turkey ready for the oven. I broke up dried bread, and Carol chopped onion. I told her about what I learned that morning.

"I'm so happy for you, Clare. You deserve this happiness. I think it's great that Joan and Susan are so comfortable with Trent. Wasn't that wonderful of him to get them their own rings? To me that shows me that he is a very thoughtful man. I'll miss having you in Lethbridge, but I think your plan to settle in Calgary is a good one. It is a great start for everyone."

"I know I'll miss living so close to you, Chris and Shannon, but we're not too far. Trent already said he wants a big house so we'll have a permanent guest room. I hope you'll be able to visit often; I don't want Shannon growing up only seeing us once a year. She wouldn't know us, and we wouldn't mean anything to her. Hopefully she'll have a playmate at our house shortly. Trent and I both agreed that it will probably be a good idea to wait around a year before we start a family. We want the four of us to have time to get used to living together, before we add a baby." Carol looked at me, grinning, and I knew she was bursting to tell me something.

"When we gave Shannon her bath this morning I used the home pregnancy kit that I brought with me. It was positive!" I think we both squealed and then met in a hug.

"I'm so happy for you guys. When are you expecting?"

"I'm pretty sure this baby will arrive in the middle of September." We began to talk about how our lives would be changing over the next year. Carol told me, "I'm not sure what I'm going to do with my practice. I don't think I want to work full time after this baby arrives, but I don't think it is very fair to tell the other doctors at the clinic that I don't want to work evenings or week-ends, when they have to. I guess Chris and I will have to figure out what we want to do. Don't tell Joan and Susan about the baby yet; I'd like to tell them tonight at supper. Do you think we'll ever have another Christmas like this?"

"I can't imagine that another day will be as full of wonderful surprises like today has been."

Trent and Chris returned with Susan and Joan. They had gone out into the desert and rode their bikes. Chris used mine; it was only a little small for him. They must have had fun -- at least that was our guess from the amount of dirt they brought home.

"Let's meet in the pool," I suggested. Everyone ran to get into bathing suits, and it wasn't long before the pool was full. Shannon even came in. It turned out that she was a real water baby.

Carol and Chris said that every time they took her over to Nicholas Sheran pool, she'd cry when they took her out. That pool is set up really well for babies. There is a warmer water, shallow pool that all the babies seem to love. If the baby gets chilly, the soaking pool is nice and warm.

Chris had his video camera out; he wanted proof that he was swimming in a pool on Christmas Day. Christmas dinner was wonderful, as much for the company as the food. My best friends, Carol and Chris, and my fiancé, and my children; and all of us were looking forward to a year of changes.

After supper, we went out in the backyard to show Joan and Susan a surprise. A couple of weeks earlier when I was shopping with Mansi, she asked if I had my piñata and candies. I knew what it was, but I didn't know the connection with Christmas.

Mansi told me, "After supper, we usually let the kids play with a Santa piñata. They really have fun doing it. Do you want me to show you where I like to buy them?" So off we went, and I ended up with two piñatas, one in the shape of Santa and the other a donkey. I had hung them up, like Mansi showed me, and they were waiting for Joan and Susan. They were hopping up and down with excitement.

I made them wait a minute, while I spread a blanket underneath. Soon they were both blindfolded and holding their sticks. Trent lowered and raised the piñatas while they tried to break them open. Chris had the video rolling. Joan had asked him to get it when she saw what their surprise was. She wanted to show her friends back in Lethbridge

We all got silly and took turns trying to hit the piñata. Joan was the first lucky one. Her donkey fell apart and the candy landed on the ground. They had fun jumping under it, gathering the candy.

Trent then put Susan on his shoulders, helped her swing, and Santa finally spilled his goodies. Once all the candy was gathered up, we went back in, and plopped down in front of the TV. Both Joan and Susan struggled to keep their eyes open, but failed. Chris and Trent each carried one of them to bed, and tucked them in. While they were doing that, I turned the Christmas tree lights on, turned off the lights and lit the candles. I brought out champagne glasses and set them on the table. "Trent brought it with him last night."

When Trent and Chris returned, Trent poured us all champagne. He proposed a toast, "I want to tell you all that this Christmas will always live within us. I proposed to Clare, Joan and Susan, and was accepted. We had your company, and then Carol and Chris, you learned that what you hoped for was true, a new baby is on the way. May we always be together, if not in body, then in spirit." After the kisses and hugs, we settled back and enjoyed the atmosphere.

The next day, of course, was Boxing Day, but we found out that Americans don't know what it is and that most people go to work that day. We found it very strange, since in Alberta, many companies shut down entirely between Christmas Eve and January 2. Trent and I had already had that week booked off, so we decided to have a traditional Boxing Day. We invited Kele, Mansi and the kids. I made all of our traditional Christmas food that was rounded out by some very spicy appetizers that Mansi prepared. Afterwards, they declared that the idea of Boxing Day was most civilized.

New Year's Eve arrived too soon. We drove Carol, Chris and Shannon to the airport for their flight back to Lethbridge. The next time we saw one another, there would be lots of changes.

In no time, they boarded their plane and we headed back to my house. We brought home pizza for the kids and their baby-sitter. Trent and I were going to a New Year's Eve party at the faculty club. We thought it would be a great time to announce our engagement.

I wore the new dress I had bought. The minute I saw it I just loved it. Spaghetti straps went over my shoulders, and were attached to the gathered top. The only way to describe it was like a string bikini top. From that flared yards of silky, peacock blue fabric which swirled with every movement. I felt wonderful and sexy. When I looked in the mirror, my engagement ring captured the light from the candles.

We had a wonderful time at the party. On the drive there we had decided we'd tell people, individually, about our engagement. I really don't remember telling a soul. Mansi was the first familiar face we saw, and when she saw our expressions, the first thing she did was glance at my hand.

"I knew it. I knew that you'd finally ask her Trent!" From that moment on, we received congratulations, kisses and hugs from all sides. Everyone wanted to know what our plans were. Most knew that we were from different cities, so most people were asking who was moving. When we told them that both of us were, almost everyone thought it was a great idea.

The head of our faculty asked us both if we were giving up our research. Trent told him that we thought we'd combine our projects at one site, and continue on. He made a point to saying that we weren't going to rush back to work because we wanted lots of time to settle in as a family.

Driving home, Trent told me that he had an idea about what our timetable could be. He thought if we went to Calgary for Spring Break, that we could house hunt and decide where we wanted to live. If we had a new house built, then it would be ready when he was finished at the university here. That way he'd have somewhere to live until we joined him at in the middle of June.

I decided that I'd leave for Canada a month early. I needed the time to get ready for our wedding and moving into the new house. Of course I didn't want to be separated from Trent too long. While we were, Trent would be very busy, rearranging his work. He didn't anticipate any problems at the Edmonton end, and he was pretty sure U of C would be happy to accommodate him, under the same conditions as he worked under at U of A..

The next afternoon I started one of my infamous lists. Actually I started three; one for Trent, one for myself, and one for the girls. Trent's wasn't too bad, since we couldn't put down too many details, but we managed to decide on his departure date, we specified what we were looking for in a house, and I decided that I'd leave it to either Trent or his mother to make wedding arrangements.

She had been very warm and friendly when Trent called her Christmas day to share our news. She told me how happy she was that Trent would have a family once again. She wanted to know all about Susan and Joan, and from her reaction I wasn't worried the slightest that they wouldn't be accepted by their new grandmother.

My list had a lot of things on it, but I couldn't be too definite, because I had to see if the university would agree to my plan of leaving early. I put lots on the girl's list; school records, doctor and dental records, and schools to check out in Calgary.

I found going back to work difficult. My thoughts centered on the upcoming months, not the present. After I dropped more than my share of equipment, I took an early lunch, went for a brisk walk and returned more focused. Trent came home with me every night so we could have supper as a family. We took some evenings for ourselves, and generally spent them eating out at a nice restaurant, and then going back to his place. After lounging in the Jacuzzi, we'd retire to his bed and make love, made even more wonderful knowing that we had the rest of our lives to make love

We seemed to talk an awful lot about when we'd have a baby, and what the baby would look like. Afterward, we'd wrap ourselves in cozy robes and sit in front of the fireplace. Trent told me that he wanted to buy more of the Gibbard furniture.

He's used to me, and picked up paper and pen. "I'd like both Joan and Susan to have new beds. Do you think they'd want four poster beds, or another style?"

I suggested that we let them pick out their own beds. Trent surprised me, and said, "I don't think that we should get them twin beds. We might as well get them queen size so when they leave home they'll be able to take their beds. Plus it gives them lots of room for stuffed animals and friends during sleepovers. I've always had a queen-size bed, and liked it. What do you think about dressers; how many would each of them need?"

"I don't remember where I saw this, but there is a new system out called California Closets and they design the closet space so it can be used more efficiently. The picture I saw included lots of drawers, and different layers for hanging things. I think what caught my eye is that everything can be adjusted as kids grow. What I can see is that system in each of their walk-in closets. That way a lot of room in the bedrooms isn't taken up by dressers. You know what I've always loved? Window seats! My aunt's window seat lifted up and provided a lot of storage. That along with the closet system would give the girls lots of room so they can keep their rooms tidy. I don't care if they throw their things into drawers or storage bins; I just hate looking at a mess."

Trent remembered hearing about California Closets too, and said he'd check into them, both from here and in Calgary. It seemed that every time we talked about what we wanted in a house, it became clear that we were going to have to build. We looked at one another, and said simultaneously, "Chris."

CHAPTER 25

When we flew back to Canada in February, we carried not only our luggage, but our dreams. We had put down on paper everything we wanted in our house to give to Chris. He was flying up from Lethbridge to meet with us later in the week.

Rather than stay downtown in one of the bigger hotels, we decided to base ourselves in the Crowchild Inn, which was central to the areas we wanted to look at. Joan and Susan didn't want to come with us until there was something specific to look at, so I took advantage of a kind offer from a cousin of Trent's who lived in Silver Springs, just down Crowchild Trail from the hotel. We dropped them off at her home, and started our tour.

We knew to start with, we just wanted to drive around all the areas close to the university and become more familiar with them. It quickly became apparent that we would have to buy in a new area if we wanted to build a custom home. We drove through a new portion of Varsity Estates, and the houses were of the style we liked, but there weren't any views and they weren't far from Crowchild Trail so traffic noise was a potential problem.

We drove to the top of Edgemont, where there were some wonderful view lots. The mountains looked wonderful, but my first thought, after living in Lethbridge, was to wonder what the Chinook winds would be like up there. We stopped the car when we saw a woman out sweeping her steps. "Excuse me, we're looking at lots, and I was wondering if you'd tell me how you find the wind up here," I asked her.

She looked at me, and said, "The wind isn't too much of a bother in the yard, but what drives me nuts are the windows. They rattle like crazy. Last month, our furnace pilot light went out. The service man told me that if the wind is blowing at the right angle, it creates a down draft. Our heating bill is pretty high, too, because we have so many windows, to take advantage of the view. My husband and I think that we'll sell the house this spring."

"Thanks for the information," I told her, and then we walked back to the car. We both agreed that we'd pass on the wind

We drove around more of Edgemont, and came across a street that wound down a hill. The lots didn't have views of the mountains, but they backed onto a wooded ravine. We walked around each of the eight lots, and when we each finally gave an opinion as to our favourite, we had picked the same one. It was the last lot at the bottom of the hill, so we'd have neighbors on one side only. We thought if we needed the lot to be slightly bigger to take the house, it probably wouldn't be difficult to buy some of the land to the south of us.

We suddenly realized that we were ravenous, and found a wonderful little Italian restaurant in Silver Springs, called Mario's. We both had Veal Marsala that was exquisite. One thing that we missed in Albuquerque was good Italian and good Chinese food. We dragged ourselves from the restaurant, with the promise we'd be back before we left. The owner told us that there was a new area opening up, called Scenic Acres.

It was just west of Silver Springs, so we checked it out. We both thought the views were great, but the houses being built there were small and on very tiny lots. Our house wouldn't fit in. We picked up Joan and Susan and showed them the lot that we really liked. Both of them were excited about the ravine in the back. By the time we were having dinner at the hotel, we had made our mind up. The next morning we went to the sales office and put a deposit down on the lot, only after Trent made sure that we could expand the lot, if necessary.

Chris arrived the next morning, and brought with him some preliminary sketches. We drove straight out to show him the lot, and he agreed that the house we had in mind would sit well on it. We continued on to the sales office, and told the salesman that we'd take the lot, but that we'd be building to our own design. His face fell, and he told us that they normally didn't do that.

Trent wasn't used to dealing with unsure people, and insisted that the man call his supervisor for an afternoon meeting. Once that was set up, we took Chris for lunch at Mario's. We insisted that he have the Veal Marsala -- we couldn't resist having it again ourselves. We had Chris's plans spread on the table, as well as the revised list we brought with us. Neither Trent nor I could find much to change in the plan; we had him add walk-in closets for the girls and the guest room, window seats, and we added a special extra in our bedroom, a fireplace.

The rest of our visit to Calgary was a whirlwind of activity. We tried to make as many choices about appliances, flooring and lighting, as possible. We chose the contractor for the project, and Trent dealt with the city to add an additional six feet to the side yard. We found out that Joan would be picked up by bus and taken to the junior high down the hill. Susan would take the bus too, but she'd go to an elementary school that was brand new and in the district. We all fell asleep on the plane, and were happy to get into our peaceful home. Our work routine continued as before, except for interruptions by phone calls from Chris or the contractor.

CHAPTER 26

Easter week was glorious in Albuquerque. The sun shimmered through the air and filtered through the leaves as it entered the Church. We were there for Palm Sunday, and for the first time, we carried real palm leaves in the processional around the block and back into the church

The sun warmed our shoulders as we stood outside the church, listening to the prayers offered before we re-entered. I've wondered about this symbolic procession and re-entry. Obviously it is meant to remind us of Christ's procession to Calvary, but why the re-entry? For some reason that Easter, the importance of this symbolic re-birth became startlingly clear.

Somehow, my decisions were re-affirmed and I knew that Joan, Susan and I were starting a new life once again. We had suffered death; Robert's desertion and the wrench of letting Patrick go. We had grown to know one another fully as our new selves, and we were ready to accept the new life offered through love.

Easter Sunday Mass affected me emotionally as I listened to the hymns sung in Spanish. How I wished that Trent and I could have a wedding Mass, but because I divorced Robert, that was an impossibility. I found it ironic that now, when I was entering a marriage with the full knowledge of myself and my love for Trent, it couldn't be celebrated through the sacrament. When Robert and I were married, I was a young woman who cowered under his authority, and that masqueraded as love. Which will be the true marriage? There was no doubt in my mind.

Of course we all had fun looking for Easter eggs. Earlier I asked Mansi how you hide candy when there are so many bugs around. She took me shopping, and showed me bags of plastic eggs. They opened and you placed the candy inside. Thank heavens. I had visions of ant trails making a map to the candy, or cockroaches fighting to drag some off with them.

Even with the plastic eggs on hand, I kept the lights on that night - an added precaution against cockroaches. I hadn't hunted for Easter candy since I was a child, but Trent insisted that he'd hide them. He flew down on Good Friday to be with us on the long weekend.

He brought pictures with him, so we could see how the house was progressing. The album began with shots of the lot and moved onto the point where the basement was poured. I was surprised to see, from the rest of the pictures, that all the framing and roofing were done. I found it easier to start thinking of the interior once I saw the exterior shell up.

Trent and I poured over the paint wands I borrowed from the local paint store to make sure we were happy with our original choices. I was lucky that Trent enjoyed being involved with such decisions. I remember doing the same thing by myself when Robert and I built a house, except he wouldn't give me a clue. The task wasn't enjoyable because I was so worried that I'd pick something that he wouldn't like. That would give him another excuse to yell or hit.

Trent and I both were fans of blue, and decided to paint our bedroom Wedgwood blue, and paint all the casings white. We decided to use the colour throughout the house; not necessarily all the walls, but somewhere in each room.

Joan and Susan laid on the floor trying to decide what colour they wanted for their bedrooms. Joan had a vision for her room, and it was one of romance. She chose a darker shade of blue for the walls, and a lighter one for the casing. She decided that she would choose the canopy bed, and already talked about the material she wanted. I guess she inherited her talent for sewing from me, and planned on sewing lots of pillows. Susan was determined that her room was going to be sunshine yellow.

Too soon, Trent was gone. We knew that this time we'd not see one another for six weeks. Trent had too many organizational tasks ahead of himself, as well as the actual move of his lab. Phone calls came every night, at times just to talk, and others that reported on the house's progression.

Joan and Susan both came home from school excited. They told me that there was going to be a big party at the school. I asked them what the party was for and they told me it was Cinqo de Maio. I knew that meant May fifth, but didn't know the significance of the date. The girls told me that it was a celebration of a Spanish victory.

May fifth dawned, and the girls wore their new white dresses to school. All the parents who could were in the church to watch the students quietly file into the church with their white candles. My two blondes were easy to spot in the crowd.

Once Mass was over, the parents were served juice and cookies, and talk turned to the end of the year celebration. I was saddened to realize that it wouldn't be long before we were saying good-bye to our new friends. I already had extracted a promise from Kele and Mansi that they would fly to Calgary for the wedding, and I think Trent and I both got them excited about the idea of skiing, so they'd have to make a return trip during the winter.

Of course, with end of the year come exams. Susan's day pretty much continued as usual, only the frequency of quizzes picked up. Every night we spent half an hour working on all her spelling lists of the past year. She was a very good speller, and remembered almost all the words. We practiced math together, and although it wasn't her favourite subject, she studied without complaint.

I tried to vary how she learned adding and subtraction. I would pull out my grandmother's wooden button box. My mother used them to teach me, I used all the old buttons to teach Joan, and now they were being used again for Susan. The buttons were very old, and not like the buttons of today. When she started to get restless, we'd stop math and sort the buttons. First we sorted by colour, and then by size, and sure enough, soon we were adding and subtracting again.

Joan's homework was more complicated. Studying math with Joan led to fractions. Both of us found it boring to just memorize, so soon Joan was once again studying buttons. She had social studies to go over; while I was helping her, I was again happy that I was teaching both Joan and Susan their Social Studies through correspondence school. Why it is based in Barrhead, I do not know, but that was where our teaching packages came from and where we sent the completed assignments.

The courses were very well done, to my mind, and were easy to teach, and easy for the kids to follow. Throughout the year we learned together, and I remembered some long forgotten facts about Canada and the world. The contrast between their Canadian and American courses was striking. The American courses dealt only with the United States. The Canadian program, while it focused on Canada, also compared it to other countries. Perhaps that explained why my kids knew almost as much about the United States as their classmates. Granted, the American students knew minutia about New Mexico, but they knew very little about the rest of the country. Most in Joan's class couldn't locate states such as North Dakota, Idaho or Montana. I suddenly realized that the saying "out of state, out of mind" wasn't a joke.

The last day of school arrived, and we all attended the graduation Mass for the Grade eight class. For American school children, grade eight is their final year of junior high. Afterward, I gave both Joan and Susan address books so they could get all their friends' mailing addresses. Joan managed on her own, and I helped Susan out.

They each gave their teacher's little soapstone carvings, which Trent sent down. Joan and Susan's teachers had a surprise for them; one of the mothers had embroidered them each a Mexican blouse. She did a lovely job, creating a memory that will be kept and will always remind Joan and Susan about their friends.

In the early spring, I had written Halona's mom, and asked if she could possible make some bead bracelets for the kids' teachers and their special friends. Halona brought them with her when she arrived the day before, so Joan and Susan gave them out. Halona was down for a week, and when we left Albuquerque the next week, she'd come home with us.

I was kept busy going through all the things we had accumulated in the past year, trying to decide what to take and what to leave. Plus, I spent some time taking Halona around Albuquerque and out into the desert. It was sort of funny how some locals would come up to her and start speaking Spanish.

She'd look to me at first, so I'd explain, and after a couple of days, she finally would just blurt out, "I'm a Canadian Indian."

Halona loved the pool and they spent as much time in it as possible. That was something that they would definitely miss. Trent arrived at Kele and Mansi's the night before the movers arrived to pack. I wasn't expecting him, so it was a huge surprise. Mansi had been in on the secret, and had arranged for a baby-sitter so the four of us could go out for a last Mexican dinner. We did it properly; time was of no importance as we had first one course and then eventually another.

I knew how much both Kele and Mansi had meant to both Trent and me. They made us feel welcome, they were our guides as we lived in a new culture, and they were our friends who gave us love and support during what was turning out to be the most important year in our lives. They gave us many levels of themselves. Kele offered his friendship, and his professional respect. Mansi was there to listen to my hopes and dreams and my fears. During Trent's time at the university, they instinctively pulled him into the midst of the living, and in doing so, he was open to the possibility of a relationship with me. What else can we ask for in friends?

Trent and I spent one last night in my hacienda. We took candles out to the pool and set them in clusters

The flames were reflected in the still water, wavering only when the water was disturbed. Trent came to me and slowly undid the ribbon that tied at the front of my blouse, and slipped it further down my shoulders. While his lips trailed down my neck, he found and undid the zipper of my skirt.

I stood naked in front of him, proud that I chose to be his wife, and he freely chose to be my husband. His shirt slipped easily over his head, and soon his slacks joined my skirt, my blouse and his shirt. We stood apart, looking on one another under the silvery moonlight. As one, we moved to the edge of the pool and slipped in. Languorously we moved through the water until we reached the wide stairs at the shallow end. I lay back onto the stairway, allowed my body to float freely under his touch. My body and soul were content.

CHAPTER 27

The flight home was filled with memories. All of us had an incredible year in Albuquerque. Not only did it provide the opportunity for Trent and I to renew our friendship; it allowed us the time to see that friendship develop into love. We were privileged to become friends with Kele and Mansi. Joan and Susan developed many friends, both at school and in the neighborhood. They were both able to speak quite a bit of Spanish at the end of the year, and were very comfortable in the homes of their Hispanic friends.

I am sure that the year spent in New Mexico will have a positive impact on their lives. They learned that they are flexible and able to adjust to different cultures. They also learned the most important lesson; no matter what background people come from, they share our desires. We landed in Calgary on a glorious June day; the sky was the perfect blue to form a magnificent background for the mountains. The tip of an occasional mountain was still capped with snow.

The girls and I were almost squirming in our seats during the drive from the airport to our new home. Although Trent sent us pictures, they weren't the same as being in the house. As we came to the bottom of the hill I held my breath; will it be as I imagined? It was. The cedar had been painted, and I was happy to see that it went with well with the brick.

Trent made opening the door an occasion. He asked the girls to cover their eyes and wait. He swept me off my feet and carried me over the threshold, and then he did the same for Joan and Susan. Laughter and squeals followed us through the house. We all went into our bedrooms first. I took one step into the bedroom and came to a complete halt. I held my breath as I surveyed my new bedroom. Our four poster mahogany bed stood proudly against the blue wall. Trent had already bought some linens in a marvelous Waverly print that not only picked up the blue in the walls, but the deep roses, and reflected the richness of the mahogany. Bedside tables sat on either side of the bed and looked as I imagined. They were big enough to hold the necessities: Kleenex, a book, and alarm clock.

I went through our closet and into the bathroom. The most important feature was the Jacuzzi; of course it was big enough for two. Chris had done a wonderful job, and placed a window beside the tub that looked out to the woods. No need for window coverings. We went onto the deck through our bedroom French doors. Chris designed a deck that was one level at our bedroom, and then went down two steps for the rest of its length, across the entire back of the house. We walked along the deck to the family room, which sat at right angles to the deck. Trent surprised me with a brick fireplace in the family room. He used a wonderful green marble on the raised hearth. The kitchen was as large as I envisioned, and I had a walk-in pantry. Finally, coming home with groceries wouldn't be an exercise of rearranging the entire kitchen. The girls' voices called for us.

We went into Joan's room, "Mom, Uncle Trent, this is perfect. This is the bed I've always wanted. Look at my closet! I have tons of room." She threw her arms around us, and then led us out into the corridor and down the hall to Susan's room.

"This is just the yellow I wanted. It makes me feel sunny." All of us stood in Susan's room, admired her choice of yellow, and agreed that it would hard to be sad in that room. We finally went back to the family room and sat on the floor.

"I didn't want to pick out any furniture for this room until you were here. I know we talked about what type of furniture, but I couldn't decide. I've some set aside that we can look at tomorrow, and if you like something, I've arranged for it to be delivered. I think we should go to the store first thing in the morning, so we can be comfortable tomorrow. If you want, Clare, we can also go to the linen store so you can pick out the rest of the sheets and towels for the house."

I stood and stared in amazement at my fiancé. How did I get so lucky? Trent was so understanding he knew that we'd want to sleep in our new home that night, so he bought the necessities, and yet he was sensitive and knew that I'd want to pick a lot of the linens and furniture. What more could I ask for?

My arms went around him, "Trent I love you. Let's get up early tomorrow and do all of those things. The sooner we finish these chores, the sooner we can nestle in."

We all suddenly collapsed around eight o'clock that evening. Susan fell asleep watching the TV, and Trent carried her to bed. While we were tucking her in, Joan went by on the way to her room. "I'm sleepy too, Mom. I'm going to sleep, in my brand-new bed. Night."

"Night, Honey," Trent and I said in unison. Without words, we drifted to the family room, turned off the TV, turned the lights out, washed the glasses, put them away, and then went to bed. We lay in one another's arms, talking about the day. I guess we fell asleep, since when I woke up, the sunrise began to paint the sky with its morning pinks. We all quickly converged in the kitchen for a quick breakfast, hurried with showers, dressed and were ready to go.

If I had to, I don't think I could tell anyone every store we visited that day. All I know is that by the time we were home that evening, that we were expecting a furniture delivery before 7:00, and that the once empty family room had to cleared of all the bags we hauled in from the car. I had just finished unwrapping the last of our purchases when the doorbell rang. An hour later, we sat in our reclining chairs and surveyed the complete transformation of our family room. Comfort was our goal, and I will report, that we accomplished it.

Thankfully, by the time Trent's mother came down for a weekend visit during Stampede Week, the house was organized and we could spend our time talking about wedding plans. She was prepared with three different scenarios for us to choose from. The first involved a traditional wedding in a church performed by a minister, who was a family friend. I really didn't want to get married in a church unless it was a Catholic Wedding Mass, and I tried to explain myself. I saw Diane nod with understanding, "That is one of the reasons I thought of the alternate plans. Please don't think you'll hurt my feelings if you want to change anything, or if you don't like anything. It is your wedding."

I sat down beside Diane. "You have been absolutely wonderful helping like us like this. Thank-you for what you just said; that's how I feel too. I can't stand it when people don't say what they mean. What are you other scenarios, Diane?"

"Since our friend, Trent's 'Uncle John,' is a member of the Winter Club, he suggested that the wedding and reception could be held there. There is a spectacular view of both the city and the mountains. Another plus, it isn't far from here. What do you think of that idea, Clare?"

I looked over at Trent, and saw in his face the excitement I felt. "That sounds perfect. I didn't want to be married by a judge, but at the same time don't want to have a church wedding."

Diane smiled and told us, "Well, I guess that means I don't have to bother you with the third suggestion -- a judge. Do you have any particular date in mind? John told me he is free anytime after July 20. He did say he'd need to know the date as soon as possible so he could confirm with the Winter Club." Trent got up and brought the calendar over, so we could finalize a date. We both agreed we didn't want to interrupt the August long weekend, and at the same time, we both pointed at the following Saturday. August 11, 1984, would be the date we'd marry.

Diane told us, "That will give us enough time to have the invitations printed and mailed." She turned to me and asked, "Clare, have you decided what you'll wear?" I admitted that I had given it some thought from time to time while in New Mexico, but that I hadn't come to a conclusion.

"I don't want to wear a traditional wedding dress, since both Trent and I have been married before, but I would like to keep a formal theme. I love seeing Trent in a tuxedo; to be perfectly honest, I really don't know." Diane had a surprise for me.

"Trent's godmother's daughter is a dress designer and I talked to her before you arrived back in Canada. Of course I gave your good news, and then I asked for her advice on what she thought would be an appropriate dress style. She told me she'd think about it, and would get back to me. Well, two weeks ago a parcel arrived for me, and when I opened it I found five beautiful dress designs."

While I sat there with my mouth hanging open, Diane popped open her briefcase and handed me a sketch pad. It was absolutely incredible that each design looked as if it were designed for my body. When I said the same to Diane, she confessed, "When I was down in Albuquerque, I made sure that I took pictures of you from all angles, and then gave them to Erin, and from those she put together these designs. Do you like them?" All I could do was sit next to Trent and look at each design over and over.

"This is incredible. Erin managed to create five designs that I absolutely love. The hard part will be choosing which to have made."

While I continued to flip from picture to picture and back again, Diane and Trent went out onto the deck to check on the girls and bring some lemonade in. The first design appealed to my romantic nature, it was what I have always called a Juliet gown. The bodice curved low across the breasts, and from there, the gathered material fell to the floor in soft folds. I visualized such a dress in the softest of velvets, made in the deepest of jewel colours. I found it difficult to imagine the dress in an appropriate summer material, but I was far from ready to eliminate it.

The second design was very elegant. The sleeveless dress was accessorized with a bolero jacket. The dress was deceptively simple, shaped against breasts, waist and hips. It would certainly be adaptable to other occasions. I wasn't sure if I was still in good enough shape to wear such a dress -- I guessed the mirror and I had an appointment that evening.

The third design was for a short dress, simply held by spaghetti straps over the shoulder. The dress fell in an A-line to the knee. I didn't think I was ready to move away from a long dress, even though I wasn't wearing a traditional wedding gown.

The fourth design was stunning, with a full, long skirt that fell from an empire waist line. I would definitely be able to wear it to some events, but not many.

The fifth design was stunning as well, and wasn't a dress. Instead Erin showed a full, long pleated skirt, a wonderful blouse with a plunging neckline, and a wonderful cummerbund. As soon as I saw it I could picture the material it cried out to be made from. I saw the skirt made of ivory lace, over layers and layers of satin. The lace would be ivory, with small darker ivory florets scattered across the field until the border.

By the time I had gotten that far, Diane and Trent came back in with our lemonade. Trent wanted to know, "Have you decided on which you like the best?"

"Come and sit next to me so I can go over each one with you." I told him what I had thought of each one, and by the time I got to the fifth design, I finalized my decision. "I love them all, but there is something about the skirt and blouse that seems so very right. Do you like it Trent?"
"I can already see you in that and I know that you'll look gorgeous." He turned to his mom, and asked, "Is Erin still in Edmonton, Mom?"

Diane nodded and told us not to worry about location; Erin had already decided she'd fly down for the initial fitting and fabric selection the next week, and then go back to her studio to run up a base model. Then she'd be back the following week for a further fitting, and then she'd fly back to Edmonton. Apparently she was giving this her top priority, and it would be ready in plenty of time.

Diane thought that my choice of colour was right, and now that it was decided, we could choose flowers and decorations. Trent had some chores he needed to do before we went to the Winter Club, so Diane and I went down to the local florist to get a general idea of flowers available, and to be perfectly honest, neither of us particularly liked what we saw. Diane suggested that we should wait until she had an opportunity to talk to her florist in Edmonton to see who he'd suggest that I check with in Calgary.

CHAPTER 28

"I called John this morning and told him that I was coming here and he told me to call him back as soon as I could give him a date. He told me . . . Oh, hi John. I was just telling Trent and Clare that you were expecting my call. Yes, August 11. How is that date for you? Yes, okay, we'll meet you there. See you at two."

Diane turned to us and said, "John said that he'll meet us at the Winter Club this afternoon. He's already arranged to meet with the Food and Beverage Manager, and we'll be able to settle all the details then. Have you thought of what time of the day you'd like to have the wedding?"

Trent and I looked at one another, then at her and shrugged our shoulders. "It seems like a good idea if we had the wedding when it was still light enough for everyone to appreciate the view, but if the view of the downtown is so beautiful at night, it would be nice to have that as well," I told both Diane and Trent.

Diane reminded us that it wouldn't really be dark until ten in the evening, and with that reminder I could see a plan form. "If we have the wedding ceremony at seven, the sun will still fill the room with natural light, and we'll all be able to enjoy the view of the mountains. The view will be constantly changing." I paused and looked to see what Trent's thoughts on my suggestion were.

"I love the idea, honey. I guess the next things to decide are the guest list and the menu. Mom, have you drawn up a preliminary list?"

Diane pulled a sheaf of papers, and for a brief minute I thought that maybe they were all needed for a guest list, and I began a quick panic. Trent saw the look on my face, laughed and pulled me close. "You look like an army just arrived in your backyard, and you're expected to feed them all!" he laughed.

Diane handed the list over to Trent, and we looked at it together. "You did a wonderful job, Mom. Everyone who needs to be here is on this list, other than the personal friends of both of ours." Trent found his pen, and we began adding to the list. Carol and Chris, Carol's mother, Ann and John Ferris, Lora Migs, Halona's family, Kele, Mansi and the kids, and then we added colleagues from work, both in Lethbridge and Albuquerque. Those two stages in my life were extremely important, for without them I wouldn't have met with Trent again. By the time we were finished, I gasped at the number, 350.

"Isn't that too many, it will be awfully expensive." As soon as I blurted that out, I felt like an idiot, of course that wouldn't be a concern for Trent or his mother.

Diane smiled at me, and winked. "Don't worry Clare. I know that you've had to very careful with your salary. I think you did a wonderful job, but now you can relax and plan what you want without worry. This is your wedding day we're talking about, and for the two of you it is the beginning of a second life. Not everyone is so lucky. Do you have any ideas of what you'd like included in the menu?"

"I really haven't thought about it. Trent do you have any specific ideas?"

"Not really, let's wait until this afternoon. I'm sure that they will have suggestions for us."

It wasn't long until it was time to go up to the Calgary Winter Club. Joan and Susan came with us so we could show them all the facilities they'll be able to use, once we're members. Trent had been smart, and as soon as he was in Calgary, he had put our name on the waiting list. He was told that it would probably be another six months or so, but we'd be busy until then anyway, considering all the changes that we were going through.

The drive to the Winter Club, took only five minutes, and we were quickly sitting in the Food Services Manager's office discussing menus. He was very helpful in giving us various menu selections. Uncle John spoke up and said that their chef roasted the best Prime Rib in Calgary and that gave us our starting point.

I was emphatic that this was not to be a buffet -- that we wanted our guests served properly, and I also requested that the chef who cut the meat gave each person a nice thick piece rather than shaved pieces. Trent chimed in and said that he wanted to make sure that there were platters with additional meat on each table.

Diane made an excellent suggestion, "You know, everyone has salad at these events, and I know I get tired of seeing salad at every event I go to. Why not have two appetizers, such as escargot and vegetable crudités?" We all agreed with her, and then all we had left to discuss was desert, wines and liquors.

"I've always found that a crème caramel is a wonderfully light desert to end a meal. Most people just want a small sweet that won't make them feel as if they overate." Apparently the James family shares my taste for crème caramel, and that decision was made.

During a break in the conversation, Mr. Adams looked at us and told us that he had never seen people make decisions so quickly. He told us of brides and their mothers who agonized over which vegetable they wanted, and that could fluctuate from week to week.

Trent told Mr. Adams that he wanted extra staff working during our reception in order to make sure that our guests did not have to wait for anything while trying to flag down a waiter. Mr. Adams looked at Trent, but before he could say anything, Trent quickly told him that of course he'd pick up the cost of the extra staff.

He went on and told Mr. Adams that he wanted enough waiters so that each would be responsible for only two tables. Diane told Mr. Adams that the family silver would be used, rather than their standard dishes. She also told him that her housekeeper would of course help out in kitchen to clean and repack the silver.

I was as stunned as Mr. Adams; to be perfectly honest I didn't realize that a family would have such numbers of silver bowels, dishes and platters, and coffee and tea pots. I was obviously moving into a totally new social group. Trent told him that he'd be in touch in regard to wine and liquor choices.

We went home and quickly settled in the family room for tea. We were all quite satisfied with our day's work. My dress was picked, and the site and menu for the reception was organized. We really didn't have too much left to organize.

Trent and I had decided that we'd each have one attendant, as well as Joan and Susan. Trent decided that he wanted Kele as his best man, and there was no question in my mind that Carol would be the Matron of Honour. If it hadn't been for her support and love from the day I left Robert, I wouldn't now be planning my marriage to Trent.

I phoned Carol in Lethbridge, to ask her if she'd accept -- a pure formality, and to discuss what she'd wear. When I told her about the dress I picked, I also told her that Erin offered to design complementary dresses for her and the girls. Carol was thrilled at the idea of having a dress designed especially for her. She decided to come up to Calgary when Erin came for my first fitting so that Erin could decide on design and colour. Of course, her pregnancy had to be worked into the design.

It was only ten days later when our family room was covered with fabric samples and sketches, under which could be found two giggling girls and two beaming women. In the ten days since I had made my choice, Erin had produced the pattern and a mock dress. When I tried it on, there were only a few minor adjustments to be made. I wanted to be able to breathe with complete comfort, so I had Erin let the waist out just a tad, and I had her lower the neckline.

Erin used Carol's height to guide her dress design, and had a design ready for her to try on. Erin's design for Carol was similar to mine, but rather than a full skirt, the skirt fell straight to the ground and the blouse wasn't as full. Joan and Susan's dresses were one piece and reflected my dress.

We all poured over the fabric samples trying to decided on colour and texture. Carol and Susan shared colouring; they both had blue eyes and blond hair. Joan and I had blue eyes and black hair. These facts gave Erin a starting point; she asked, "Why don't we choose Carol and Susan's colour; perhaps a light peach shade, and then a darker peach colour for Joan's dress and Clare's cummerbund. See, this shade would go wonderfully with the ivory you've already chosen Clare. It would be wonderful for Joan, with her black hair. Then we could use this, no, this shade for Carol and Susan. With their lighter complexion the lighter shade would be better, yet the whole wedding party would tie together, from a colour point of view." She passed the various colour samples around, and everyone was happy to agree with her. "Have you thought of flowers yet, Clare?" asked Erin.

"Diane and I went to the florist earlier and didn't really see anything that we liked, but mind you, I didn't have any specific colour in mind. Diane is going to consult with the florist she uses in Edmonton for a suggestion of whom to consult here. Do you have any idea's Erin?"

"I was at the Muttart Garden awhile ago when they were having an orchid show, and I saw some beautiful orchids that were creamy, with tinges of salmon and coral. Perhaps those with some other flowers would be an idea." She opened her mouth to speak, then stopped, and turned to me. "Are you set on carrying flowers? I have an idea." I told her that I was flexible and wanted to hear her idea. "Instead of carrying them, what about having a few tucked into your cummerbund?"

"That is perfect. That way I would be able to walk holding Joan and Susan's hands." I was really happy with the idea, after all Trent had included the girls in his proposal, and this would be symbolic of a new family forming.

Carol piped in, "I like the idea of flowers tucked in the cummerbund."

Once again, we had made a decision and that allowed us to finish up the wedding planning. The time before the wedding flew by, filled with dress fittings, confirmations of RSVPs, consultation with Mr. Adams regarding the placement of the dining tables, consultations with the florist to order our flowers, and those for the reception and thinking about music at the reception.

I don't like going to events where you are expected to make conversation and then can't do so because the music is so loud. Trent and I agreed on a string quartet and I was able to book the quartet that was recommended by the Calgary Symphony. When I spoke with them, I told them that we wanted them to play during the wedding when I entered, during dinner and then soft after dinner music, that people could dance to.

CHAPTER 29

We spent a lot of time at the airport during the week prior to the wedding. Kele, Mansi and the kids flew up on the Thursday, so we'd have at least one night to catch up. Everyone looked wonderful, and Kele brought something special with him. When I had left Albuquerque, I left him with all my data and conclusions, and Kele had blended our research to produce the finalized report. This he handed to me.

Along with it was a letter from the American Secretary of Agriculture. He thanked Kele and I for our efforts, praised the joint venture between Canada and the US, and was especially grateful for the results. We were able to decrease the amount of water needed by the barley by thickening the membrane and reducing osmosis.

We caught up on all the news about our colleagues in Albuquerque, and we shared our news. Both Kele and Mansi loved Calgary, and when they saw where we were having the reception with the fantastic view of the Rockies, they said they felt right at home. We didn't have time to show them around the city, so they took my car down to the zoo.

They thought we were joking when we told them it would take them most of the day to see it all. By the time they dragged themselves through the front door at 4:00, they knew it to be true. Everyone was hot and sticky, but happy. Thankfully we had enough bathrooms so everyone could immediately have a shower.

That night was lovely. The kids all had pizza and then settled in for a movie night while the four adults sat on the deck and barbequed our supper. I had bought Porter House steaks at the butchers in the afternoon so I could show Mansi and Kele how good our beef is. They thoroughly enjoyed it, along with the baked potatoes and Garlic Bread, which they never had before. They were very happy to learn that they'd be sampling Alberta Prime Rib on Saturday.

We sat outside until 11:00, and they were amazed at how the twilight lingered. We finally went in and woke Neil and Emily so they could go back to the Crowchild Inn with their mom and dad. Our girls were half asleep, and didn't argue that it was time to go to sleep. We went through the house turning the lights off and locking the doors, and then went to our room. We snuggled together.

"Clare, you know we only have two nights left to sleep in sin?", Trent teased me. "I don't think we should waste the opportunity, do you?" he whispered. My response was to slide down his body, kissing him as I went. My mouth was tickled by the curling hair on his flat belly. That hair thickened as it moved downward and it was a path that called me. I lay between Trent's legs and wondered at the velvet skin that covered his penis. That contrast between softness and hardness is exquisite to my lips and tongue.

By that time, my own body was preparing itself for him. When his mouth encircled my nipples, they stood erect and felt on fire. Trent had discovered that I had quirky erogenous zones. As he slid he hands gently along my sides, my whole body responded as one. It was if he had his hands on my breasts, my sides and inside me. I had a circle of pleasure that became unending until we moved as one to become one.

Trent knew how to read my body, and made sure that I experienced the ultimate expression of love, before he allowed himself to join me. We lay quietly on the bed, allowing the evening breeze flow over our bodies, cooling us off. We talked of the wedding plans, and of our luck. Both of us had lived with the extremes of joy and hurt, and for some reason, we each allowed one another to once again provide love in our lives.

Friday evening we hosted a rehearsal supper for the bridal party. We had a wonderful supper in the dining room and then moved into the banquet room and decided on the details for Saturday. The florist would be there in the morning to create a wedding bower, so we decided where it would best be located. We decided to put it in the far corner so there would be a bit of an entrance.

We all were tired after the rehearsal, and everyone decided to make it an early night. We all headed for our rooms; the girls each disappeared into their rooms, and Trent and I went to ours. I was in the closet making sure that all my clothes for the next day were ready, when I heard Trent calling Susan and Joan in. They hopped into bed with him as I came out of the closet.

They sat around some jewelry boxes, and prompted me, "Mom, hurry, hurry, Uncle Trent says we can't open them until you're here." Joan told me. I snuggled next to her, and waited to see what Trent had up his sleeve. With grave formality he gave Joan and Susan their gifts, and then to my surprise, he handed one to me.

Joan quickly opened her box, and stared in silence at a gold necklace with an understated pearl setting. All she could do was whisper, "Thank-you, thank-you, this is beautiful."

Trent blushed and told Joan the story that went with the necklace. "This necklace was given to my mother, from her grandmother, whose father gave it to her when she had her first child. Your new grandma thought that made it just perfect for you, and we hope you'll wear it tomorrow." He turned to Susan, who by then had her present open, and saw that it too was a necklace, this time pearls were in a silver setting.

"Does this necklace have a story too?", Susan asked Trent.

"Yes it does. This necklace belonged to my great-grandmother, and was given to her by her father when she had her second baby, my grandmother. I'd like you each to wear these necklaces tomorrow. To me they seem just like the right thing as we start our new family. I'd also like you both to think of something; I feel funny now, when you call me Uncle Trent, that was great earlier, but now, well, I wondering, do you think you'd like to call me dad?" His answer was delivered by two little girls flinging themselves on him.

"Oh Dad, I've wanted to for a long time.", said Joan as she kissed him. Susan told him that she'd already been calling him that in her dreams. Everyone was so excited that we almost forgot that I had a present to open. Joan handed it to me, and asked me to open the box. Snuggled into royal blue velvet was an intricate gold necklace, set with rubies and diamonds. I looked and Trent and he nodded.

"Yes, this necklace has a story as well. This necklace was given to my great-grandmother on her wedding day, from her father, and she wore it during her wedding, and then she gave it to her daughter, who then passed it on to my mother." Trent took a deep breath and looked at me, and I could see that he wanted to say something, something he wasn't sure that he should say, and then I knew and could say it for him.

"Nina wore this when you married her didn't she?" Trent nodded, hiding his glistening eyes. "I am thrilled to wear this necklace at our wedding, Honey. I know how much you loved Nina, and it was that love that eventually allowed you to love again." While we hugged I saw Joan tug at Susan's nightie, and with that they said good-night and went to their own rooms. "How to you know when the right time is to do these things? Those necklaces for the girls are not only beautiful, but highly significant. That is one of the things that I love so much about you, not the just the gifts, but that you even think of such things."

"I think I got that from my dad. When I think of my parents as I was growing up, one thing that was a constant was remembering the looks of pleasure on my mom's face whenever dad surprised her with a little gift. He was always imaginative, and thought of very special gifts that meant a lot to mom. She obviously didn't need things, and at the beginning of their married life, dad couldn't afford to spend a lot on presents.

"I remember one fall, when mom and dad, and Marion and I walked along the river valley. We started at the Groat Road Park and walked as far east as the paths took us. By the time we came to the end, Marion and I were so tired we couldn't walk back. Dad led us back to the nearest street, found a phone and called a taxi. He had the driver take us back to our car, and we drove home.

Once we were home, Mom was busy with us as we had a bath. I guess dad decided that Mom was too tired to cook supper, and yelled up that he'd go for Chinese food. Marion and I always had long baths, and had great fun painting each other with finger paint/bath gel.

"We had just put on our pajamas when we heard dad come in. Mom followed us downstairs, and when she joined us in the kitchen, dad brought his left hand from behind his back. He held a bouquet of fall leafs. He found leaves of each colour that we had enjoyed on our walk. I can still see Mom walking over to him, with misting eyes, and snuggling into his arm. I can still hear Dad say, 'Honey, it was such a perfect day, I wanted you to have something to remind you of it.'

"When I first moved out of the house, I was looking in a trunk that was in the basement, for some of my things. I didn't find the dissection kit, but I found those leaves pressed in between pages of my dad's Chemistry book. I found other things too: love letters, little pictures that dad thought mom would enjoy, and daintily little pieces of jewelry. The jewelry wasn't particularly valuable, but they were important to dad, because they belonged to his mom. He always presented them to mom with a little card, on which he explained why he gave her that particular piece at that particular time.

"He loved to surprise mom with little things when they were totally unexpected; not holidays, any day when he wanted to show mom how much she still meant to him. I remember how dad would remember little things that mom would say in passing, and from that surprise her with a present.

"Mom told me once that she was watching a program about horses when she mentioned that she'd love to learn how to ride properly. I remember what dad did. Two weeks later, he took us all for a ride into the country, and all of a sudden we turned down what looked to be a private road. That road led us to a riding academy. They were waiting for mom, and she had her first of many, riding lesson. Mom didn't stop smiling for a long time after that. Anyway, dad always knew just the right thing to do to show his love."

I murmured against his chest, "I'm so lucky that you learned that from your dad. I wish he were still alive because I would have loved to known him. I know one thing I'd say to him and that would be thank-you. Thank-you for the sensitivity and love he gave to you." We lay there in one another's arms and drifted off to sleep.

CHAPTER 30

I remember waking up early in the morning, and when I padded off to the bathroom, I peeked out the window. The sight was what I hoped to see; the last tinges of the sunrise were fading into the clear blue sky. I heard the gentle rustle of the bushes in our backyard, and that was a pleasant sound. I didn't want guests getting overheated. You just never know what kind of day you'll get in August, but quite often they can be unbearably hot.

I was going to go back to bed, but something drew me through the house. My hands slid over our bed as I walked out to the hall. I pushed open Susan's door and tip-toed into her room, and knelt beside her bed, gazing at her mussed hair, and her pouting lips. "How did I produce such a gorgeous little girl?" was the question that ran through my head.

I knew I couldn't take all the credit; she had her father's colouring, but her nature was formed by me. She was a very loving little girl, and I thought that it was her physical nature that saved me at times during those early years on our own. I don't think we realize how much we can find that our bodies have a built in body-hunger. There were times when I could hardly sit still and calm, and then Susan would throw herself onto me for hugs and kisses and tickles. She needed that physical contact, but I needed it as much or perhaps even more.

Once I realized that it was the physical contact that was soothing for us, I started giving the girls regular massage after we all shared a hot bath. We filled the tub with so many bubbles that they spilled over onto the floor. I didn't care. We'd giggle, we'd talk about our plans, but most importantly, that was when they most often told me how they felt.

When the water finally cooled off, we'd dry off and get into our jammies, fix ourselves hot chocolate and then play a game, read, or watch a movie. Those memories stayed with me as I drifted into Joan's room. I felt saddened when I remembered that at first Joan was uncomfortable with being stroked or having a massage. It took awhile, but I realized that for Joan, physical contact wasn't always pleasant. She never knew what her father was going to do; was he going to hold her as his little girls, or would his hold be on a scapegoat

I felt guilty that the contact between Joan and I was tense, because I never knew if when I held her on my lap, Robert would complain that I was babying her, or if he'd complain that I didn't show him enough attention.

When I first started giving Joan massages, she'd squirm away. Once I clued in, I'd tell her that I was wrong and so was her dad. I took the responsibility for not standing up to Robert, and told her that it wasn't her fault. I told her that every little girl deserved to cuddle on her mom and dad's lap. Slowly she relaxed until she enjoyed the massage, and our bubble baths.

As Joan changed from a little girl to a pre-teen, I could see more of me in her, beyond the obvious colouring. Neither of us has a very large mouth or lips, but when we set our lips in certain way, there isn't any doubt as to our mood. Joan and I are both stubborn, and for us to change our minds, there has to be lots of good reasons.

Unfortunately, Joan shares another trait with me, and I hope she'll loose it soon. During my marriage to her father, I learned not to argue with him. To stop myself from saying anything that would make him mad, I'd bite my lip, and turn my head away. On car trips I spent many an hour with my lip between my teeth, and my head turned as I blindly looked at the scenery pass by. I didn't even realize that she was copying me until after we moved to Lethbridge when I no longer needed to do it.

Joan continued to bite her lip and turn her head despite the fact that I told her that it was safe for her to tell me anything; how she felt -- good or bad -- and what she had done. When I consulted with the psychologist, her recommendation was that I continually remind Joan of that, and to allow her to see me, occasionally, when I was dealing with negative emotions.

That was more difficult to do than I had imagined. The first time I tried, Joan became very upset and tried to take blame for my feelings. We cuddled on the couch and I tried to remember what our counselor had said. "Honey, you haven't done anything wrong, how I'm feeling has to do with work, and sometimes it makes you feel better to mutter about them. I just had a rotten day at work; everyone wanted me to do things for them at the same time, and there wasn't any way I could get it all done. I feel better now that I've told you. Do you know why?"

A little voice told me no.

"I realized that those people were being silly, since they all knew what was being asked of me. They should have done that work themselves until I was available. I feel better about myself because I know that I did the best that I could."

Over the years we had many such conversations, and slowly the silences lessened. Occasionally they still show up, and when they do I know that something important is brewing in her life. Looking at her long black hair spread over her pillow, I suddenly realized that Joan hadn't done that for a long time. In fact, almost from the time Trent came into our lives, Joan had become more open. I'm sure that is because she sees a man who is able to express his feelings; sadness, happiness, hope, and above all, love. How much he has given us already.

Today was the day when we would celebrate that sharing and love with our family and friends. I tip-toed out of her room, and walked down the hall, and slipped out onto the deck. The air was still cooled from the night, but felt refreshing. I walked along the back fence to check on the flowers.

The sunshine marigolds were living up to their name, each individual fold was opening to the morning sun that glistened on the dew that sat ever so lightly upon them. Some Sweet Peas were still blooming as the plants climbed up and along the corner of the fence. The Snapdragons stood proud in the pale sun, their pinks, yellows, corals and reds creating their own painting.

While I was pinching a Snapdragon open, I heard a snap. Looking up and over the fence quickly, I saw two dark eyes looking back at me. A fawn stood frozen, I think it was pretty sure I was harmless, but it was still dependent on her mother, who calmly strolled out from under cover of the bush. The fawn went back to grazing when she saw her mother look at me and then ignore me.

What a wonderful sight for a wedding morning; trust and love were their bonds, just as they were for Trent and I, and Trent and Joan and Susan. This was what I had been searching for, and for some reason I was lucky and I found it. The deer and I shared the morning stillness for quite some time, until a horn blared down on John Laurie Blvd. The doe calmly looked at me, looked around, gathered her fawn and disappeared into the trees.

That was my sign that it was time for the day to move ahead. I puttered about the kitchen, making a new pitcher of juice, grilling the bacon and cutting the bread so it was ready for French toast. It wouldn't be long now until everyone showed up, and it wasn't. The smell of the bacon drew the sleepy heads out of their beds. Soon the toast was sizzling on one grill while the bacon finished on the other. Joan and Susan set the table, and soon we were all sitting down for breakfast.

We all couldn't stop grinning. I'd look at Trent and smile, the girls would look at me and smile, and they'd look at Trent with hunger and love. There was no doubt in my mind that they looked forward to the wedding that would make him a "real" part of the family. I think each had a secret fear in the corner of their hearts that he'd leave us, as their father had. This day couldn't have come too soon for them.

CHAPTER 31

The only thing wrong with a wedding in the late afternoon is how to fill up the day. Joan, Susan and I were picking Carol up at the Inn to have our hair done, but that wasn't until 1:00. The girls helped me pack my suitcase for the honeymoon. Trent and I discussed it quite a bit; whether or not to take Joan and Susan with us. Trent was happy to bring them along, but I wanted to be selfish and have him all to myself. Carol came to the rescue, without even knowing it.

"When you guys are on your honeymoon, why don't Joan and Susan come back to Lethbridge with us. That way, they'll have a chance to visit their friends and help look after Shannon. We'd love to have them!"

When I asked Joan and Susan they had given an unqualified yes for an answer. So, they helped me pack my bathing suit, shorts and tops, and dresses. After we were done mine, we went into their rooms and packed their suitcases. By the time we were all finished and I went back to our bedroom, Trent had finished the dishes and had his suitcase opened on the bed. He was trying to decide if he needed to pack a tie and a jacket, and then decided he'd better take them, just in case. The rest of his things reflected mine. We were going to Kihei, on Maui. Family friends offered us their beachfront home that was well away from other homes. While Trent hadn't been there, he showed me pictures that his mother brought down with her from her visit. I mentioned the pool's isolation, and started laughing while trying to look Trent in the eye.

"You do have a fetish for pools, don't you?" He grabbed me in his arms and I ducked out from them, telling him that he'd have to wait until Hawaii before he could start his honeymoon; after all, we weren't married!

Since we were both packed and had some free time, we called to the girls and they joined us for a walk. I told them about the doe and her fawn from that morning, and we decided to walk in the general direction they had gone in. We didn't see them, but you could see depressions in the tall grass where it looked like they had laid. Magpies swooped down in our direction; we were obviously too close to their young. As we went further into the trees, a rustle beside the trail announced a very large Jack rabbit that bounded out so close to us, it almost tripped Susan up.

It wasn't too long until we were all hot and decided that it was time to return to the house. Walking through the door, we saw that Diane had arrived just before the caterers, and was now busy directing their activities. They were Diane's idea; she told us from her experience, the bride, groom and wedding party usually forgot to eat during the day, so she went ahead and called the caterers and organized lunch for all of us, as well as for Carol and Chris and Mansi and Kele, and of course, all the kids.

This caterer obviously had children of her own at home, and knew what kids actually wanted for lunch rather than what some adult thought would be "elegant." One end of the table groaned with Kraft dinner, with and without added wieners. For those who wished their wieners cooked in the traditional manner, a chef was tending them over the barbeque. As well, various pizzas spread down the table.

So, what did the men grab? That's right, pizza. When I saw the piece that Trent was eating, I decided that I had to try it out. I fell in love with Ye Olde Pizza. Their pizza was thin crust dusted with cornmeal, and the cheeses were layered on, the pepperoni loaded on top, and then it was baked in their special oven. When we returned from Maui, we'd be trying out their restaurant.

The adults were good, we left enough pizza for the kids, and tried all the tasty dishes that were laid out. The selection was just right; the dishes were filling but light, and very tasty. I enjoyed an asparagus, mushroom and Gouda cheese casserole that just slid down my throat. Wonderful homemade bread sat among the dishes. Kele and Mansi were very impressed with the luncheon. It was a treat for them to have things that weren't in their normal diet

Mansi was going to leave Canada laden with recipes. I saw her in the corner with the cook, getting the asparagus casserole recipe. It would be interesting to see how many she ends up with when they return to Albuquerque in a month. Before they had made their plane reservations, they had decided that if they were coming to Canada, that they wanted to see as much as possible. So while we were in Maui, they'd stay at our place, and see all the local sites. When we got back, we'd all convoy up to Banff, along the Banff-Jasper Highway to Jasper. While mountains are nothing new to them, I thought they'd be amazed at the Columbia Ice Fields. I was sure they'd want to go up on the glaciers. They'd have a pretty good chance of seeing wildlife along the road, too.

We sat quietly relaxing in the dim family room, preparing ourselves for the rest of the day. Mansi looked at Trent and I as we held hands, sitting on the couch. "I am so happy for you both. I remember Kele coming home for supper one night and asking if I remembered meeting the Canadian scientist who was visiting. I'll confess I did, but forgot your name, Trent. Anyway, when Kele told me that his funding came through for the study, and that you were coming down, he also told me that the two of you had known each other while in Edmonton.

"Almost right away, he started making comments that Trent was single, and of course you were, but that you had two children. I remember going out to the university to bring you something that you forgot, Kele. I tried to keep the children very quiet and well behaved, because I thought that a bachelor wouldn't like having them around. Instead, Clare, the next thing I knew, Trent had them outside chasing a Frisbee around. He really seemed to enjoy them. After that I think both Kele and I started getting the same idea, and this was all before you were there. And now look where we are, sitting in your country, waiting for the two of you to marry."

Then Mansi started crying a little and speaking Spanish very quickly. Kele must have thought we were worried, for he said, "She is crying because she is happy and is saying a special wedding prayer for you."

Mansi and I came together, hugged and drifted out of the room and down to my room. Carol followed behind. Mansi convinced me that it was time for me to relax in the tub, and afterwards she pampered me. First Mansi gave me a massage, and then I had to rouse myself enough to sit up so she could give me a pedicure, and a manicure. While she filed my nails, we laughed, reminiscing about having a girls' day like this around our pool. I was so lucky that Mansi, as Kele's wife, came into my life and quickly developed into my dear friends who helped me in every way possible.

When all that was done, I still hadn't finished being pampered. Carol took over and blew my hair dry, and then started with the curling iron. She needed stamina for that part, because my hair is so thick. Eventually the job was done and we took a cool drink break before putting my hair up. We went out onto the deck and sat along the edge that was now in shade, and managed to drain a full pitcher of lemonade.

Quiet settled over us. It was as though the birds were having a siesta, and all the cars came to a halt. I suddenly felt myself start to fade and struggled to keep my eyes open. My body was so relaxed that it demanded that I sleep. I stood up, and told Carol and Mansi that I had to have a nap, and asked them to wake me in twenty minutes. I was asleep the minute my head hit the pillow. When I finally woke, I sensed that I had been asleep for a lot longer, and confirmed that feeling with a glance at the clock. I sat up so quickly that I had to sit for a minute so I wouldn't fall. I realized that the house was very quiet; the quiet was suddenly broken by the door opening. Trent stood in the doorway. For a moment I had the terrible fear that he was going to tell me that he changed his mind. I shook my head, clearing it.

"Hi, Sleepy. Mansi and Carol decided that you needed the rest, so they've been busy making sure the girls were bathed, their hair washed, curled and their nails done. We had quite the beauty salon in operation in our kitchen. Then they shooed Kele and I to the free bathrooms to shower, shampoo and shave. We were pronounced clean and respectable, so we're going to head up to the Winter Club."

I tried to jump up, when I heard that, thinking we were late, "Don't worry we still have an hour to go, Kele and I just thought we'd get there early so we can check on everything. I want to make sure the florist delivered all of our flowers. And I told Uncle Jim that we'd meet him up there about now. Just think, the next time we'll see one another we'll just be minutes away from being married." With a kiss and a hug and an "I love you," Trent was gone.

CHAPTER 32

Carol came in and sheepishly grinned at me, "I did come in and you didn't wake up when I called you, so I figured that you really needed to sleep more so you can enjoy the rest of the day. The only thing left to do is out our dresses. I think Mansi and I will get yours on first, then I'll pull your hair back."

With that I felt my housecoat pulled from my shoulders, and then felt the silkiest blouse fall over my shoulders my breasts. My strapless bra left most of my breasts bare to the touch of the silk. It felt wonderful; sexy and cool. Next I felt the crinoline fell over my shoulders and settled on my hips. Already my waist looked smaller.

I moved over beside the bed, where Carol had climbed up so she and Mansi could carefully ease my skirt on without catching the layers of lace. I held my breath and closed my eyes, and asked that they turn me so I was in front of the mirror. When I opened my eyes I saw exactly what I had envisioned when I first saw Erin's designs. She had layer upon layer of the most delicate lace, until the skirt was wonderfully full.

All that I needed to do was put on the cummerbund; Mansi picked it up, and from behind me, settled it into position, and fastened it. Looking in the mirror, I saw myself with my best friends beside me on this, the most important day in my life. I wanted to see them dressed, so I spun around and sat down on the little stool while Carol pulled half my hair back, and arranged the curls down the back. Then I urged them into their dresses. Shortly afterward, we turned and faced the mirror, and suddenly there were three transformed women standing before us.

Mansi went to make sure the girls hadn't forgot their necklaces, and were all ready to leave. She yelled down the hall that the limo was just pulling into the driveway. Carol and I turned to one another before joining the others. "I don't know what my life would be like now, if you hadn't helped me from day one. How can I ever thank-you for that day and every other that has followed? They've all lead to this very day."

Carol hugged me, and whispered into my ear. "I was so lucky that I was in a position to help; I don't think I've told you enough how much I've valued your friendship. I know you thought my life was perfect, but I was missing someone very important from my life, a best friend."

We each gave a quick squeeze, and then went down the hall to the foyer, and out the door. Mansi jumped in the limo to help Joan and Susan get in without ruining their dresses, and Carol stood behind me, holding my skirt up off the ground as I bent into the limo. Carol arranged my skirt, and then climbed in. Five minutes later we were at the entrance of the Winter Club, and reversed the whole procedure. We went in, and then up the wide staircase, to the formal beginning of my new life, Joan and Susan's new life, and Trent's new life. For some reason, fate had delivered us to this moment in time. We were all willing and ready to begin the rest of our journey.

Carol entered and joined Trent and Kele. Mansi opened the doors of the ballroom, checked that the musicians were ready, and at her nod, they began Elgar's Wedding March. Our guests rose and, with Joan on my right and Susan on my left, we slowly walked, hand in hand, to the arbor where Trent stood waiting for us. The four of us turned and faced Uncle John, who stood in his vestments.

At first all I was aware of was Trent's hand holding mine, and as I gradually relaxed I began to hear John. "Dearest friends, today is one of the most special days in the lives of these four wonderful people. Each has separately negotiated tragic events in their separate lives, and was strong enough to allow themselves to once again experience God's love, through their love for one another. I have been lucky to spend more time with Trent during the past few months than I had in a long time, and if I know anything in this world, it is that he loves Clare as fully and completely as God intended when he deemed that the marriage between man and woman was so sacred that it was a sacrament.

"Trent enters into this union with great anticipation of not only being a husband to Clare, but a father to Joan and Susan. As we've shared a meal and time this summer, I feel as though I know them. Trent not only told me who they were and what they looked like, but most importantly, what their dreams and hopes were, and what their fears are.

"Jesus' father Joseph, may not be portrayed as prominently, or as interestingly as Mary, but I ask you to think about how important Joseph was in the life of his son. Had he not accepted Mary's announcement, had he not protected Mary throughout her pregnancy and delivery, had he not been a role model for Jesus as he grew, we wouldn't be sitting here celebrating the marriage of Clare and Trent.

"Trent loves both Joan and Susan, and he wants to be their protector, he wants to be their father. I could hardly wait to meet Clare, after hearing so much about her, and we've had a couple of chances to meet and talk privately. She has opened her heart and mind to allow love to once again bloom. Most of us do not know the amount of courage that takes. Whenever she talks about Trent, her eyes flash with love and protection. I know she'll always hold his heart within hers, and will love Trent with every fiber of her being.

"If each of these two people had their way, neither would ever again feel pain; either mental or physical. However, they know that life's river doesn't run straight and smooth, rather it runs over rapids, and at times diverges and then rejoins to continue on. Therefore, when they both say they'll support and love one another through good times and in bad, I know, and, indeed we all know, that they are truly prepared to follow through on today's promises.

"Clare and Trent have invited you, their guests, as witnesses to their marriage, and their promises to one another. When you came to this wedding, you also offered your support to them as they grow through their marriage. Clare and Trent, please turn to one another and as you take your vows of marriage, look into each other's eyes. Trent, do you promise that you will love and protect Clare, throughout your life?"

"I do."

"Do you promise that you will always consider Clare's feelings, will you be gentle with her love? Will you respect her knowledge?

"I do."

"Will you promise that you will love Clare, not only in the good times, but most importantly, in difficult times?"

"I do."

"Trent, place the ring you hold on Clare's finger, as a symbol of eternity, and of your love."

"Clare, you have heard the promises made by Trent. Do you accept them?"

"I do."

"Clare, will you freely love and protect Trent, during your life together?"

"I do."

"Clare will you continue loving Trent, for the rest of your life, not only during good times, but in bad?

"I do."

"Clare, place Trent's ring on his finger, and while doing so, remember that rings are symbols of both love and eternity."

"God recognized marriage as a freely entered into relationship, by a couple, who when they are ready to make a commitment, do so in the presence of God, in the presence of their family and their friends. Clare and Trent have done so today, and in God's eyes are husband and wife.

"Today another commitment was made. Joan and Susan, come and stand next to me. I know we didn't practice this last night, and that is because it was a surprise. Trent, do you promise to love and protect, for all time, Joan and Susan. Do you promise that you will help them develop into young women confident in their own being, in their abilities, and in their feelings? Do you promise to listen to them, when in times of confusion it may be hard to express themselves? Do you promise to ensure that they continue on the path that their mother has set them upon; being considerate, empathetic members in the family of man?"

"I do."

"Joan and Susan, will you promise to continue loving Trent, and will you let him help guide you?"

They both shyly looked at one another and then Trent and as one said, "Yes."

"Trent told me that when he proposed to Clare, that he also proposed to Joan and Susan, and gave them rings as well. He wishes to continue that to the end, therefore Trent take Susan's hand and put her ring on, and now take Joan's hand and put her ring on.

"Joan and Susan, I don't know if you know why a ring is a symbol for love and eternity, so I'll tell you. When you look at a ring, you can see no beginning and no end, it continues on forever, as will the love in your family. Ladies and gentlemen, I take great pleasure in pronouncing the formation of a new family, Trent and Clare, and their children, Joan and Susan. May God look over these precious bonds of love."

CHAPTER 33

We turned and then Trent scooped up Susan, Joan held his other hand, and we walked through the well wishes of our friends. Diane began to gently shoo our guests to the sitting room, to allow the tables and chairs to be rearranged. I think we had just finished a brief chat with all our guests when the dining room doors were opened by Diane, and she directed our guests to their tables. Before they were all seated, most drifted over to the picture windows to admire the already changing view. The sky was suffused with soft corals and yellows, and the silhouette of the mountains emerged more clearly

I was surprised to see Mr. Adams, quietly directing the waiters. He hadn't said that he'd be there, but I imagine he wanted to make sure that everything ran smoothly, considering the extra expense that Trent willingly assumed. Shortly all of our guests were enjoying their escargot stuffed mushrooms.

While I ate, I looked around and was so happy that Trent had decided to hire more waiters. We were all eating at the same time -- no one's food was getting cold. The waiters were instructed not to whisk the plates from the table, but instead were to wait until everyone was finished with each course. Next, the jumbo shrimp were presented properly, in silver bowels nestled in ice.

I took the opportunity to enjoy the table setting. Diane's silver certainly lifted the dinner from your ordinary catered event. The candles that burned brightly on each table were reflected in the silver, creating a wonderful effect. A lot of people were surprised while they were enjoying their shrimp. The waiters set out, on each table, a platter of shrimp, should people want more. They did, and the platters were empty when they returned to the kitchen.

The main course arrived, and I was happy to see that the meat had been cut like we instructed. I know the men were happy to see a healthy portion on their plate. Uncle John was certainly right when he said that this chef was a master at Prime Rib; it was wonderfully tender and mouth-watering in flavour. I saw a lot of our guests taking advantage of the meat platters on their tables; I know I did.

The crème caramel was a perfect ending to the meal. When tea and coffee was served, Kele rose to speak to the guests.

"It is hard to believe that it is just over a year ago that my wife Mansi and I had the privilege of welcoming Clare, Joan and Susan to Albuquerque. I had already made a Canadian friend the previous year when Trent came down to the university to share his knowledge. I didn't know that in a small way, I'd be responsible for their lives crossing paths. I do know that when you are suddenly living another culture, it is comforting to spend time with someone you know, and who has more local knowledge than you do.

"At first I thought that would be Trent's role, but quickly it became apparent that there was much more than that between Clare and Trent. I loved sitting with Trent when we had our lunch; he always had new stories about places he had taken you and about Joan, Susan and yourself. Mansi and I were privileged, along with Carol and Chris, to share your happiness last Christmas Eve when you announced your engagement. I would ask everyone to offer a toast to the happiness to this new family, to our dear friends. Salud!" Trent and I sat in silence to appreciate the hopes of our friends.

Then Trent rose, "Kele is so right. I, along with Kele, didn't know that when the newest Canuck showed up, I'd end falling in love again, not only with a woman, but with two little girls as well. I certainly didn't expect to be engaged by Christmas and then married by this summer. If I recall correctly, my most pressing issue of that time was thinking about where I'd go for holidays.

Clare and I agreed before today, that we wouldn't ignore Nina and Julia; that we wouldn't try and pretend they didn't exist. Clare was most emphatic that we should include them in today's celebration, for it was the deep love that I had for them that allowed me, eventually, to risk pain in order to regain what I shared with Nina.

"Most of those here today were at my wedding to Nina, many held Julia within days of her birth. You also grieved with me, when they were taken from us so suddenly. My grief was so intense because my love for them was so deep. It was hard to imagine that I could once again feel that way, and once I acknowledged that I did, I kept it hidden from Clare.

"Should I take a chance and tell her how I felt and risk her sending me away? I wrestled with that question every night, and with each night the struggle lessened. Perhaps Nina was helping me see that all Clare told me about her years since we were last together were her way of saying that she, too, was longing for love.

"I would find myself playing with Joan and Susan, and for the while I'd feel guilty. I felt ashamed that I was enjoying playing with these little girls when I no longer could with Julia. Slowly, my guilt transformed into pleasure that included Julia. I'd look at something Susan or Joan did, and gently form a picture that never was; Julia doing the same things." Trent's voice started to crack, so I went and stood next to him.

"Trent is so right. Despite their absences from our lives, these people can still have a tremendous impact. Therefore, as we celebrate our marriage today, Trent and I would like to send our thoughts and prayers to those no longer at our sides."

Glasses were raised, and I think most of us were using the moment to compose ourselves. Shortly after that, the tables were moved to the perimeter, and the dance floor was cleared. The quiet music allowed people to dance if they wished, yet allowed visiting without having to shout at people to have a conversation.

Joan and Halona came up to us and Joan wanted to know how long they'd have to stay. I know they were anxious to go home so they could catch up on all their news, listen to CDs and watch Much Music. Kele was standing next to us at the time, and volunteered to drive them home. I had made arrangements with our neighbor to pop in occasionally to make sure the girls were fine.

Trent and I walked them out to the front door, and gave each of them a big hug and kiss. We promised to phone them the next day, from Hawaii. I don't know how many people that I met that night, but I'm sure that I probably forgot most of the names within minutes. We danced, we visited and planned visits later in the year with many a new relative. By 11:30 most people were sipping coffee and tea, rather than drinks, and it was obvious that it was time for us to leave so our guests could go home.

It was too difficult to say good-bye to each guest, so Trent went to the microphone. "Clare and I want to thank-you all again, for celebrating our wedding with us. We're leaving early this morning for Maui, so we decided that we'd better get a short rest. Thank-you and goodnight." We exited to applause and good wishes.

CHAPTER 34

Clare, Chris, Mansi and Kele drove with us to the Airport Hotel, where we booked a suite. They stayed only long enough for a quick drink and more hugs and kisses. In a moment we were alone for the first time since what felt like years ago; that morning. Trent stood behind me and his arms encircled me as his lips gently nuzzled my neck and my ears. "Was today everything you hoped for, honey?" I heard whispered into my ears.

"It was just perfect. Everything went perfectly, thanks to your mother. She is incredibly organized, isn't she? I think she could throw anything together at very little notice. I only had to worry about getting myself and the girls ready. When I went to phone the club this morning, she intercepted me, and took care of whatever it was herself. Before I met her, I worried whether she'd like my little family, and she's been so welcoming. You were a very lucky little baby to born to your mom and dad. I would have loved to have met him. When the girls and I were walking toward you, I had to fight the urge to run and throw my arms around you. I could feel the girls trying to walk faster; they wanted to be next to you as quickly as possible, too. How long is it until our flight leaves?"

Trent looked at his watch, lasciviously smiled at me, and said, "We still have two hours, time enough."

"Time enough for what?" I tried to ask innocently.

"Time enough to make love to my wife instead of my mistress!" With that uttered, Trent bent to the task of unbuttoning the many little buttons that studded my back. His fingers brushed against my neck as he started at the top; the next button led to lips on my neck. I stood perfectly still and listened to my body. Thrilling signals were sent to down my back, back up to my nipples, and to my thighs. I managed to stay still until Trent undid the last button, slipped his hands under my blouse, and slid it down my arms. I had to turn to him. There I stood, bare to the waist, enjoying the sight of my husband's hungry looks.

It was my turn; I moved closer and began to slowly undo his studs and cufflinks. I had to step even closer to undo his vest, and as I did so, I felt his hot breath down my back, I felt his stiff muscles as he stood controlling himself. My hands drifted down his chest and belly, seeking the clips on the side of trousers. Once they were opened, my hands traveled once again over his belly and chest, and across his shoulders to push his shirt to the floor.

We each stood there, half bare, and as if by agreement, we moved to the bed. As we stood beside the bed, Trent grabbed my waist and searched for the zipper on my skirt. Once he lowered it, I stood there before him, with the filmy panties and garter belt I had chosen for him. His face gave me all the approval I needed, all the encouragement I needed to begin to strip for him.

I spun around and presented my back, while I bent over to loosen a stocking. I sat on the bed, and slowly pulled off a stocking. I raised the other leg to him, and he obliged me, loosening the other stocking and slowly pulling it off. He took both legs and placed them over his shoulders, while he bent to the mysteries of the garter belt. Once it was removed, Trent set me in the middle of the bed, and bent to remove his socks and then his trousers. For a moment he stood, naked, ready to come together with his new bride.

We still didn't speak; instead we spoke through our bodies. Trent bent his lips to the task of discovering my entire body, with delicious results. I hardly knew which body signals to pay attention; first my nipples insisted on my acknowledgment, then my sides started sending tiny messages to my clitoris, which demanded precedence.

I had to move; I straddled Trent and began an assault on his body, my hands and mouth making him ready to join with me. Suddenly urgency was the key. We turned to one another. Now was the time, and I opened my legs to him, urging him into me. Our movements echoed one another's until we both climaxed in delight of one another.

We lay in bed curled side by side, and gradually began softly talking about our day, and how in love we were. We dozed for just awhile, and then pulled ourselves from the bed, and into the bathroom. After a long, sensuous shower, we dried off, and changed into our traveling clothes. We had the hotel porter take our luggage over to the airline, and followed behind it. An hour later we were sitting in our first class seats, awaiting take-off.

We landed in Honolulu five hours later and took the Wiki-Wiki bus over to the inter-island terminal for our twenty minute flight to Maui. We were soon waiting with our luggage next to the carousel, looking for our driver. A minute later Trent raised his arm to signal a young man walking by with our name on a sign. I had forgotten that Trent told me the Newman's limo and driver were at our disposal.

In no time our luggage was in the trunk and we were relaxing, enjoying the scenery as we drove from the airport to Kihei. We passed through cane fields, and we passed through tropical plants, and we saw the bottom of Haleakala, the major volcano on Maui. The top was covered with clouds, as often it is. Trent and I had already decided that we'd make the early morning pilgrimage to see the sunrise from the top of the "House of the Sun."

We drove through the town of Kihei, past condominiums, and more condominiums. I haven't seen so many Canadian flags in a foreign place before. Our driver, Kaena, told us that so many Canadians visited the Kihei area that the merchants wanted to keep them happy and to acknowledge their importance.

Kehei ran along the beach, stores and condos mauka and tourists makai. We were just past the last store, when Kaena turned makai (to the sea), and in minutes was pulling up the front driveway of our honeymoon haven. It was indeed paradise, and that opinion was formed purely on the outside view. A green lawn ran down toward the sea, until it became tangled with round-leaved plants that grew along the line between sand and soil.

It was the beach I headed for, even before going inside. I expected wind, but the August air in Hawaii hangs still and heavy. My skin hungrily absorbed the water that was borne on the air after leaping off the waves. I felt Trent come up behind me, and he slipped his arms around me.

We swayed together, looking out on the grandeur of the ocean, until I stirred and whispered, "This really is perfect. How are we ever going to thank the Newman's?"

Trent's reply told me everything I needed to know about his god-parents. "The best thank-you we can give them is to enjoy our time here and live happily ever after. They were wonderful when Nina and Julia died, and so worried that I'd never again have a love in my life. To them, you are a miracle come to life, and they couldn't be happier. In fact, they've already told me that they'd like us all to visit them here in the New Year. Come; let's go check out the house."

We walked up the lawn, and by the time we went in the house, I was very hot. We weren't used to the humidity. The house gave us an oasis of cool, refreshing air. The foyer of the house was done in marble, and it led into the living room. All of the exterior walls were continuous Jalousie windows. The late morning sun highlighted the peach walls and the wonderfully printed fabrics.

We left the living room to investigate the rest of the house. The dining room and kitchen were across the hallway, and when we went through the kitchen, I couldn't help but notice that everything any chef could possibly want was there. The dining room was furnished in mellow teak, and the simple style echoed the serenity of the house. At the back of the house were the bedrooms, all four of them, and the bathrooms. The master bedroom took up one corner of the whole house. It had its own lanai and an incredible view of the ocean. The king-size bed was placed to ensure that those in it could view the ocean. We walked onto the lanai, and saw to our delight a Jacuzzi surrounded by a jungle of tropical plants, which made a delightful screen. We went back in through the bedroom and back to the kitchen.

Kaena was just coming in with the last suitcase. "My wife Leilani and I live in the apartment over the garage, and we look after the house and the grounds. Leilani makes all the meals, and would like to come down this afternoon to discuss menus with you. The two of us do the house and yard cleaning, but if you want privacy, we'll wait until you call us."

Trent and I looked at one another, and then he said to Kaena, "We'd love to meet Leilani, and we can give her an idea of what we'll want for food. I don't think we'll worry about having her cook breakfasts, and we'll probably do most of the evening meals. We're on our honeymoon, and, since I have two new daughters waiting at home, I think the thing we'll enjoy most is privacy."

"Mrs. Newman told me that you were on your honeymoon. Leilani will call this afternoon to see when you'd like her to come down. We've stocked the fridge with enough things for a few days. We thought you might like Azeka's Ribs for tonight, so they're in the fridge, and the rice cooker is set. The rice will be ready at 6 o'clock."

"That sounds great, Kaena. We were told to make sure we had those ribs, at least once, while we were here. Perhaps you'd tell Leilani that if she came down around four, I'd appreciate it. That is, of course, if it is convenient for her."

I hope that sounded right; I've never had staff to give directions to. I looked to Trent for some indication that I was right, and he gave me a nod. He walked out with Kaena, and made arrangements about the cars. Trent and I wanted to go out on our own, so he decided we'd use the Newman's red Mercedes instead of the limo. While Trent was outside, I went into the bedroom and began unpacking. In no time, that chore was done, our toiletries were in the bathroom, and it looked like our own bedroom. I stripped off my dress, and decided that I either had to go for a swim, or have a shower. While I wandered around the bedroom nude trying to decide, Trent came in and stripped off.

CHAPTER 35

"Come on. Let's go to the beach. There is a chest down there with everything we'll need; towels, lotion, beach mats, and even books." He started out the door without stopping to put a bathing suit on.

"Hon, don't you think you'll need your bathing suit? As far as I know, nude sunbathing isn't legal here."

Trent paused at the lanai door, looked back at me and laughed. "We are at the end of this stretch of the beach and there is a sign posted, saying, private, nude beach, and we're going to take advantage of that."

We ran down the lawn, found the chest, pulled out everything we needed, laid it out on the sand and ran to the water's edge. At first the water seemed cold to our feet, but in no time, as we progressed a little further in it felt warmer and warmer. I took a deep breath and plunged under. It was warm, and I loved being washed back and forth by the small waves.

This was how the ancient Hawaiians swam; in intimate harmony with nature. Trent surprised me, I thought he was behind me, but he circled me underwater, and grabbed my thighs. We laughed as we tagged one another and I scolded him. Even though I love the water, that didn't mean I wasn't keeping an eye open for sharks. Without my glasses, I was sure they could swim right up to me, and I wouldn't see them until they announced their presence.

We stayed in the water for twenty minutes or so, until we decided that it was time to get some sun. That wasn't as easy as it sounds. First we lined up the various lotions; SFP35 (for those private areas that hadn't been exposed to the sun much, SFP 25, for slightly more exposed skin, and then SFP15, for our skin that was already tanned. Of course we had a lot of fun, applying it, but after the time taken to apply it, we only stayed there for a half an hour. Neither of us wanted to start our holiday burned. Besides, it was almost time to meet with Leilani.

We showered together to get the sand out of some places that are most uncomfortable if sand remains. I threw a dress on and went to the kitchen. Leilani was a beautiful young woman and we quickly felt comfortable with one another. She helped me decide on groceries, letting me know what local products we'd most likely want to try. By the time she left, her list was rather long and she told me, she'd shop in the morning and have it all put away before we came back in the afternoon. As soon as she was out of the door, Trent came in to see if I wanted to go into town and see what was there.

He was ready to go, all I needed to do was comb my hair, and we were gone. It was fun driving with the top down, and the air rushing over us, cooling us. We wandered in and out of T-shirt shops, scuba shops, and more tourist shops. While in one of the scuba shops, Trent started talking with the owner, and the next thing I knew, he'd arranged for some private lessons, in our pool, with the idea of a diving trip to Molokini before we left.

When I was in university, I planned to take scuba lessons at the pool, but changed my mind when I saw the cost. I couldn't afford the $160.00. I was happy about the lessons, but wasn't entirely sure about diving in the open ocean; however, I was willing to consider it. When we left the shop, it was with prescription goggles for me -- not much use diving if you can't see in front of your face. Plus, I wanted lots of warning if there were any sharks within sight.

We barbequed our supper on the lanai, and the ribs with rice were fantastic. I was quite sure that I'd be happy eating them every night of our honeymoon. We didn't even worry about our few dishes; we sat on the lanai listening to the hush as the waves quietly made room for the next. The sky was brilliant with stars that stood out like stars do when we look at them away from the city

We strolled down to the beach, but it wasn't uneventful. We were only half way there, when something jumped right in front of me. I'll admit it; I did let out a little scream. It was only when the toad moved that we were able to see it. Then it seemed like the lawn was alive with them. I walked in front of Trent on the way back to the house. I didn't want any toads attacking from behind.

I think I jumped a couple of feet straight up when something touched my leg. I whirled and saw Trent holding a long piece of sea grass. I would have stolen it from him, but that meant I'd have to go back, so instead I ran into the house. He was just behind me, still holding the stupid grass, and he chased me around the house. I turned tricks on him and hid in one of the bedrooms, held my breath and stood still, until he came in looking for me. When I jumped out of the closet it was his turn to jump.

We hugged and laughed. We walked through the house, locking the doors, and turning the lights off. We were already lulled by the quiet and peace of the island, and joined in soft sensuousness. I remember lying next to Trent, enjoying the breeze on my body as it floated down from the ceiling fan. Then I was running and running; but where was I? A little boy stood at the edge of the water, and before I could get to him, he walked out into the waves.

I ran as hard as I could, but even when I came to the shore I couldn't reach him. The further out I went, the further out he went. How could that be? A two year old child couldn't swim like that, how was he staying afloat? I thought I had him, but when my hand reached to the spot he had been, he was carried further out. He looked at me, steadily and clearly, and called, "Bye-bye, Mommy." And he disappeared. I stood there looking at my empty hands; they once held something, and now no one else can see that he exists. Am I any more certain? I became aware that Trent was sitting up in bed, shaking me.

"Honey, wake up, wake up Clare." Suddenly I knew I was awake. "What's the matter, can you tell me?"

"I'm not sure. It was a dream, and I remember there was a little boy standing by the water. He said good-bye, I think." I didn't really know what to say, it wasn't clear even to myself.

Trent pulled me next to him, and then I woke up to the sound of the mourning doves. I felt somewhat exhausted, but attributed it to the past few hectic days. I fixed our breakfast; fresh papaya with lemon, and English muffins. "Let's drive up island to Lahina this morning Clare. We don't want to spend too much of our time in the sun right away, so we could get our sightseeing out of the way." I guess I didn't answer right away. "Are you too tired to go today?"

"I felt a little sleepy when I first woke up, but I'm fine now. I'll throw our bathing suits and towels into a bag, just in case we want to stop along the way. Why don't you get the car, and I'll run down and grab the lotion."

Off we went for a wonderful tour of the island. In Kihei, there are both tropical foliage and desert plants. I certainly didn't expect to see cactus, let alone cactus the size of a bush. We drove through cane fields, and we drove along the highway as it rose and fell as it followed the coast line

The biggest challenge in Lahina was finding a spot to park. Once that goal was accomplished, we decided against immediately wandering through the shops, and instead went through the whaling museum, and then we went to a historic home. After that, we found a lovely, small restaurant that was cool and shady, and allowed us to watch the boats coming and going in the harbor. We dawdled over our lunch, since it was so much fun watching all the people going back and forth.

Eventually we left and made our way to the shopping complex behind the museum. The tourist items didn't interest either of us too much, but we were in heaven when we rounded a corner and found an art gallery in front of us. We entered and fell in love with six paintings right away.

We were drawn to the brilliant colour, and the scenes of rural, Mediterranean islands. The artist, Igor Medvedev, created glaring light bouncing off the bright red doors, the clear blue roofs, and the white walls. We must have stayed in the gallery for an hour or more.

By the time we had left, Trent and I had bought two of the paintings and had another one on hold. We didn't want to risk damage to the paintings, so we arranged with the gallery owner to have them packed professionally and sent home to Calgary. They would be there when we got home.

While in the gallery, I mentioned to Trent that I was getting hungry, and wondered if we were going to drive home for supper or eat somewhere in Lahina. One of the clerks overheard us and mentioned that the luau at the Sheraton Ka'anapali was well done. We thanked her for the information, but when we were walking to the car, decided that we'd rather drive home have a snack, lay in the sun for awhile and then make supper.

We grabbed a snack, hopped in the car, and in forty minutes we were back home. I looked in the fridge, and it was obvious that Leilani had already done the shopping; the fridge and cupboards were bulging. She left a note, telling us that the mahi-mahi was fresh that morning, and that it would be good to have within a day. She thoughtfully left instructions on how to cook it.

Once again, we went through the lotion process, and were pleased to note that neither of us had any burned areas, and decided we keep with our cautious schedule. The ocean was very calm that afternoon, and we floated on our backs, looking at cloud shapes in the sky. The mahi-mahi was delicious cooked over the barbeque, and we enjoyed another tranquil evening.

Neither of us were night owls in Canada, but here we found it hard to keep our eyes open past 10 o'clock. Another night of gentle love led to being lulled to sleep by a combination of our satisfied bodies and the soft night sounds. I remember being awakened abruptly during the night by a loud thumping sound. I sat up in the dark, heard it again, but couldn't figure out what it was. I listened for another ten minutes or so, didn't hear anything, so went back to sleep.

Next I remember thinking, that little boy is too young to be at the beach by himself. I looked all over to see where his parents were, but I couldn't see them. Who would abandon a child, like this? I walked up the beach one way, and then the other. The only adults in sight were so far away, I couldn't see their faces. I walked to them anyway; they must be his parents. By the time I was at the parking lot, they had driven away. I looked back, and the little boy was gone. I swiveled my head back to the car, and there he was, waving at me from the back seat.

The next morning, I told Trent about the noises I heard during the night, and we went outside to investigate. We walked around the house, and finally saw what had awakened me. Just outside our bedroom window, a coconut tree arched gracefully toward our window, and sometime during the night four coconuts fell to the ground. "That must have been what you were dreaming about last night. You woke me up tossing and turning, and moaning. You said something about being hurt." Trent looked at me quizzically.

"I don't remember that, I remember sitting up in bed listening for the sound. Oh, well. If I hear it tonight I'll know what it is."

"Did I tell you that the scuba instructor is coming over at 11? Are you ready to give it a try?" he asked me.

"Yes, I think it is really exciting, but I have to tell you that I'm not sure that I'll want to dive at Molokini. I could always sit on the boat and watch, if I'm afraid of going in."

"Honey, you know you don't have to do anything that you don't want to. We'll just take it one day at a time. No one is pressuring us to go further with this than we want."

We had lots of fun during our first lesson, I was happy that I didn't get any feelings of claustrophobia like some people I knew. Trent had a ball, and took to it right away. The instructor called him a natural.

CHAPTER 36

The next week followed a pattern. A leisurely breakfast, followed by a walk down to the public beach, and then into the pool for our lesson. I felt more confident with each passing day. The day before our one week anniversary, we decided that we'd go to the top of Haleakala. We set our alarm to ring at four-thirty in the morning. We dressed quietly, and with barely a word or two, loaded the car with the picnic we packed the night before.

The early morning held a stillness that we were reluctant to break, so we rode in silence as we climbed higher and higher until we were arrived at the gate of the National Park. We paid our entrance fee and used the facilities. The ranger told us that we were on schedule to see the sunrise. With breathtaking suddenness we were at the summit. We slipped our jackets on, and walked up to the observation point. There were only four others there, and there was a sense that this sunrise was meant for us alone. As we stood waiting the arrival of the sun, the moon's silvery light, softly illuminated the astronomical observatory with a ghostly whiteness. We turned from them, and with astonishing suddenness, a dome of light began its ascent. The top layer of light began as an almost black purple, and with each minute, more and more pink began to show.

We stood in silence, appreciating the colours we were shown by nature. Nature can conceive more variations of one colour than we can possibly begin to imagine. While we were treated and amazed by colours that seemed to come right from the ocean, the morning darkness began to vanish with the arrival of buttery, yellow light that surrounded an intense, almost white lemon colour. We were lucky not only to see this sunrise, but we could watch the full moon gradually loose it's light and fade.

The silence was unearthly. Six people watched this spectacle, without a word passing among them. It seemed sacrilegious to speak, before this display of the power of nature. Our contemplation was interrupted by a carload of noisy tourists, who profaned the silence and peace with their shouted obscenities because they were late. Those of us who had shared this unique experience communicated our displeasure with silent looks of reproach; those looks were not understood.

The spell was broken, and we six scattered to begin a new day, full of awe for the spectacular sunrise, for Mother Nature, who can so peacefully display her power. While Trent and I walked to the visitors' center, I told him, "Now I understand what Mark Twain said about this sunrise, 'the sublimest spectacle I ever witnessed.'" We walked along in silence.

"Can you imagine all the things that Mark Twain saw, and then calls this the most spectacular. We're lucky we didn't have to spend a life time exploring the continent, before we were treated to this. Where did you hear about Mark Twain?" Trent asked me.

"I picked up what I thought was a magazine, instead it was basically a beautiful book of photographs. I guess it was a part of a series, this one was called, *Hawaii Maui: Island At The Crossroads.*"

As we walked along, we picked up pieces of sharp, jagged edged lava with the thought of taking them home with us as a souvenir. At the visitors' center, there were samples of the different types of lava. The lava we held in our hands was called A'A'. There was pahoehoe lava, which flowed and as it cooled, formed wrinkles and ropes. There were samples of lava that reminded us of spun sugar, so thin and glistening they were. The Hawaiians called this Pele's Hair, and the name seemed so right.

Trent and I were slowly warming up from the cold morning air. The climb from sea level to the top of Haleakala is the highest, in the shortest distance, in the world. The ranger told us this when he came over and pointed out a small herd of feral goats that were heading into the crater. Their descendants were brought to the islands by early settlers, but they thrived when they escaped, as their descendants do to this day

Unfortunately, the ranger told us, they are very destructive to the native plants and animals of the islands. As he headed over to another couple, he turned and told us, "You might not want to take that lava home. Pele gets angry with those who take part of her away from the islands."

Trent and I sort of shifted the lava from hand to hand, and when we went outside to head up to another observation point, we looked at one another, and as one, we dropped the lava to join the other parts of Pele that lay at our feet. The crater itself was fascinating: I expected to see just a black hole. Rather, the colours were astounding. They didn't just come from plant material, but from the minerals that Madame Pele threw up for the Hawaiians.

The mineral content is very high, which can be seen in the greens, the coppers and reds that bathe the crater floor. I was also expecting just a hole, and we were both very surprised to see the many cinder cones that rose from the crater floor. While I was looking at the largest, Pu'u OMaui-Haleakala, I could envision bolts of the softest velvet draped over furniture, it's folds absorbing the light and it's ridges bouncing subtle hues upon subtle hues to delight our eye.

The image of cloth brought to mind the legend we read the day before about why this volcano was called Haleakala. It means the house of the sun, and legend tells us of Maui, who wanted to help his mother with all her chores. She didn't have enough light during the day to finish making her tapa cloth, so Maui lassoed the sun and kept it at the summit so his mother would be able to finish making her tapa.

The goddess Pele was responsible for the volcanoes of Hawaii, it is said that she was trying to get away from her evil sister, Na Maka o Kaha'i, the ocean. The only way she could do this was by forming land in the middle of the ocean. Pele and Na Maka o Kaha'i were the daughters of Haumea, Mother Earth and Wakea, the Sky Father.

We learned that the Hawaiians, through their legends, were right about the order in which the islands were formed, and basically how they were formed. In the early days of Polynesian settlement of the islands, the Polynesians wanted to placate Pele, who was still angrily forming new lands to stay away from her sister. The volcanoes were destructive, and the Hawaiians wanted to stop them. They tried through human sacrifice.

Today, Hawaiians still leave sacrifices to Pele, sacrifices of fruits, vegetables and flowers. These are folded in Ti leaves, and placed next to a hot vent, where prayers are said, asking Pele to accept the offerings.

Trent and I walked in silence to our car, thanking nature for the sunrise of a new day, thanking nature for allowing us to begin a new life. The drive down the volcano is very different than going up because you focus on the ocean that seems almost directly below you. We were both hungry on the drive down, and kept an eye open for a restaurant, finally coming upon one, halfway down to sea level.

Outside the air was much warmer than on top of the volcano, and the flowers burst forth all around the rustic building. We had already been up for enough time that we felt like having lunch, not breakfast. Obviously this restaurant was used to that, they started serving lunch at ten o'clock. Our table looked down to the sea, and while we were sitting there I saw a movement from the corner of my eye. I nudged Trent, and we both saw someone hang gliding. Our waitress saw the expressions on our face and explained.

"This is a very popular spot for hang gliding. Some people jump from a cliff not far from here, and some, from almost at the top of Haleakala. Can I get you anything for dessert?"

Instead of automatically saying no, I asked to see the menu. When she brought it back, she suggested a particular dessert. Trent and decided we'd split it. I think our eyes must have popped when she brought it to the table; it must have been four inches tall. Trent and I started our attack. We broke through the first layers of black raspberries on top of whipped cream, the top of the puff pastry, down into the custard level and more raspberries, until we found the bottom layer of puff pastry. This was pure heaven in our mouths. There seemed to be a certain magic in sitting eating this dessert after watching the sunrise, and seeing gliders float down from Haleakala. After tea, we managed to rouse ourselves enough to pay our bill. We decided on the rest of our descent, that rather than go straight home, we'd venture inland to see the 'Iao Needle.

This pointed mountain rose straight from the floor of a valley lush with tropical plants; flowering and giant ferns. We followed the short path that led us past some interpretive sites, where local women demonstrated the crafts of the Hawaiians: tapa making, braiding of plants to form ropes, and taro farming. They also explained the importance of the valley and the needle. The ancient chiefs were buried in the valley and the valley holds much mana, or sacred energy.

Trent and I found ourselves overwhelmed at the forces of nature we'd seen in such a short time, and in such close proximity. The valley sat shrouded in a heavy stillness of contemplation. We didn't arrive home until early afternoon, and we were both too tired to contemplate anything more strenuous than a nap in the shade of our lanai. I phoned Leilani, and told her that we wouldn't need anything until lunch the next day. We stripped off our clothes, spread our towels out on the lounge chairs, opened our books and promptly feel asleep.

The sun woke us up. We had been asleep long enough for most of the shade to disappear. We decided to cool off in the water, and played in the waves for what seemed like an hour, then went through our sunscreen ritual. We had enough tan in those certain spots that we could eliminate the SFP35, so only needed two bottles. Another afternoon passed, as we alternated lying in the sun, and playing in the waves. We practiced scuba diving a little further off shore, where the ocean lay calm. There wasn't too much to see right in front of the house, but Trent called me over to a spot he found next to some of the rocks, at the far end of the beach. I was amazed when I joined him and saw the profusion of colour. Yellow Tangs, with their sharp noses and flat bodies swam by in schools. Puffer fish, tiny as they were, would put on their defensive display and puff up to three times their size as they swam back and forth in front of an entrance to their little square of coral. Huge, silvery, flat fish swam by in schools, striped angel fish swam by lazily, unconcerned with our presence.

When we swam back to the beach, I pretty well had my mind made up. I was going to scuba dive when we sailed to Molokini, sometime before we left. Despite our nap, the early morning rising and all the activity of the day caught up with us, and we went to bed early. I think I fell asleep before my head hit the pillow.

I became aware of once again being at the summit of Haleakala, but I didn't look like myself. I was wearing a skirt of tapa cloth; a small boy clung to my hand. He stood naked and shivering. I laid him across my lap and painted his body with ochre. I could hear that I was speaking, but it wasn't English; it sounded like a prayer. I sent the little boy away from my side, and as he stood watching me, I bent and began wrapping poi, flowers, nuts, mangos and papaya in Ti leaves.

The little boy began to cry, and I saw myself open my arms to him. He crawled into my lap, seeking both warmth and comfort. He nursed, while I saw tears form in my eyes and fall onto him. The little boy and I sat in silence, until suddenly I saw myself pull him from my breast and walk closer to the edge of the volcano, his hand in mine. I was surprised to see the volcano active, molten lava bubbling, stinging steam rose, making our eyes water. No, she isn't going to! I saw her pick the little boy up, and hold him over the lava.

I woke up screaming and thrashing. "No, no you can't do that. It won't stop the lava. Please, he is your son, don't drop him, don't! Patrick!" I felt Trent's arms around me, and heard comforting sounds, but I couldn't calm down. My heart was pounding in my chest. Not only was it pounding hard, but it was racing. I could hardly get a breath of air. I felt tears streaming down my cheeks.

I don't know how long Trent held me and tried to comfort me, but finally I was able to choke out what frightened me. "Honey, can you remember any of your other dreams that you've had this week." I nodded yes. "Can you tell me about them? It might help." He held me close to him, and when I finished he asked me, "Do you have any idea of what your mind is trying to tell you?"

"It's Patrick; I see him in dangerous situations, but then he is safe. But I've always abandoned him, he is always by himself, until the very end. There are times when I can logically stay my heart. Yes, it was probably best for him, but when I can't then I blame myself. What was wrong with me, that I gave him to strangers? I don't even know if he is alive. What if he's been in an accident and killed? How will I know?"

"Honey, do you remember what we said at the wedding about those in our past who were no longer with us. I have a feeling that you just weren't talking about Nina and Julia. Without even thinking about it, I think you were trying to say that Patrick wasn't with you. Does that make sense to you?"

"I think so, but why would I have these dreams now, when I didn't since after he was born?"

"I don't know honey, but when we get home, maybe it would be a good idea to make an appointment to talk with someone. I don't want you going to sleep worrying about these nightmares." I fell asleep while Trent rubbed my back.

CHAPTER 37

In the morning, Trent asked me if I remembered having a dream last night, I guess he didn't want to worry me, in case I didn't. "Yes honey, I do remember, and I actually feel a little better remembering, even though it hurts. When I woke after the other dreams, I felt vaguely uneasy, without knowing why. I think you are probably right that it would be a good idea for me to see someone at home, but for now, I'd rather not worry about it. Are we having another scuba lesson today?"

"Yes, I told him to come over around eleven. I thought maybe we should have him take us out where we were snorkeling yesterday, sort or a trial run. What do you think?"

"Yes, I think I'd like that. Yesterday, I almost convinced myself that I want to when we go to Molokini." I phoned Leilani and told her that we'd want lunch at one; I didn't feel like cooking today.

The instructor told us that he had planned on getting us in the ocean today, so he was pleased that we had made the decision ourselves. I felt safe so close to the house, and had a great time exploring around the coral and rocks. I saw Trent wave me over, and when I swam over, I saw that Dan was pointing out a moray eel. I didn't get too close; I wasn't taking any chances. We followed Dan, like little ducklings follow their mother, as he led us out, ever deeper. The smaller fish stayed closer to the top and we began to see different fish. Of course I was busily scanning the area for sharks.

I didn't see sharks but I saw large, multi-coloured parrot fish that swam in iridescent schools. We also swam among Blue fin Trevally, which are beautiful. Their backs are a lawn green, while their bellies are peacock blue. Soon, it was time to head to shore, and as we rose in the water we once again saw Pyramid butterfly fish and Moorish Idols. By the time we waded ashore, I knew that I had one question to ask of Dan. "Are there sharks at the dive site at Molokini?"

"I won't lie and say no, but remember, they stay at the bottom, and the water is very deep. They are also very used to divers and they haven't bothered anyone for years and years. If you want I'll be beside you every minute, so you feel safer." His dark eyes stared into my blue ones, and he knew that I was fighting with myself, but really wanted to dive there. He stood quietly waiting for my answer.

"If you're with me, then I'm going to dive." Trent laughed, and I knew he was relieved that I made the decision. I think he knew I'd regret it once we were home if I didn't at least try.

We asked Dan to join us for lunch, and we sat on the lanai, while he told us about Molokini. We learned that it was what remained of the edge of a volcanic crater, the rest of which was under water. It is a favourite diving spot because of the numbers of different fish in the area, and the calm seas. We set a date for our dive, and then said good-bye to Dan. While Leilani finished with the dishes we decided what we'd have for supper, Ono fish, and then she went up to her apartment. Trent and I took off our suits and headed down to the beach to lie in the sun; we'd be going home without tan lines.

We were in the middle of our last week on Maui, and were starting to miss Joan and Susan. I could hardly wait until we brought them to Hawaii. They are both water babies. Trent told me that he'd made reservations for the luau at the Sheraton Ka'a'napali for that evening, so in mid-afternoon, we dragged ourselves out of the sun, showered and changed into our dressier Hawaiian clothes.

I bought a muumuu by Reyn Spooner, and the material was fantastic. It felt like silk against my skin, the turquoise colour was luminous, yet subdued, and enhanced with softly shaded flowers. I wore it low off my shoulder. Trent was wearing a Spooner Aloha shirt, made of similar fabric to mine, but coloured in incredible shades of grey, highlighted with turquoise.

We drove north, along the ocean, passed through Lahina, and just down the road to our destination. The hotel was situated at the very end of the beach. As twilight quickly gathered, a conch horn was blown by a young man as he made his way through the complex. We followed him out onto the beach, and with the gathering crowd saw the tiki torches lit, and watched the young man climb up to the top of Black Rock Cliff.

He stood quietly, his arms outstretched as he offered a lei to the sea; he studied the sea and when the dying light silhouetted him, dove into the water below. We held our collective breaths until we saw his head break the water. Young women in ancient dress, led us to the luau. I was slightly uneasy that we had been roped into a cheesy tourist event, but while it was not everything I wished for, it was much better than I hoped for. The meal was adequate, and the dancers were excellent. I just wondered how authentic they were; was all this just for tourists? We left when the dancing was completed, and drove with the top down, back down the coast to Kihei. We talked of our dive, which was the next day. Trent told me that we were sailing out to Molokini on a true sailing ship.

The next morning we met Dan at the dock, and I was surprised to see that we were the only ones. I looked at Trent who gave me a grin. "I asked Dan to hire the boat just for us, so we have his guidance all the time, and it seemed more romantic. The sail out to Molokini lasted about forty-five minutes, and when I saw the other boats pass us, I was happy we were on our own. Many in the other boats seemed bent more on being rowdy and drinking, than enjoying the sail and the dive.

When our ship weighed anchor, most of the commercial boats had disgorged their customers who hadn't quieted down yet. Our captain had placed our ship slightly away from the others. Dan helped us on with our gear, donned his own, and then he slipped into the water, without my asking, to check out the shark situation.

He reported back to me, "There aren't any near us; they are all over where the others are diving, because their staff has been touching them. They are staying down near the bottom." He and Trent both looked at me to see what my response would be.

Instead of talking, I acted and walked to the dive platform and slipped into the water. Trent followed and soon we were diving side by side, down, further than ever before. I became so enamored with the fish and, believe it or not, a tiny shark that glided our way that I relaxed and thoroughly enjoyed the dive. Dan motioned for us to follow him and he pointed out the coral hollows that some eels were claiming as home. He held his fish chart in front of him, and pointed to the variety of fish we were seeing. Soon it was time to ascend.

Trent went aboard first, and then helped me get in. Dan brought up the rear. We rehashed the dive as we sat on deck, enjoying our lunch, and decided that we'd dive again, once we let our lunch digest. Laying on deck, the sun and the lulling motion of the ship put us to sleep. We must have slept for an hour. We were awakened by the noise made by the divers from the other ships as their ships left the shelter of Molokini. Dan checked to see if we wanted to go for another dive, and with our yes, we got busy and ready.

The water felt wonderfully cooling, and this dive was even more enjoyable, since there was only one small other group still diving. We were diving for quite awhile, when Dan lived up to his promise, and pointed out a couple of what I thought were huge White tip reef sharks. He signaled the question about getting out of the water, but I shook my head. They were swimming to the bottom of the ocean, as if getting some time away from people. I didn't throw all caution to the wind, though. I stayed closer to Dan. On board, we saw the other ship setting sail for home. Trent told me that the boat was ours for the entire day, so we weren't in any hurry to leave. We warmed ourselves on deck, had fun talking with Dan and the crew, and decided on one more dive before anymore divers arrived. We didn't stay under as long, we felt the currents getting stronger, and I felt somewhat uneasy.

Getting into the boat this time was more difficult. Every time I put my leg up to the stair, the ship would rise and I couldn't reach it; I knew these short legs would cause me trouble. Trent and one of the crew pulled me up high enough so I could reach the step. I managed to give my shin a good whack on the way, but I was in. We decided that the sea was getting quite choppy and that it was time to head for shore.

Dan followed us in his car, as we once again hugged the shoreline back to Kehei. We waved goodbye at the Y-intersection. Trent pulled into the property, and turned with a questioning look at me. "Are you glad that you decided to dive?"

"I am. I think I would have kicked myself once we were home if I didn't. Mind you I did end up with a bruised shin anyway. I'll confess that I felt a little panicky when I couldn't reach the stair. I guess that means next time, we'll have to make sure there is a longer ladder on board."

CHAPTER 38

We kissed and hauled all of our stuff onto the lanai. When I looked in the kitchen I saw the rice cooker ready light on, and saw Azeka's ribs waiting on the counter. Leilani made a great choice for supper. The house was spic and span, since Kaena and Leilani took advantage of our absence for the day to clean. Trent fired up the barbecue and in no time we were sitting by the pool eating the ribs, rice and salad. The ribs were delicious, our hands sticky and we were more than content. We finished supper and didn't even bother taking the plates into the house. We decided that we'd go for a swim. The pool water was as warm as bath water, and we stayed in for a long time. We floated on our backs, looking up at the darkened sky, a velvet background for the stars as they appeared. We raced from one end to another, until I finally let him catch me.

"What are we going to do when we're back in Calgary, and we don't have a pool or an ocean to make love in?" Trent asked me as he came up from behind me.

His actions suited his words, saving me from coming up with an answer. I stood in the water that just came up to my hips and enjoyed the play of the slight breeze on my skin as I felt the heat from Trent's body, warm my back. He was ready to make love to me; his penis pushed against my back as he caressed my shoulders. His hands moved to cover my breasts and they warmed under his touch. How long we stood there I do not know, but I finally turned to him and, sank down into the water so I could please him

The half wall that separated the Jacuzzi from the rest of the pool was the perfect height for me to perch on, while Trent entered me, and we slowly moved in rhythm, until we couldn't stand the pace, and moved back and forth, faster and faster, harder and harder, until finally our bodies gave in to the climaxes they had built towards. "This reminds me of the first time we made love in your pool in Albuquerque. I think we have a water fetish or something."

"I like the water, because I can move around easier and try things I can't on land. Besides, I've always loved the sensuousness of bathing, even if only by myself. I love the feel of the bath gel as my hands slide over my body. The warmth of the water lets my muscles relax, and then they are open to all the sensations. Once we're home the Jacuzzi will have to be our substitute pool."

Trent told me, "We know we can always come back here or go somewhere else warm and private. One of my uncles has a beach home in the Bahamas and another has a spot on Kauai."

"You never fail to amaze me. No wonder I heard someone say that I was marrying you for your money."

Trent looked at me. "Who would even say such a thing? Not someone at the wedding, surely?"

"No Trent, I was in the bathroom at the university, before we moved back to Canada, and I heard two women talking. I didn't recognize their voices, but they certainly seemed to know a lot about us. I didn't let it worry me, since I knew it wasn't true. I'm glad I fell in love with you just the way you are, without having all that hanging over my head. I knew I'd follow you anywhere, no matter what; whether you were rich or poor. I can't say it isn't fun to have friends and relatives with homes like this. You know how much I've enjoyed our time here. But, I confess I'm getting ready to go home. I've never been away from Joan and Susan. Plus I want to start creating our family life together."

"I'm missing them too honey. Have we bought all the things we wanted to take back, and are we even?" He was already aware that it worked best if each daughter got an equal number of gifts.

Besides their gifts, I wanted to pick up something special for Carol and Chris, Kele and Mansi, Halona, and Diane. The next morning, Trent and I were up early and went shopping.

One jewelry shop provided almost all the gifts that I still needed to buy. I finally went back to the same store that I bought Joan's new bathing suit and bought a matching one for Halona. Once all the gifts were purchased, we had to buy one more item; an extra suitcase to take everything home in.

It only took us an hour to do all of this, and then we headed back to the house. We decided to spend the rest of the day at our own, private beach. Our tan lines were almost gone, and we were down to just one bottle of lotion, SFP 15. The lazy day rolled on to its own rhythm; play in the waves, dry off in the sun, read, have a bite to eat, something to drink, and then the cycle would start again. It was too much of an effort to dress and go out for supper, so we threw some pork chops on the barbecue, tossed a salad, and munched on some wonderful, homemade bread. That evening we sat in the Jacuzzi, leaned back, and looked at the stars as they rose in the night sky.

We didn't say much, until Trent said, "I'm looking forward to going home tomorrow. We don't have to be in Honolulu until 10:00, so what time do you want to leave here?" I opened my mouth to answer, but before I could, he asked another question. "Do you want to go into Honolulu early in the morning? The reason I'm asking is that I just thought that you might want to explore Oahu, there is a lot to see."

"Can I think about it for a minute? I would like to see around, but if we're coming back with the kids, should we do that this trip?"

"There are something's that you'd want to see that the girls probably wouldn't care about: the Punch Bowl Cemetery, the Arizona Memorial and a general trip around the island. It isn't all the same. I was thinking that when we bring Joan and Susan, there are a lot of things that they won't want to miss: Sea Life Park, Hanauma Bay, the zoo, and of course, the Polynesian Village on the North Shore. It takes up an entire day if you want to see the whole thing and go to the evening performance. What do you think?" Trent asked me.

"I think I'd like to do those things you mentioned, and then leave the others for our next trip. What time do you think we should leave?" Trent pulled himself from the Jacuzzi, padded over to the phone, and next thing I knew he had his hand over the phone and was asking, "How about a flight at 9 tomorrow morning?" I nodded, and he confirmed with the ticket agent. "We could have left earlier, but we won't be rushed for time, and after all, this is a holiday, we don't want to get up too early."

With our arrangements for the next day settled, we decided that we had better finish our packing, and went from room to room, checking for our belongings. Not long afterward, our suitcases stood in the foyer. Our day in the sun shopping and packing suddenly announced itself, and we headed for bed. We kissed good-night, and fell asleep. I don't remember setting the alarm, but that was the next thing I was aware of as it woke us to the early morning darkness. We silently passed one another as we traded places in the bathroom, and then in the closet. It didn't take us long before we were finished, and called Leialani, as she asked us to the night before. She was down in an instant, and started bustling around the kitchen.

She insisted that if we were going to have a busy day before we left Hawaii, we needed a paniola breakfast. When she served our breakfast, I could see why it was called the cowboy breakfast; it was huge. Rice layered the plate, then came chili, then scrambled eggs, and to top it all off, a thick slice of Spam.

I hadn't seen Spam since I was a little girl, when I remember mom and dad frying it up. I liked it then, and after that long break, the taste brought childhood back, with just one fork full. Kaena and Leilani ate with us, and then it was time to leave. Kaena had already packed our bags into the limo. All that was left to do was to leave. I hugged Leilani, telling her that they were most welcome to stay with us if they wanted to come to Calgary.

Leilani dropped a plumeria lei over my head and another over Trent. It was time to leave. Trent and I walked down to the beach for a last look, and we each took a flower from our lei, dropped it on the water, and watched to see if it returned to the beach. The plumeria flowers returned, as would we, according to tradition.

We turned our back to the ocean, walked to the limo, and got in for our trip to the airport. Trent and I held hands and talked about the magical time we had on Maui. I reflected on the changes my life had gone through in the past two years. This was certainly the last thing I would have dreamt about after Robert left me. At the time I didn't think anyone was watching out for me, but I guess I had to go through all that to prepare me for the opportunity I had in Albuquerque.

In what seemed like no time, Kaena was pulling up to the airport. He took our bags to Aloha Air, Trent checked us in, we said good-bye again, and then we boarded. On our drive to the airport, Kaena told us that there would be a limo waiting for us at the airport in Honolulu, and the driver would take us wherever we wanted to go for the day, and then to the airport.

CHAPTER 39

The flight only took twenty-five minutes, and that included the taxiing time. We collected our bags from the Inter-Island terminal, and about one minute after Trent retrieved the last one, a chauffeur came over, and inquired if we were Dr. and Mrs. James. Since we were, we followed him as he pushed a cart, filled with our luggage out to the limo.

Trent told him that our first stop would be at the Punch Bowl. He told me that the National Grave of the Pacific lay within the depression, and that many of the casualties of the Pacific war lay at rest in this cemetery. Emotions swirled about, each jostling for prominence. The early morning calm was a peaceful background for the rising emotion I felt. Row upon row of dead young men. Surely, there must be another way

The tall monuments that stood as sentinels at the bottom of the valley called out to be touched. I found my fingers tracing young men's names as the list of casualties wound around the columns. The names changed; the young deaths forged them together. How did mothers and wives endure saying good-bye to their loved ones? How did they carry on, day to day, not knowing where their husbands and sons were, not knowing if they were well, injured or dead? I placed myself in their shoes, and the pain that caught at me was staggering. I literally had to put out my hand out to steady myself, against the solidity of marble. While I caught my breath, I marveled at what I knew the of these men's experiences. From where did they draw their courage to go forward in battle, not just once, but day after day?

I let my mind turn to those who survived the war. So many men, who, as a necessity in war, shut their emotions deep within themselves. They were a generation of men, often condemned for their coldness, their emotional reserve. I wonder, if perhaps, that was how they survived what they experienced, whether in the Pacific Theater or in the European or African Theater.

With sudden clarity I remembered something I used to think when I was little. When I became aware of what mankind endures in the face of war, I wished that I would die early in a war; I didn't think I had the strength to survive. As I grew up, I realized that there is a certain point when we have to stand up and prevent evil. I grew up learning how long it took to run home from school. When we had a test at the beginning of the Cuban Missile Crisis, if you couldn't get home in ten minutes, then you would have to stay at school, when the alarm rang.

I remember running home with my brother, Joseph, running as fast as we could. We were both afraid that if we didn't make it fast enough, we wouldn't be with Mom and Dad. Today don't remember exactly how long it took us; but it was under the limit, to our great relief. I do remember the sound of the air raid siren going off for a practice evacuation of the city. We took our elderly neighbor with us, and went out to her son's farm, somewhere near Strathmore. I remember reading air raid instructions: what food to have ready, blankets, lamps, candles and portable radios. The thing that scared me most was the listing of the cities that they expected would be targeted in Canada. Calgary was on the top of the list.

At the time, I didn't realize, that it was most likely a function of the alphabet; I thought it meant we were the first to go. All these thoughts and feelings flooded through me, as turned up the ever rising stairs. I walked alone. I was thankful that Trent left me on my own; that way I could wrestle composure from my jumbled emotions.

When I reached the panels that depicted the battles of the Pacific Theater, I had a semblance of composure that allowed me to read and view the panels. I stood amazed at what was accomplished by the Allies; while at the same time was horribly aware of the cost. How many children were left without fathers and how many of those young lives were shaped by that singular fact? It didn't end with just those children; it affected their children and on and on it continues. In position of honor was the chapel paying tribute to those who fell in battle.

Many sat quietly in the darkness, punctuated by candle light, sat contemplating the horror of not only WW II, but the Korean and Vietnam Wars. The dimness allowed for the dignity of those inside. Suddenly, I felt warmth next to me, as Trent placed himself next to my body, to lend his warmth to my body and spirit.

We sat quietly, and then slowly, without words, walked back to the limo. I heard Trent tell the driver to head into Honolulu through Waikiki. Soon, we were driving down Kalakaua Ave, which ran along the beach. I was amazed at the different atmosphere here. There were a lot more people, and they all seemed to be rushing here and there. We didn't stop, but continued along the coast line, passing by Turtle Island, Sea Life Park, through Waimanalo, through Kailua, and up the North Shore.

We stopped and had a picnic lunch at the State Park at Chinaman's Hat. We continued on until the driver pulled into Waimea Beach Park. We walked to the shore, and learned that not all sands are created equally; this one had particular heat storing abilities. We hopped up and down, alternating feet until we finally surrendered and moved back onto the beach. As we journeyed further up the cost, we decided that we'd definitely go there with the girls.

We made stops at the Dole Pineapple Plantation, and learned that there is a lot of difference between pineapple picked from the field and canned pineapple. We continued on and Trent asked me if I wanted to go to the Arizona Memorial. I really didn't feel up to it, so we passed it by.

We decided instead to go for supper. We ended up back in Waikiki and had supper on top of the Sheraton Waikiki. We were seated just as the sunset began its quick painting of the sky. By the time our waiter brought our appetizer, darkness had descended fully. We saw the lights that stretched along the shoreline. Fingers of light jutted into the valleys that were cut into the mountains. The setting was a romantic backdrop for our last evening in Hawaii.

Eventually we left for the airport, and went through security, and proceeded to our boarding area. I had to struggle to keep my eyes open, while we waited for our turn to board. I think I was asleep before we even took off. I woke just before we landed in Vancouver, and was thankful we didn't have to change planes. We weren't on the ground any longer than it took for passengers to gather their belongings and exit. In no time, we were over the Rockies, and then started our descent into Calgary. We hadn't expected anyone to meet us, but when we exited customs, there were Kele and Mansi.

CHAPTER 40

"Aloha, Kele and Mansi." Trent and I said in unison as we dropped their leis over their heads. Hugs and kisses followed, and then we headed out to our car. Trent drove us home, while Mansi told us that Joan and Susan were coming back to Calgary in the afternoon. Halona's mom, Lena, was driving them up from Lethbridge. I was very happy that I decided on a beautiful coral necklace for Lisa. She has been very loving toward my girls, and I was grateful for the friendship that Halona offered to Joan.

Home looked wonderful to us; it actually really felt like home for the first time. We weren't living in it waiting for things to happen. The wedding was over, and the honeymoon was over; now, real life began. We were a new family, and were all beginning a new life. I could hardly wait until the girls arrived home, and as awful as it sounds, I was ready for our company to leave.

I wanted to nest, to be isolated with my family. Mansi was very intuitive, and so I wasn't totally surprised when she told us, "Kele and I hope we won't disappoint you, but while you were gone we took the trip to Banff and the Ice Fields. We decided that we'd love to see more of Canada before going home, so we changed our reservations. I hope it's all right with you; we leave tomorrow afternoon." Before I could answer, I saw the expression on her face, and realized that she knew what I wanted. All I could do was hug her, and thank them for coming to Calgary for our wedding. Mansi came with me, as I unpacked our suitcases. She asked if we had picked up a wrong bag; she didn't recognize the black, soft-sided, bulging bag. I laughed and told her that we needed it for presents.

"No opening that one, until Joan and Susan are here.", I laughed while playfully slapping her hands away from it. It didn't take us long to create a mound of laundry. We took it to the laundry room, but waited until I could add the girl's laundry to the pile. After lunch we heard a car pull up the driveway. Trent and I were out in a shot; both very happy to see Lena's car. In particular, it was great to see Joan and Susan untangle themselves from the back seat and rush toward us.

All of a sudden everyone was talking at once; mind you it was a little hard to hear Joan and Susan, since their faces were buried in our necks. Finally the hugs stopped long enough for us all to go back into the house. We herded everyone into the family room, where we had all the presents sitting. I must admit it did look like Christmas. Joan and Susan and Halona were busy opening all of their things, while we handed out the presents to the adults. I think the person most surprised by their gift was Lena; she was totally shocked.

"Oh, this is absolutely beautiful. I've never had anything like it before. You didn't have to do this; it was fun having Joan in the house again. Halona was thrilled having her on the reserve." While Lena was talking, Trent went behind her to fasten the necklace. The coral gleamed against the coppery sheen of her skin.

"I'm so glad that we picked this necklace, Lena. We debated between this one and a turquoise necklace. That coral looks even deeper against your neck. I think it is just the right length too, but if you want to change it, any jeweler can easily do it." Lena went over to show Halona her new necklace, and came back amazed at the mound of gifts growing around Halona.

"Did you two spend all your time shopping? I can't believe that you brought so much for Halona and I. How can I ever thank-you?" Lena asked as she sank onto the couch beside me.

"Don't you know that you already did, when you and Halona were so kind and friendly to Joan? Joan had such fun when she went with you to the reserve. And now we're good friends too!"

I leaned forward and picked up the presents we bought for Carol, Chris and Shannon, so I could show them off. Halona agreed that our choice of a coral pin and matching earrings were perfect for Carol. We bought an exquisite eel skin wallet that held a gold money clip for Chris and some cute summer clothes, that would fit Shannon next summer. Neil was very happy with his goggles, flippers and snorkel. Emily wanted to blow up her Killer Whale, but we persuaded her that it would be much easier to take home if she didn't. Instead she put on her new bathing suit, and Susan put on hers, and the two of them ran around the house like twins.

Trent and Kele went to the photo store so they could have our pictures developed that afternoon. When they returned we spent a lot of time looking over them, and telling everyone about what we were doing, or where we were in each. Trent phoned the Wok Inn and ordered Chinese food for supper. We sat around the dining room table enjoying one another's company, and when we finished supper, Lena told us that she and Halona had to head back to Lethbridge.

As we walked outside I saw Trent hand Lena an envelope. Joan and Halona went upstairs to gather things together, and then we saw them into their car, and waved good-bye. I asked Trent what he had given Lena, and he told me that he didn't want her worrying about the cost of insurance for the necklace, so he had already insured it for the next ten years. I didn't have a choice. I had to kiss him and thank him for being so thoughtful; I'm sure that Lena probably hadn't any idea as to the cost of her necklace, and wouldn't have thought to have it insured independently.

I was going to give Lena the presents for Carol and Chris, but decided that I wanted to give them myself. Kele and Mansi surprised us when they told us that they were going out to the airport hotel shortly. Their flight left early in the morning, and they didn't want us getting up early. Trent and I immediately told them we'd drive them out, but even as he was offering, a taxi drove up

"We don't think you really want to go anywhere tonight, tonight is the first night of your new life. Give us a kiss good-bye and we'll leave before Emily starts to cry. She loves being here with everyone, especially Susan." With that, Mansi ran upstairs and came down with Neil and Emily. With surprising swiftness, we were alone: Joan and Susan, Trent and I, and our life was ready to begin.

We had two weeks before school started, and we lazily passed our time. We all bought new bikes, and started making a habit of going for an evening ride along the bike paths that connected Edgemont with the surrounding communities. A few of the hills were a bit of work, but we managed them with our new ten speed bikes.

We saw a lot of deer, gophers and rabbits, and occasionally spotted a skunk in the sparsely developed areas. We hoped the skunks would stay where they were, but I guess we couldn't complain too much. After all they were there first. On hot afternoons, we'd go to the Winter Club for a swim and to lounge outside on the grass.

One thing the girls and Trent had to gradually get used to was that the fact that he wasn't a visitor in our family, but a part of it. That meant he began to discipline the girls. It wasn't anything major, just little things like reminding them to do their chores, keep their room's tidy; normal, day to day things. They didn't do anything such as talk back; rather, they'd look to me to see if that was really what I wanted. I decided the best thing for everyone was for me to leave them to settle things themselves. I was sure that we'd have to weather more serious concerns as time went on, so it was nice to start with such little things.

It was fun to do back to school shopping with another adult. I didn't have to make all the decisions. The girls had a ball because we had to get them almost everything new. Their clothes from our time in the States weren't warm enough, and even if they were, Joan and Susan had grown a lot over the summer. We bought jeans, we bought shoes, dresses, dresses, underwear, running shoes, nighties, sweat pants and tops, and we bought sweaters and we bought coats.

CHAPTER 41

After one particularly tiring day, we arrived home and I collapsed into my chair. I noticed that I had a message, and checked it. It was Carol, asking me to call her at a Calgary number. That was puzzling, because she hadn't phoned to say that she was coming up. I dialed the phone.

"Hello, Carol? How come you're in town? Is everything okay?"

"Yes, everything is great. My doctor thought it best that I have an ultra-sound to check on the growth rate of the baby, since I'm getting so big, particularly these last two weeks. Plus, I have what I think is exciting news. While you were gone, I talked to some doctors in Calgary, and yesterday they phoned me, to see if I'd come up and see their clinic. That is what I did this morning, and over lunch they offered me a position. Obviously they know I'm pregnant, but that actually works out very well. There are three other female doctors who are planning children, and none of them want to work full time, so we'll work our schedules out to accommodate the babies. The men aren't excluded either. One of the male doctors, has a wife working on her doctorate who is expecting in eight months. He is planning on staying home with the baby for six months at least. None of us will make as much, but we've all decided that we'd take flexibility over the money. Chris and I have talked about this for the past while, and when I phoned him before I called you, we decided that I would accept. We're moving to Calgary!"

"Oh, I can't believe this. It's great. Trent and the girls will be thrilled too. What about Chris? What will he do?"

"Actually that won't be a problem, one of his friends has been bugging him to join their firm, and he had a tentative meeting with them already We were just waiting to see what I was going to do. So we're all set. Would you guys mind company next week. We need to look for a house, quickly."

"Of course not! We'd love to have you stay. We have some things here for you, anyway. What time do you think you'll be here?"

"I'll be there around five-thirty. See you then."

Trent had come into the room when he heard the excitement in my voice. "Was that Carol?"

"Yes, and they have the best news. They're moving to Calgary as soon as possible."

Trent and I were both happy that the Adams were going to be close. Once Carol arrived, we didn't waste too much time with supper. I threw some pork chops on the barbecue, tossed a salad, we ate and then left. We drove all around our neighborhood looking for houses for sale. Carol and I were sure of one thing, and that was that we wanted to be able to walk back and forth to each other's houses.

There were actually a few homes for sale on our block, but they weren't big enough. We saw one that looked promising so we stopped and checked it out. It was a new house that was almost finished; we could see that the walls hadn't been painted yet, and there weren't any rugs. Carol saw that as a positive, since she didn't want someone else's colour choice. We were lucky; when we went around the back, the deck had been built, so we could peek into the family room and kitchen. Both were nice and big, and from what she could see, was the style that Carol liked.

While we were discussing the house, Carol's only negative comment was that it was a little far from the house. She said that just as I was going down the deck stairs, which gave the opportunity to see a path running past the backyard. When I turned to point it out, Carol was sitting on the step, taking a breather. "Why don't I run down this path and see where it leads?"

I didn't have to go far before I saw something familiar. I realized that this path intersected the path we walked all the time. It was only a few more minutes to our house. I turned around, and told Carol the good news. Carol dug into her purse, found a pen, and when we reached the front of the house, wrote down the builder's number. She phoned right away, and the agent agreed to meet us there an hour later.

We went home so Carol could rest for a bit and phone Chris. After their conversation, Carol told us that as far as Chris was concerned, if she liked it and the price was right, buy it. We kept our fingers crossed, and within the hour, accompanied by Trent, we met the builder, and went inside. The layout was exactly what Carol and Chris wanted, and it was a spacious house, with four bedrooms upstairs and a den on the main floor

I was sort of surprised at four bedrooms as well as a den, but realized that they would both need offices. Trent went around the house with the builder while we poked in the kitchen counters, and tried to make sure there was enough storage space. We even started to talk about colour for the flooring and walls. The builder went outside and left us to talk with Trent and get his opinion on the construction of the house.

"I think the house has been well built, it is obviously up to code, since it has just been built. There may be a few things you'd want to add, but they can be added later without any problems. I think you could make him an offer lower than the asking cost. There are quite a few houses for sale in this area, and with the economy the way it is, he should be happy to find a buyer for this house. There aren't that many people who buy houses this size."

"What do you think if I make him an offer of 150 thousand? That's five thousand less than list.", Carol asked Trent.

"I'd offer him 145 thousand and then see what he does. He'll probably give a counter offer, and then you can either accept it or try another offer. I think he wants to sell this house, and he'll still be making a profit it on 145 thousand. If he hesitates, tell him that he'll get a bonus of two thousand if he has the rest of the house completed in one week, $1000 if it's ready in two weeks and nothing if you can't move in by then. He can only say yes or no, and then if he says no, then we'll regroup and make a counter offer."

Carol looked at Trent and said that the bonus idea was really good, because she really wanted to be moved in before this baby arrived. Trent went outside and brought the builder in, and helped Carol tell the builder what her offer was. At first I thought he'd say no, but as he thought, Trent explained the bonus concept, and the builder quickly accepted the offer. He told Carol, that so long the flooring she wanted was in stock in Calgary, that he could have the house ready within the week. Carol told him that she'd be at his office in the morning to sign the papers.

As soon as we were home, Carol called Chris and told him he was the proud owner of a new home. He decided to drive up that night so he'd be here in time for their appointment in the morning. Once the girls were in bed, Carol and I sat in the kitchen flipping through the colour wands that the builder had with him. Carol was immediately drawn to the corals. The furniture she had already would go well with the colour. Just before midnight Chris and Shannon arrived.

We all went to bed right away so we could recover from the hectic day, and prepare for the next one. We were all up together for breakfast; Joan and Susan were up early so they could play with Shannon. Shannon stayed with us for the day so Chris and Carol could devote their day to making the many decisions necessary. We were all sitting on the back deck, enjoying the shade, when Carol and Chris returned, tired but pleased within themselves. The paint was chosen, the rugs they liked were in stock in Calgary, the lino for the kitchen and bathrooms was also available. The builder assured them the house would be theirs August 30.

Chris told us that he had already talked with movers in Lethbridge, and they were just waiting for a date. They'd be ready to move them. In one day, everything had fallen in place. Now, all that was left to do was go back to Lethbridge, and sort out all their things for the move. What was coming, what was being given to Goodwill, and what was just okay for the garbage heap. Early the next morning they went back to Lethbridge, with plans to be back in five days. We spread the remainder of our shopping over that time, I didn't have enough energy for anymore all day shopping sprees. Actually, I took one day off, and Trent took them; I just couldn't get enough energy up to even consider it.

It was fun helping Carol and Chris move in their new home. Since the movers did all the hard stuff, Carol and I spent most of our time unpacking. That was a job I liked; to me it is almost like Christmas, opening lots of packages and not knowing what is inside. I find that many items generate memories that are fun to share. Shannon wasn't at the house, she was down the path, with Joan and Susan, so she wouldn't get stepped on. The movers were gone by mid-afternoon, we continued unpacking, and the guys moved furniture around for us, until Carol was happy with the arrangement. We slowly followed the path to our place, placed a pizza order, and waited for it to be delivered. Shannon was happy to see her mom and dad, who took her to their new home right after we ate.

CHAPTER 42

The girls kept practicing the route to where they caught their school bus. Their back packs were packed, and unpacked, and were ready long before they were needed. Finally the first day of school came. I drove them, since there were a lot of forms to fill out, and there wasn't a full day of school until the next day. It was hard to realize that Joan was now in Grade Six, her last year of elementary school, and Susan was in Grade Two, no longer new to school, but an old veteran. She even told me herself, "You don't have to walk me to my classroom, Mom. I can go with the teacher."

The next morning I walked with them to the bus stop, and was firmly told that my presence wasn't needed. Joan was rather indignant that I could even think she needed me there, or needed to be reminded to look out for Susan. I promised myself that I wouldn't make the same mistake the next morning, and while I walked back to the house I suddenly realized that I hadn't been like that when Joan was first in school. I tried to convince myself that I was more concerned because we were living a big city again, but that didn't seem to make sense. After all, we had lived in Edmonton when Joan started school.

Trent was waiting for me on the deck so I joined him, and enjoyed the fresh squeezed orange juice he had ready. We looked at one another, and laughed, as we both realized that for the first time since our honeymoon, we were alone. The glint in Trent's eyes was matched by that in mine, and we ran down to our room, stripped off, and flung ourselves onto the bed. The still cool, morning air drifted in, and cooled off our bodies. We had the luxury of time, and slowly began the preparation of each other's bodies, readying ourselves to surrender to one another's rhythms. Slowly, slowly, we moved together, until it was no longer possible to hold back. As if we had both be given silent signals, our bodies moved, faster and harder, trying to merge our bodies into one.

We fell asleep, and when I finally stirred I saw that it was already eleven-thirty. I woke Trent, we hopped into the shower, and walked over to Carol and Chris' house. They must have been busy while we were otherwise engaged.

The house looked as if they had been there for a long while. Chris had already been to the grocery store, for he was busy preparing our picnic lunch, which they had invited us to the day before. Trent took the plates and cutlery out to the deck, and soon we were seated around their picnic table.

Carol had a hard time sitting still, she was up to the kitchen, then she was up to check on Shannon, then she was up just walking around the back yard. I was about to say something, when I realized why; under her chair was a large puddle, getting steadily larger. Carol was sitting quietly, with her eyes closed, and her hands massaging her belly. "You're in labor aren't you?" I asked. Carol nodded.

"Last time I didn't rupture my membranes until just before Shannon was born, this definitely feels different. I had a really strong contraction when my water broke. In fact I feel another one starting to build." Things moved quickly after that. Chris knelt next to Carol, helping her with her Lamaze breathing, Trent was putting a shower curtain on the car seat, and then came back to help Chris get Carol to the car. I went in the house and got her hospital suitcase, and joined them out front. Carol was in the car, just peaking with another contraction as I slid behind the wheel.

Trent went home, taking Shannon with him. I had curious sensations during the short drive to the hospital. I felt uneasiness, not excitement, and I wasn't thinking about Edmonton, or when the girls were born. I couldn't even say what I was thinking of.

Carol had three more contractions before we were at the hospital, and I was pretty sure it wouldn't be long until another Adams lived in the new house. Chris was with Carol, but I had to stay in the waiting room. Then it was my turn to be restless. I'm sure that I knew the entire maternity floor and could tell you what each sign said. Happily, I only had a two hour wait before Chris came into the waiting room, beaming with pride

"It's a boy! He's 7 lbs.6oz. He has lots of black, curly hair. Carol feels great, and she told me to come and bring you up to the nursery so you can see your new 'nephew.'" I was happy to follow him, and I was glad that my premonition was right; I felt all along that this was a boy

We had just come up to the nursery window when suddenly, I broke out in a sweat and felt as if I were going to faint. My breath was shallow and quick. I reached out my hand to steady myself on Chris's arm.

He looked at me with alarm, "My God, Clare, you're as pale as a sheet. Here, sit down."

He knelt before me until I could speak, "I'm sorry I don't know what's wrong; it just happened. Maybe I got too hot today, or it's just all the excitement today." A nurse went by, and Chris called to her.

She stopped, took my pulse, asked me a few questions, and then found me a cold ginger ale. I felt much better in just a short five minutes. Chris helped me up and we looked into the nursery. A nurse was just putting their little guy in a bassinet. Chris pointed to his son, and she brought the bassinet to the window. He was adorable, and I think he looked like his father.

"Have you picked out a name for him, yet?"

"We have a few in mind, but we didn't want to make up our minds until we saw him. Let's go and see Carol."

"I'll just stay a short while; I know how tired she'll be." We passed a phone booth, so I popped in to give Trent a call. I knew he'd be waiting. He, too, had thought that the baby was a boy, so he was happy to be right and even happier to know that both baby and mom were well.

"Congratulations Carol, you have a beautiful son. Are you feeling all right?"

"Surprisingly, I feel really great, I thought because he came so fast, that I'd be sorer, but I'm not. Don't you just love his black curls?"

"Oh, I envy them. I can hardly wait to feel them, they look so silky."

Chris piped up to ask if Carol had an inspiration for his name, once she saw him.

"I think he is very handsome, just like his dad, so I think Kevin suits him. In Irish Gaelic, it means handsome. What do you think, Honey?"

"I think that Kevin was my favourite from our short list, so Kevin it is. What about his middle name? I think Bryce goes well with Kevin."

I piped in, "Kevin Bryce sounds like a very strong person. I like it."

Carol told me, "When you go home you can tell everyone that our son's name is Kevin Bryce Adams. You look tired out Clare, why don't you head home? Chris can take a cab home later tonight."

I was too tired to argue, so I just said good-bye. By the time I was home, Joan and Susan were waiting for me at the front door, full of questions about the baby. They decided it was nice to have a little boy to help look after, and they were full of questions about what he looked like. We moved into the kitchen, where I saw, with relief, that Trent was in the middle of making supper.

"Are you okay honey? You look really tired."

I admitted that I was, and quickly accepted his suggestion to rest until supper was ready. I closed our drapes, and since I felt chilly, crawled under the duvet. I must have fallen asleep before my head hit the pillow.

It wasn't a restful sleep. I had strange dreams full of jumbled images of babies. I could see Kevin, but suddenly he wasn't a baby anymore, he was a little boy going to school. I saw myself running after him. I tried to yell that it wasn't right that he was going away, but every time I came closer to him, he would suddenly be a long distance away again, and I could never catch up with him.

In these dreams, Joan and Susan would show up as little babies, and then as their current age. They seemed to be running between Kevin and I -- they could reach him, but not I. Things became really confusing because the scenery kept changing. We were in Hawaii, then Edmonton, then Calgary and finally Lethbridge. While the dream occurred in Lethbridge, the light changed to storm darkness, the wind whipped around us all.

I don't know why, but we seemed to be in Indian Battle Park, and no matter how hard we tried, we couldn't leave the river valley. We couldn't go to our home. I remember struggling to make a path so the kids could follow me up, but just as I was at the rim, ready to climb to safety, a gust of wind would push me back, and I'd fall, hitting Joan who stumbled backwards into Susan, and finally we all rolled over Kevin.

I must have shouted, because my next conscious awareness was of Trent, shaking me awake. I sat bolt upright, and shrank into his arms. Trent kept asking me what was wrong, but I couldn't tell him. I couldn't remember any of the details then, just an awareness that I was falling down a hill.

Trent eased me back, crawled in next to me, and gave me his body warmth. I was shivering uncontrollably. I don't remember falling asleep, but I must have, for when I woke, the night darkness had settled in. I could see light shining under the bedroom door. My limbs lay heavy against the mattress. My mind couldn't focus on anything in particular, and, once again, I fell asleep.

I was amazed when I next awoke. A new day was starting. My body felt heavy and sore, like after you battle the flu for a week. I slowly eased out of bed, staggered into the bathroom, and ran the water for a hot bath. I slid in and felt the hot water ease my muscles. I lay there trying to figure out what had happened the day before. I couldn't explain why I had felt ill in the hospital, I couldn't explain why I was so exhausted that I slept all evening and all night. I didn't leave the comfort of the tub until the water felt chilly. I wrapped myself in a fluffy robe, and walked down the hall to see who was home. Trent was just closing the front door, and looked happy to see me.

"Morning, Honey. Are you feeling better today? Do you have the flu or something?"

"I don't think so, and yes, I do feel better today. I'm still a bit tired. But, I think that maybe just all the activity of the past couple of weeks was catching up with me. Did you talk to Chris last night?"

"Yes, and he is flying high. He is thrilled about Kevin. He also said that he'd come just before noon so he can take Shannon up to see her new brother and her mom. Joan and Susan helped me with her this morning. Before I was even up, they had her changed and had her in the high chair. All I had to do was cook us all eggs and toast. Shannon ate them up, and had fun trying to drink her juice. She still gets quite a bit on her bib, but she managed to drink a fair amount of it. It was fun you know, it's been a long time since I've made breakfast for a baby."

After breakfast, I dressed, and then Trent and I took Shannon for a walk along the path system. We didn't realize that we'd gone quite a way until Trent looked at his watch and saw that it was already eleven-thirty. We turned around quickly, and sped up for the return walk.

Chris was waiting on the deck and Shannon started babbling at him. After she played with her dad, I took her upstairs and changed her into a cute sun-dress so she'd look cute in her first pictures with Kevin

The afternoon was quiet until Joan and Susan came home from school. They told us about their new friends, their special art teacher, and what they did that day. Joan was happy to find out that one of the girls from her class who got off the bus after Joan, didn't live far away at all; in fact she lived on the other end of Carol's circle. We learned that her friend's name was Jennifer Wright, that she had long brown hair, and that she was a member of the Winter Club. She had taken swim lessons all her life there, and was in the same level as Joan.

Joan could hardly wait to be a full member so she could take lessons with Jennifer. My mind worked in typical mom fashion; that meant we'd be able to take turns driving. Joan asked Susan if she knew Jennifer's little sister, Amy, who was also in Grade 2. Susan shook her head, and Joan told her that maybe she was in one of the other Grade Two classes. She promised to take Susan with her when she went to visit Jennifer.

Chris arrived shortly afterward and the girls took over Shannon's care. Joan was a real little mother; she was very patient with Shannon, and kept an eye on Susan while she played with Shannon. We had made sure we had a toy box full of age-appropriate toys. They kept her entertained until supper was ready.

As we sat around the dining room table, Chris updated us on Carol and Kevin. Carol was feeling great and was happy that Kevin was nursing well. He latched on well, sucked well and burped with vigor. She told Chris that she planned on being home in two more days; earlier if she could convince her doctor. Chris told me that Carol wanted to know if I had any more dizzy spells, like the one I had the day before.

Trent looked alarmed, and turned to me. "What happened yesterday? I didn't know you weren't feeling well."

I told him that it wasn't a problem; I had merely been overheating. The way he looked at me told me that he wasn't convinced. "That is why you went to bed early last night, isn't it?"

I admitted that he was right, but told him that he wasn't to worry. In truth, I really did feel fine. After supper Trent and I walked with Chris back to their house and helped him set up the nursery. They had just started when Carol went into labour. The crib was assembled, but that was all.

I had fun doing the rest. I thought back to the fun and anticipation I had while readying Joan and Susan's nurseries. In no time I had the room arranged like Carol wanted, and got to work filling the dresser drawers with nighties, little T-shirts, summer sleepers, diapers and blankets. Baby clothes were even nicer now than when I had the girls. Everything seemed to be softer and lighter weight.

I put the Winnie the Poo sheet and matching quilt on the mattress. I fixed the bumper pad in place and set up the mobile over the crib. I hugged a teddy bear for the longest time, before placing it in the corner of the crib. I maneuvered a reclining chair into position, sat for a moment, and regarded the view Carol would have as she nursed Kevin.

The nursery window overlooked the ravine, and I could easily see the tops of the trees with their already yellowing leaves. I stocked the change table and then called the guys in. Chris was amazed that I had it exactly how he knew Carol wanted it.

I laughed, "That was one of the first things that Carol and I talked about when we first came into the house. Chris, I think Trent and I will go home now. I want to check on Shannon, and I think it is probably a good idea if you get all the sleep you can during these next couple of nights." He smiled and agreed, and walked us downstairs to the door. Trent and I strolled home, and talked about our new "nephew" and how excited Chris was.

Two days later, as Carol had predicted, she brought Kevin home. Joan and Susan could hardly wait for the end of the day so they could see him. The minute they were off the bus, they ran into the house, out of the house, and up the path to Carol's. I trailed behind, not having quite as much energy. Trent would follow once he had Shannon in the stroller.

The girls each took turns sitting in the recliner, holding Kevin like the precious bundle that he was. Carol looked wonderful and was moving easily, not like someone who had just had a baby. Trent arrived with Shannon and her bag of belongings. We weren't rushing her out of our house; Carol wanted to have her home so she wouldn't feel left out.

CHAPTER 43

Our lives settled into a pattern. Weekdays flowed along according to the school schedule. We'd all have breakfast together, the girls would catch the bus, and Trent and I did the chores together. It is amazing how nice it is to fold laundry when you are doing it with the man you love.

Usually we left the house around eleven and drove over to the university. The new building in the Research Park was almost completed, and we could go into our labs. We tried to make sure that everything we ordered was on its way, and we tried to anticipate if there was anything that we had neglected to order.

At times I would be shocked at the prices listed on our order forms. It wasn't uncommon for many of the instruments to cost twenty-five thousand dollars, and there were quite a few that cost more than that.

After the lunch that we usually ate on campus, we would spend an hour or two interviewing potential employees. Trent and I both demanded that our associates be passionate about their work, but that didn't mean that we expected people to work unreasonably long hours. Obviously, there would be the odd times when certain experiments would require extra time and effort, but on the whole we wanted everyone happy.

We were paying top dollar for the top people in their fields; not for people whose only interests were work to the detraction of their families. We wanted our people to be with us over the long haul, and we decided to make their situation as fulfilling as possible.

Neither Trent or I would be working full time for at least a year, and that influenced us, as well as a deep philosophical belief. I took it upon myself to write an employee information packet, and in that I articulated our philosophy of work and how we saw work and family relating. As a part of that I developed our maternity benefits. More and more women were working in the sciences, and that fact alone determined the need for a well-thought-out plan.

I decided that women would be able to take up to a year off; the first six months with full pay and the remainder at three-quarters pay. Six months isn't enough time to spend with a newborn, it isn't enough time to regain both your physical and emotional strength.

I felt strongly that new dads must be considered as well, so I decided that new dads could take a month off with full pay. That way, he'd be home to help his new family settle in.

With those issues out of the way, it was important that parents feel as comfortable as possible when they did return to work. In my mind that definitely meant quality daycare. I could easily remember my terror when I didn't know what I was going to do with Joan and Susan when we first moved to Lethbridge. What if I hadn't been as lucky as I was? What would I have done? I would have had to put them somewhere while I worked, I didn't have a choice. I was so lucky that I had wonderful women looking after my children, but that didn't stop me from missing the girls.

I was determined that any employees with children would not have to go through the same thing. I told Trent that we had to use an area on the main floor that we hadn't dedicated to anything else as a daycare for our employees, and other employees in the Research Park and the university.

I think I surprised him with that idea, but when I explained my reasoning, he quickly agreed. "You are right, it will be so much easier for the moms and dads if they don't have to stop anywhere on the way to work to drop their children off, and if they want to have lunch together, it will be easy. I guess that means we'll have to decide where the playground will be; can't have a daycare, without outside fun."

"I'm so glad that you saw what I want to do so quickly. There is one more problem I'm thinking about. You know as well as I do that kids get sick a lot when they are little. I remember when I was in Lethbridge; I'd have to leave Susan with Lora, even when she was sick. I don't think that was fair to either Lora or the other children. But I could never think of any other solution. I think I might have an answer, or at least two. I'm not sure which is best, and which is the most economical."

I must have stood looking at Trent while I tapped my pencil against my teeth for too long, because he finally prompted me to share my ideas. "I was wondering if we had a roster to either nurses or nurses' aides who could go to the home of the sick child and look after him or her; how that would work out for the child's parents. I would think that they'd be happy knowing that a qualified person was looking after their child, and that we covered the cost. The other way to go, from what I can see, would be if we had a separate day care for sick children. The advantage of that would be that a sick fussy child would be able to see their parents, and vice versa. My concern with that plan is that if there is more than one germ going around, then there will be cross infection. Personally, when the girls were little, the last thing I wanted to do when they were sick was to bundle them up and drive off in awful weather. I think the first option is best, what do you think?"

"Honey, both of your ideas sound good, but I'm like you. I think the first one is easier on the child, easier on the parents, and best for the other children in the daycare. Why don't you phone the provincial government and find out which department is in charge of daycares so you can get all the requirements. How do you want to go about creating a roster of nurses?"

"I'm not sure yet, but I have a few ideas. I'm going to do some calling, and that will give me a clearer idea."

We usually worked until around three, and then headed home. That gave us an hour to ourselves before Susan and Joan were home from school. Quite often we took advantage of that interlude to make love. It was certainly enjoyable not only because we weren't waiting until night when we may be tired, but we didn't have to worry about the noise level.

By the middle of October I had solved the dilemma of nurses. When I mentioned it to Carol, she told me that they had a list of nurses who dropped off their resumes, and she told me that quite a few of the nurses at Foothills hospital were looking for more hours, but without a set commitment.

I liked that idea best, since among all the doctors at the clinic, they knew a lot of the nurses and could give me an idea of whom they most trusted. I phoned the hospital administer and asked for permission to post a notice. He was very cooperative, and told me that he loved my idea.

Within two weeks I had interviewed almost forty nurses. Many of the nurses worked in peds, some were older, and some were new graduates. I was lucky that those who were young all came from large families and had experience with children. When I drew up my list and showed it to Carol, she took it to the clinic, and each nurse was known by one of the doctors, who gave their stamp of approval.

I now was able to write thirty-six letters, inviting these nurses to join our daycare nurses' roster. I decided that, to keep this group on call with fluctuating need, I'd pay each nurse for one shift a month whether or not they worked. They all happily accepted.

I worked though all the government red tape, met all the requirements, hired a daycare director and staff. I didn't have any trouble getting applications when I put the ad in the Calgary Herald. I insisted that all the staff either had formal training in childcare or their own children. Those who didn't have formal education in the field would be required to take a first aid course that included infant CPR. We would also give them time off, with pay, to attend classes, so they could attain their certificates.

If I were going to open a daycare, it was only under certain conditions. The child-care workers had to be professional, and I expected to pay them as professionals who were entrusted with our children. The children would come to an environment that not only stimulated their bodies and minds, but would also care for their psyches. This was important work, not menial work.

Unfortunately most of the outside world didn't agree. To them, cleaning bathrooms, keeping a daycare clean, and cooking are menial jobs for those untrained for anything else. Yet, what is more important than maintaining a clean, germ-free environment for babies and toddlers who constantly put things in their mouths? They don't seem to understand that providing nutritious foods, prepared for children's taste, are a necessity if children are to grow up healthy. Which of these things wouldn't they do for their own children? Didn't they make sure that their children played with toys that were age appropriate, safe and stimulating? Don't they know that reading books to a child and playing games with a child are more than ways to pass the time? These are the activities that all children must do to develop emotionally, intellectually and socially.

CHAPTER 44

Joan and Susan were happy. They could run back and forth between our house and that of Jennifer and Amy. After school, all the girls would go to their homes, drop off their knapsacks, and then play together until supper. It was good that Joan had a friend the same age to play with, especially now that her activities were changing.

While they still had fun playing outside for awhile, Jennifer and Joan were also happy lying around her room and listening to tapes. Before the tapes had been of children's songs, now the sound of teenage music started to float under her bedroom door. Joan asked me if she could borrow some of my make-up. When I gave it to her, the two girls would spend a lot of time in front of the mirror, practicing. Every once and awhile, they come and show Trent and I the result of their efforts.

At first they looked quite a bit like clowns, but it didn't take them long to learn how to use the makeup in a more normal way. I checked with Jennifer's mom before I gave them the cosmetics, just in case she didn't want Jennifer experimenting with them. She laughed, and told me that she thought that the girls might as well start practicing when they weren't going out in public. We both figured that by Grade Seven, they'd want to wear at least a little makeup to school. This way they know what they were doing.

I was really happy to meet Jennifer's mom, Bonnie. We thought very much alike, and as we spent more time together, we became good friends. She was just thinking about going back to work, part-time. I told her about the clinic that Carol was working in, and suggested that working there, might be an idea. She could choose what hours she wanted to work. Her husband, Jim, was an engineering prof, at U of C.

The girls, all four of them, started having sleepovers, and it worked well for all four adults. Bonnie and Jim were able to have a quiet night and morning without worrying about the girls, and it's always good for a husband and wife to have a night to themselves. They were both thrilled, and said it had been a long time since they could have long, romantic nights.

It was nice that Joan could study with a friend. Both girls were very good students, and didn't have to be prodded to do their homework. They both liked to study by asking one another questions, so before exams they holed up in either of their rooms. They were also at the stage where wandering the mall entertained them. They tried on many outfits, but didn't buy a lot. Either Bonnie would drive them to Market Mall, and then pick them up when they called, or I would.

Susan and Amy stayed close to home, and spent a lot of time in the basement making forts. The two of them loved their forts. Whenever I looked in the linen closet and something was missing, my first stop would be in the basement to see which part of the fort it was forming. Sometimes I just let it be, since I was sure that if I removed what I wanted, the whole fort would fall apart.

Susan and Amy were funny; they'd appear in the kitchen and get together a large snack, disappear into the basement, and return, for a load of books and games. On the weekend, that would be a signal that we wouldn't see them for a couple of hours. What was really funny was the reaction of Joan and Jennifer to these forts. They would pretend they were going into them to help the little girls, with something, but in no time we'd hear them all giggling together. Grade Six girls were like that, one day too old to play with their little sisters, and their "silly" games, and the next day joining right in.

We introduced Carol and Chris to Bonnie and Jim. We, the three couples, began to spend time together socially. By Christmas, there was a deep friendship among us all. We gathered on Boxing Day for a family dinner. The girls started telling Jennifer and Amy about the diamond rings they were given the previous Christmas. I don't think Jennifer or Amy could believe their ears. "Mom, would you get our rings for us, so we can show them?"

"Sure, honey. After dinner I'll go get them." I was going to tell the story of our engagement to Bonnie and Jim, but Joan beat me. So in quick order, while we finished our supper, they heard the whole story. Trent volunteered to clear the table for desert, so I went to our room and came back with the Joan and Susan's engagement rings. Trent demonstrated how he gave them to Susan and Joan, and Bonnie, Jim and their girls sat open-mouthed.

"Dad, can we wear our rings until bedtime?" Joan asked.

"Yes, Joan, but you both have to promise that we'll put them away before we go to bed tonight. When you get a little older then you can wear them all the time, like mom does."

Trent was very gallant, and served desert to us all. We excused the giggly bunch, and enjoyed leisurely tea and coffee. Carol nursed Kevin, and told how it was the previous Christmas that they found out they were expecting him.

Bonnie was amazed. "Have you guys left anything else that is special for Christmas time? Those are fantastic memories to have. All of our special days cluster in summer. It was on my birthday, July 30, that Jim proposed, and both Jennifer and Amy were born in August. I have quite a few friends whose important dates cluster like that."

After we stirred from the dining room, Carol, Bonnie and I did the dishes, while Chris burped Kevin, changed him and settled him for the night in the crib. We kept a crib at our house since they were there so much. I proposed a game of Trivial Pursuit, a new Canadian board game that was already very popular. We played as teams, and after two hours Bonnie and Chris emerged as victors.

We all had so much fun, that we decided to have a repeat game on New Year's Eve. A few days before New Year's Eve, Trent had a phone call from the Winter Club, and found out that we were now active members. We were all very happy to be able to use the facilities, and tried them out that very day. New Year's Eve passed very pleasantly, and then it was back to our routine, with a slight adjustment.

Trent and I had decided that before going to the lab, we'd spend some time in the club weight room. I found it easier to exercise that way than aerobics. I'm not coordinated enough to follow all those routines. We also played badminton, and often had the courts to ourselves. Of course we went swimming, but that had to be worked in between classes: aqua exercises, babe and mom swim, and swim and gym.

One day as Trent and I swam, he told me that he'd like to plan a spring holiday to go back to Hawaii. I certainly wasn't going to argue. Later that day, while at the lab, Trent came to my office and told me that he had just talked to the Newmans, and they told him we could have the house any time in April because they were going to be in Arizona. Trent and I pulled the calendar out and looked at possible dates. Trent said that he'd like to go for three weeks, but not spend all the time on Maui. When we talked to our travel agent, we decided to spend the first week on Oahu, then fly to Maui, and then fly to the Big Island for our last week. Trent didn't blink at the cost of accommodations. We booked a suite at the Sheraton Waikiki and a suite at the Hyatt Regency Waikoloa, on the Big Island. Of course we'd have the ultimate in luxury on Maui.

We decided that Joan and Susan were both bright enough and young enough to miss school, but we decided that we'd have them do some work each day. It turned out that our dates overlapped their Easter holiday, so in essence they were only missing eight school days.

After all the details were confirmed, we didn't get too much work done because we were looking forward to telling the girls. We knew they'd be enthusiastic. Before they were home from school, we found some of the posters we brought home with us last time and pinned them up in the foyer. I put a tape of Hawaiian music on to enhance the message. Joan and Susan burst through the door at their usual time, but instead of flinging their coats off and rushing to the kitchen, they stopped dead in their tracks. It didn't take Joan long, "We're going to Hawaii, aren't we?"

Trent scooped her up, "You bet we are. I promised you that we'd go back with you guys. There is only one little bit of trouble."

Joan looked at him anxiously. Trent laughed and hugged her closer. "The problem is, you'll have to miss some school."

"That isn't a problem dad, really." Susan told him seriously. Trent bent down, let go of Joan and pulled Susan up with him.

"I'm just teasing you, Honey. Of course that isn't a problem. Are you excited?" Both Susan and Joan squealed their happiness, and we went into the family room, so we could show them where we were going.

Our honeymoon pictures had shown them what it was like at the Newman's, and they were looking forward to staying there. Trent and I drove them to school the next morning, and went in and spoke with the principal, and showed her the dates we'd be gone. She was pleased that we had already planned on having the girls do some school work while we were gone. She told us that she'd talk to the girls' teachers, and with them, and plan what Joan and Susan should work on.

Construction of the labs proceeded, and as the case with most construction, took longer than anticipated. Chris had told us that we should anticipate that, but it was still frustrating when construction would slow because manufacturers wouldn't ship their products on time. A lot of specialized lab equipment was necessary, not only for efficient use of the lab, but to meet code standards.

We began preliminary interviews in February, and were very lucky in the number of highly qualified people who applied. From the outset, it was obvious that our approach to the integration of family life and the workplace was attracting a lot of attention. Not only did most of the applicants mention it, but when the business community heard about our program, we were asked to speak at various functions. Various media people began interviewing me, and they were more interested in the daycare than my research.

I was very surprised when some of the larger companies in town began contacting me regarding our daycare. They too, once they understood our reasoning, began to think of the added expense, as an investment in their workers. Most, though, didn't have the slightest idea of how to go about organizing a similar program for themselves. One night, after a day of two meetings with corporations, I brought up an idea that had been circulating through my head.

"Trent, what do you think about us forming a separate company that would run daycares in corporations? The people I met today kept asking me what steps I had taken, but I really can't see them following through. Their minds just don't think in the same way as ours. I thought that we could hire Bonnie as President of the daycare, and in that capacity, she'd contract our services to other companies to develop a plan and implement it. We would control the screening of staff, staff salaries, and we'd bill the companies." I finally stopped for a breath and looked expectantly at Trent.

"I think that it is a really good idea to look into. I agree that we must keep control of the staffing in order to maintain the quality that we've set up for our own. If we didn't, the public would associate our name with the daycare, and we'd suffer, as of course the children would, if a company decided to cut corners and hire staff with fewer qualifications. It would certainly be a job that would suit Bonnie, especially with her nursing background. Do you want to discuss this with Bonnie yet or do you want to do some more investigation?"

"I'm torn. I don't want to speak prematurely, but at the same time, my plans might be entirely changed if Bonnie wasn't interested in the idea. I think I'll take the chance, so I'll call her and set up a time that she could come over."

Two days later, Bonnie, Trent and I were sitting around the dining table with papers strewn over the top. Bonnie had listened to me intently while I explained my idea. When I concluded, I waited for her reaction. Her eyes were sparkling as she spoke. "I think this is a fantastic idea. I remember when you first told me about your daycare at the Research Park, and thinking that it was a shame that only a small number of people would have access to it. I would be very interested in researching the idea."

"I'm so glad you said that, because my time is starting to get stretched a bit. I was trying to think of when I'd have the time to squeeze that project in. Trent and I were talking, and thought the way to go about this, would be to hire you now, at the beginning, as an employee of the lab, purely for your pay. If the idea is feasible, then we'd form a separate company and install you as President, and from there you could hire whatever staff you need. I'd anticipate perhaps four directors, one for each quadrant of the city. I would really like to see this online as quickly as possible. Trent and I were trying to think of what an appropriate salary would be, and we wondering what you thought of $2500/month, until we actually go ahead with this idea. Of course, as President, your salary would rise accordingly. We haven't really thought of what that would be yet, but I thought we'd check into salary stats to arrive at what would be right for the responsibilities that you'd be responsible for." I fell silent waiting for her answer.

"For starters, $2500 is a lot more than I'd make if I went back into nursing full time, and I think you're right that before a company is formed, I'll have to nail down exactly how many companies are seriously interested. Don't worry if it doesn't go through, because I'm certainly not in a position where I'm refusing another job in the hopes of this one proceeding."

Shortly before leaving for Hawaii, we had another meeting so Bonnie could up-date us. She didn't disappoint me. Her research was concise, accurate, and she already had an implementation plan, which she showed us. "We already have five businesses that occupy entire buildings who have signed a letter of intent. I think the success of those daycares will generate business, purely by word of mouth. I've done some preliminary investigation into staffing, and I've written a short biography of the people I have in mind." By the end of our meeting, we decided that we would move ahead and form a corporation, and told Bonnie, to initiate talks with her short list of possible directors.

CHAPTER 45

Trent and I didn't know if Joan and Susan would make it until April 11, the day we left for Hawaii. They were both so excited that they couldn't settle down to any one particular thing. They both had piles of clothing sitting on their floor. I'm sure they added and subtracted from the pile at least once a day.

Chris drove us to the airport in time for us to catch our early morning Wardair flight. The kids almost went nuts before it was time to board, and were thrilled once we did. The travel agent booked the front bulkhead seats for us so there was plenty of legroom, and actually space to move around. Our area was somewhat separated from the main passenger space, and was nice and quiet.

Joan and Susan loved being able to ring the attendant to get a cold drink. The attendant surprised them when we were almost there, with Hawaiian fruit drinks, garnished with pineapple, kiwifruit and an umbrella. They insisted that I take their umbrellas and keep them safe in my purse.

When we emerged from International arrivals, it was mid-afternoon. Our skin drank in the warm, moist air. A young woman and man in Hawaiian dress, presented us with leis. The plumeria's fragrance was as soothing as I remembered from our honeymoon. We climbed on board the rent-a-car bus, and took the short drive over to get our car. Trent had reserved a van, so when it was brought to the door, we had a lot of room for both luggage and ourselves. Trent had been to Honolulu a couple of times before and knew his way around.

We traveled along H1 toward Waikiki.

Joan burst out, "Look. That road is called like-like. It must be a good road."

Trent laughed and told her that it was pronounced Leeke-Leeke. It wasn't long before we were driving along Kalakaua Ave., which skirted the beach. Trent pointed to a three-winged building and told us that was where we were staying. He drove to the main entrance, and the doorman took the keys and started taking our luggage out of the van. We followed him into the lobby, almost falling over one another, as we looked about us. Large urns, filled with unfamiliar flowers, were everywhere. The lobby's business was conducted under a huge chandelier that swayed in the breeze that wafted in through the open doors. I was waiting for Trent to finish, when I realized the girls were no longer at my side. I headed for the beach and there they were, standing still, staring at the ocean.

"Can we go swimming mom?" they both asked in unison.

I answered them while we walked backed to Trent, who was just finishing up. "As soon as we take our things to the room, unpack, and change," I told them.

Our suite was makai, so we had a spectacular view of the ocean. The girls immediately picked up on the catamarans and told us they wanted to go on one of those. Within half an hour we had our beach towels spread on the sand, and our sun lotion spread. We went directly into the water, and the girls squealed with delighted fright as they experienced, for the first time, the pull of the tides. They delighted in standing at the wave line, and watch their feet sink lower and lower as the sand was pulled from under their feet.

It took them awhile to feel comfortable with the sand under the water that, when standing in place tended to sink beneath your feet. I'll admit that it isn't my favourite, nor are the pieces of coral that seemed to always be in the way of your feet. Trent went to hotel beach desk and signed out boogie boards for Joan and Susan and they had great fun with those. They'd lay on top, then ride the gentle waves, into shore. Finally they started to chill, so we lay in the sun. It wasn't long before the sun started to sink quickly. By the time we gathered our things, it was almost dark, and it was only five-thirty. We rode up to our room and took turns with the showers. I had just stepped out when I heard Trent with the girls out on the lanai. The sun was setting, faster than we had ever seen it, and both Susan and Joan loved the colours. They also saw the silhouettes of the catamarans when they passed in front of the sun.

"That looks just like the postcard you sent me, mom.", remembered Joan.

We wandered through the lounge and mingled with the crowds on the street. We went with the flow, while we decided where to eat. We decided to let the girls choose, and the first restaurant they saw that was familiar was their choice, Denny's. Our first meal in Hawaii was at Denny's, not original, but at least somewhat different than Denny's at home.

We had fun wandering through the International Marketplace. Both Joan and Susan were a little intimidated with the crowds and all the voices calling in different languages, so they stayed close to our sides. They both needed new bathing suits; those we brought back from our honeymoon were already too tight on them. I think that Joan wanted a more grown-up bathing suit. We found a booth that had many, many suits, and Susan didn't have a difficult time finding a couple that she liked. She picked a one piece, pink suit, with ruffles along the straps, decorated with geckos running up her tummy and down her back. Then she decided on a Hawaiian print, red, bikini. Joan didn't see one that she liked, so I told her I'd take her to Liberty House at the Ala Moana shopping Centre.

That night we decided that we'd spend most of the day sightseeing, because we didn't want the girls burning their skin. We'd be back by mid-afternoon, which would still give them plenty of time on the beach. Our first stop of the day was at Liberty House, where Joan found lots of bathing suits to choose from. She picked an aqua bikini and a high-cut one-piece covered in flowers. After that we headed toward the windward side of the island, to Sea Life Park. We all had fun at the dolphin show that featured not only dolphins, but penguins. We spent a lot of time at the underwater viewing tank, watching the eels, sharks, and other fish being feed.

Both Joan and Susan loved the main show, which featured a young Hawaiian girl who was stranded on an island with her little dog. The dolphins became her friends, and while doing that show off their jumping skills. The audience was treated not only to the show, but since they face the ocean, they can see Rabbit Island standing off shore. We were really surprised to discover that we had spent four hours there. We probably could have lingered longer, but the girls were getting anxious to hit the beach again.

We left Sea Life Park with a few additional members of the family, both girls bought toy dolphins, and we picked up some beach toys for them both. It was sort of funny that the first day in the water, neither of them worried about sharks, but when we hit the beach that afternoon, both kept looking around once they were in the water. I finally twigged to what they were doing, and reassured them that it was very unlikely for the kind of sharks in these waters to come in very close to shore. I also pointed out the life-guards, who kept a sharp eye on the water, both on swimmers and for sharks.

They relaxed and that was the end of that concern. After we went up to our room, we decided that the next day we'd go to the Polynesian Cultural Center. We were up early, so on the drive along the North Shore we could stop at various points. We stopped at Chinaman's Hat, an island that was indeed shaped like a coolie's hat. We walked along the shore to see what the night's tide had left. We gathered some nice shells, and then proceeded on.

We were torn when we reached Waimea Bay. We loved it there, the beach wasn't crowded and the waves were a good size for body surfing. We promised to come back, later in the week. We had to get going so we'd be a village in plenty of time. The parking lot was beginning to fill up by the time we drove in, but we weren't too far from the entrance.

After we entered, I found out something I didn't know about the Polynesian Cultural Center. It was founded by the Mormons and staffed by young Mormons who came from all areas of Polynesia. Most went to Birmingham Young University, which was nearby. It was arranged by country. In the Tahitian village, women demonstrated typical Tahitian crafts; young people demonstrated their dances and songs. We visited all the villages, including Samoa, and Maori. Trent was pulled on stage where a dance was being performed, and was taught the basic steps of the hula. We stayed for the evening performance and dinner. It was interesting to see both the similarities and the differences of the dances that were performed. By the time we left we were satisfied we had seen everything there was to see.

The next morning Trent signed us up to go on the afternoon sail of the Le'a'hi. It always beached in front of the Sheraton Waikiki. We had a wonderful time. Trent and I took Joan and Susan onto the forward rigging. Lying on our stomachs, we could look through the webbing and see the ocean slide under us. We were very lucky because a pod of dolphins escorted us for fifteen minutes. Once the boat turned for the sail back to the beach, the waves began splashing higher and higher, soaking us.

Just as the waters calmed, not far from shore, a huge sea turtle swam under the webbing, and then circled and kept us company until we were too close to shore, for its comfort. It was too much fun not to do again, so we booked another trip, for the next morning. It wasn't the same; the winds were light, and we were hardly moving. We didn't see any marine life, other than fish.

All of a sudden, the captain said, "Everyone overboard!"

With that crew and other passengers jumped in. Trent and I took up his offer and we dove from the back of the boat. It was incredible swimming in such clear, calm water, so far from shore. I don't know why, but I never thought about sharks while I was in the water. I could see all the way to the bottom, and saw a turtle gliding underneath me.

I was waving to the girls, when I realized the boat was a little further away that it had been. I called to Trent who was behind me, and we started swimming. I closed my eyes against the salt water, and swam toward the boat. My adrenaline started pumping when I opened my eyes and realized that not only wasn't I closer to the boat, but I was farther away. I noticed the sails were billowing finally, and realized that the wind had come up. Both Trent and I put in five minutes of hard swimming, and reached the boat. When we climbed in, we noticed that the life-ring was uncoiled. We didn't say anything to Susan and Joan; we didn't want to scare them, but looking at one another, our eyes acknowledged what had happened.

We hadn't been in any danger, but our bodies had reacted as if we were. The adrenaline coursed through our bodies. We released it through laughter, and talking with the crew. They told us that whenever they let people swim that far out, they prepare for changes in the wind. It was an exhilarating experience.

Our last night on Oahu came, and we dined as before, on top of the Sheraton. The girls were thrilled with the view, but were anxious to get to Maui. The crowds of tourists were starting to annoy them and they wanted something quieter. Bright and early the next morning we were out at the airport and caught the first Aloha flight to Maui. Kaena picked up at the airport and the girls thought that it was really neat riding in the limo. They enjoyed the sight of so many different landscapes on the way to the Newman's house. While we drove, we chatted with Kaena about what had been going on in our lives, and he told us that he had a surprise for us at the house. In a short time we were climbing out of the limo, and when Leilani came out to greet us, we saw what the surprise was. Leilani was obviously pregnant. We hugged and congratulated her and Kaena, and found out the baby was due in the middle of May.

Joan and Susan didn't know which way to run. Finally they decided to check out their own beach, saw that and ran back to the house. They were thrilled with their rooms, but only stayed in them long enough to pull their bathing suits from their suitcases, put them on and head for the beach. We told them they'd have to wait on the beach until we were unpacked. Kaena heard us, and volunteered to go with the girls so we wouldn't have to rush and they wouldn't have to wait.

CHAPTER 46

We took him up on his offer, and spent the next little while putting away everyone's clothes. As soon as possible we were down on the beach. We found Kaena in the water with Joan, and Susan was sitting at the water's edge, making a sandcastle. Trent sat with Susan, helping in the elaborate construction while I joined my water baby. I swam, I floated and as I did, I once again marveled at how my life had changed in such a short time.

I had been a single mother of two, I had to go back to school, I had to move through the layers of my job, until I could once again work to my capabilities. I didn't have a relationship with a man; in fact hadn't even contemplated one. I had said good-bye to my child. Now my life was a reversal of its former self. The only thing that hadn't changed was that I didn't have Patrick with me. Most of the time when I thought of Patrick, I tried not to dwell on him. For some reason that morning, I couldn't banish him from my mind. I guessed that it was seeing Leilani, and seeing her and Kaena's happiness that didn't allow me that solace. Even now, the questions stayed with me. Did I make the right decision, or not? What would I have done if I'd kept Patrick at my side; he was surely with me in my heart. I must have been deep in thought, for I didn't notice Trent waving and calling to me. Kaena swam over, and told me that Trent was calling me. I swam in, and Susan told me that they wanted me to see their spectacular castle, before the tide reclaimed it. They had done an elaborate job, and built a castle with many turrets, tunnels and moats. The five of us sat on the beach and watched the first turret slowly lose its base, and a tunnel collapsed. By the time we went in for lunch, only four of the six turrets were still standing.

I felt somewhat guilty that while we were outside having fun, Leilani was making lunch. After lunch, Trent took Susan and Joan off to town so he could buy each of them snorkels, fins and goggles. I helped Leilani with the wash up. Just as I was ready to let the greasy water out of the sink, I began to feel nauseous and dizzy. Leilani helped me to our room, and I fell asleep in no time. I woke up refreshed before my crew was back. I asked Leilani not to say anything to Trent, because I didn't want to worry him. Susan and Joan came thumping into the house; their feet in flippers, their eyes covered with goggles and their mouths stretched with snorkels. I laughed even though they tried to look menacing, lumbering toward me. I shooed them outside, while Trent retrieved his equipment and mine. We joined the girls on the beach and we taught them how to snorkel. We really hadn't thought we'd take Joan and Susan up the volcano; we didn't think they'd be interested. However they surprised us and said they wanted to get up early to see the sunrise. We waited until the middle of the week, and then repeated our honeymoon trip. The girls sat in silent amazement, spellbound by the show that nature once again presented.

It was an enjoyable week on Maui. We didn't go far, instead we spent our time on the beach, in the water, playing croquet on the perfect lawn, and reading and just relaxing, doing nothing. Joan and Susan had fun playing with Kaena and Leilani's little puppy. They'd all race around the beach and the lawn, and when the girls collapsed on the beach, the puppy flopped down beside them. Trent and I confessed to one another that we missed the freedom that we had on our honeymoon, as far as clothing and making love anytime. The early darkness held one benefit; the girls became tired earlier than normal, so Trent and I had the more of the evenings to ourselves. We confined our lovemaking to the bedroom and our outdoor Jacuzzi. The stars were as silvery as the moon. I had wondered in the past where the phrase, "a silvery moon" came from; the moons I grew up with were golden, orange or yellow, but not silvery. In Hawaii the moon's light didn't travel through as much atmospheric interference, and shone with more clarity. I could have stayed there for the rest of our holiday, but at the same time I was looking forward to seeing the Big Island, and the hotel. Our neighbors had shown us pictures from their holiday, but it was hard to imagine its size. So, with anticipation, Trent helped Kaena with the luggage while we stood with Leilani, saying our good-byes. We told them that they had to let us know when the baby was born. I thought Leilani was staying at the house, and was surprised when she joined Kaena in the front seat. During the half-hour ride to the airport, she kept squirming around, trying to get comfortable I assumed.

"Leilani, I wish you had stayed home, so you'd be more comfortable. You really didn't need to come into town with us."

"Actually, yes I did have to come. I've been having contractions throughout the night, and they're getting stronger, and if I'm right, my water broke at the last stop sign."

We all started talking at once. We reached the airport and hopped right out, so Kaena could get Leilani to the hospital as quickly as possible.

"We'll phone tomorrow to check on all of you. Love, Leilani." They were off, and we were off to another new island.

Landing in Kailua-Kona was an experience that seemed to take us back in time. The green mountains were familiar, but the undulating, black, bare lava fields were of a different time. Truly the land we saw before us was newly formed, emphasizing the age of that behind us. We drove through the fields of lava, in our red convertible, top down. The tropical wind flew over our head, disguising the heat absorbed by the black blanket. We stopped occasionally to take pictures of the lava. We expected it all to be the same; but in some places, it looked like thick, black, coiled rope; in other places, the small, sharp pieces of lava sat on older, smooth, rounded mounds. It was hard to believe there was a resort not far away. We didn't see anything except the blackness of the land, the diamond ocean, and a cruise ship on the horizon. The suddenness startled Trent and I; first a sign, and then the sight of palms stretching, piercing the sky. We turned off the highway, and were greeted at the entrance gate by guard, who expected us. We all fell silent as Trent slowly drove down the meandering boulevard. Flowers in vibrant colours burst from the lava, vines radiated across the black face, stretching toward the manicured golf greens. The car hadn't stopped, before the doorman had his hand on the door, waiting to offer me his help. Trent was told they'd look after the car and the luggage. We slowly made our way across the marble floor to the front desk. Each of us were issued passports that we'd keep with us at all times. Guests were issued them, to prevent sightseers from accessing all the facilities. Trent finished the business end of checking-in, and we were shown where to catch the boat that would deliver us to our room. The teak launch arrived; we were helped aboard, and settled in to be astounded. I thought it was amazing that we didn't break one another's noses, with all the arms that pointed first in one direction and then another. African cranes stood as sentinels on their island homes; colours of the rainbow flashed by the sides of launch.

Our adjoining rooms were perfect, but we didn't spend much time there. We all grabbed our suits, put them on, added our cover-ups and then tried to figure out where we were going to swim. We had a choice of three pools, and decided that we might as well try the pool that was along the launch route. We found the pool, found the guest services booth, signed out our towels, staked out our belongings on four chairs, and jumped in. The pool was different from any I had swum in before. It was narrow, and wound around islands that were peopled with Chinese statues, representing the animals of the Chinese years. I couldn't find where I belonged, so I began to swim the circuit. I thought I was in reasonably good condition, but found the swimming tiring. Once I turned the corner, I realized why. This pool had a current. It was great fun to swim past the water slides our way past the eddies of water, and float back down the pool. When we slid down the waterslides, we splashed into the water, and then popped up to the surface, floated downstream. Joan and Susan stayed in the water constantly, until I finally dragged them out. While the sun was straight above us, we covered up and played croquet. For the first time in my life, I played on proper croquet lawns. In between shots, we looked out over the ocean, that was just feet away. It was Susan who first spotted them. "Dad, Dad!" She shouted insistently.

We both turned thinking something was wrong, but instead found her, standing next to her sister, pointing out to sea. "Can you see them, Mom and Dad? See, whales!"

She was right, proven by the sudden number of waterspouts shooting up from the water. Our croquet game forgotten, we kept track of the pod as it played in front of us for what I'm sure was half an hour. Some playfully jumped out of the water; others rose gracefully, as if they were looking around for their audience. We saw flukes slapping the water, as the whales played. As suddenly as they appeared, they disappeared, and we resumed our croquet. By the time the game was completed, it was a unanimous vote for a return to the pool. How could you ask for anything better?

We had a decision to make when we finished showering. Which restaurant would we go to for our supper? We had six to choose from; Continental, Japanese, California Casual, Beef, poolside casual, and Polynesian. So far that day we had chosen according to what was closest. Following that pattern, we soon were seated at the restaurant in our building. We were seated at the edge of a waterfall, and its pool. Susan and Joan were delighted watching the fish swim up to our table, waiting to be fed. Our waiter brought the girls fish food, which they portioned out throughout dinner.

First thing in the morning, Trent put a call to Kaena, to see if the baby had been born yet.
We all sat on the edge of the bed in anticipation.

"Kaena, its Trent. Are you a daddy yet?" He turned his head from the phone.

"She had a little boy yesterday afternoon. Both are fine, and are coming home tomorrow. They don't have a name yet. I know you're busy, so we'll give you a call tomorrow, when we can talk to Leilani."

The next day we were more adventuresome and took the monorail to the large pool. Never did I envision such a pool. The pool was over an acre in size. Grottos were hidden in rock, hidden by cascading water. Once past the silvered curtain, Jacuzzis were tucked into caves. In another grotto there was a video arcade to amuse the children, when it was time for a sun break. We could hear screeches from the far end of the pool. Adults and children flew off slides and splashed into the pool. I've always been chicken to try such big water slides; but after watching Trent, Susan and Joan, I screwed up my courage. I climbed the stairway, and too soon, found myself seated on the slide, awaiting the lifeguard's instruction to go. He nodded, I gave a strong push and disappeared into the tunnel, moving up one side, down the middle and zooming up the other side. I felt my speed pick up and saw light, growing brighter and brighter. With breathtaking suddenness, I flew through the air, and crash landed into the pool.

Joan was laughing her head off. "Mom, you should have heard you screaming! Little kids don't make that much noise."

I stood in the shallow water, and made a production of trying to gather my dignity.

"This is your mother you're making fun of! Just watch my next trip down." As I spoke those words I rushed over to the stairs and stood in line for my next turn. When I looked over my shoulder, all my ducklings were in a row. I'm sure by the end of the day, my bathing suit was well on its way to ruin, but we had a great time.

Joan and Susan had something in mind when they came through the door into our room. Joan, as usual was the spokesman.

"We were wondering if we could eat in our room and watch a show that is on."

"What show do you want to watch?", Trent asked.
Tales from the Crypt, dad. We don't get it at home. It is a scary/funny show, but not really bad. Please?"

What could he say, with the two of them standing there side by side, and knowing that we could have a romantic dinner alone?

"All right, but you both have to promise to not go out of the room, not even onto the balcony, okay? Look, on the phone here, this button will connect you to the front desk, if you need us. Mom and I will be at the Japanese restaurant."

CHAPTER 47

We phoned room service, ordered their requests, and waited until it was delivered. With that accomplished we headed down to the boat landing. A warm, moist breeze caressed my bare flesh, while we waited. The boat ride took on a totally new dimension at night. Silence muffles the resort, focusing us on the visual splendors of the stars above, and the moon, when it showed itself. Too soon we were at the landing for the restaurant. We had a traditional dinner, in a traditional setting. The hostess and the waitresses wore kimonos, and knelt at our table when they laid out the many ingredients of our supper. Supper was a leisurely affair, with first one item, and then another, being cooked. Trent handled his chopsticks well enough to occasionally attempt to place a morsel in my mouth. When we boarded the launch after dinner, we sat at the stern, and went around the loop three or four times. We exited at the main lobby, and strolled through the mall housing the oriental works of art, until we were almost back to our room. We found ourselves in a little hallway, followed it and discovered we weren't far from the croquet lawns. Croquet isn't played in the evening; the grass is too damp and it would be damaged. We pursued the silence and darkness until we were well past the hotel lights, and found the gazebo we'd glimpsed earlier.

Trent went in, and reached out took my hand and pulled me in. He spun me up against the wall, and pressed up against me. His hands scooped my breasts from my dress, and he bent his lips to them, where his lips touched alternated between hot and cold. I gave myself to him to do as he may. I was too aroused to worry about others. Trent lowered his hands to my side, and slowly slid my dress up my thighs. A finger hooked my panties and slid them over my hips, and down my legs. He let go of me long enough to bend and retrieve them, and deposit them in his jacket pocket. Before he pressed too close, I grabbed his belt, undid it, felt for the zipper, and lowered it. I reached in, and freed him. We couldn't wait. The waves behind crashed onto the beach, as Trent pushed in and pulled out. I was ready so quickly, that waves of sensation flooded over me.

The sensation was so strong, it was if the waves and Trent had combined to merge with me. That power was too insistent to ignore. My breasts were hard; the mere touch of his tongue swelled them even further. Flames followed nerve pathways from nipple to clitoris. It stood hard, high, wet, and exquisitely exploded in heat and further desire. I felt Trent get larger and larger, until he joined with me as much as is possible. Our ragged breath joined the growing wind, while we sat trying to compose ourselves. We both leaned back to see the stars more fully. Away from the light, the night sky was reminiscent of a moonless prairie sky that displayed so many stars that you'd think they were a blanket. How long we sat there, silently holding one another's hand, I couldn't say. We sat in silence, as if both of us were afraid to shatter the moment. A man and woman's voices were heard in the distance. We heard them more clearly and sat up straight, made sure we were decent, and wandered back toward the hotel. Perhaps the other couple would be swept away by sensation, as had we. We both suddenly got the giggles, and could hardly speak.

Once we could, I said to Trent, "I've never felt like that before. I don't know how to explain it; the best way I can think of is to say my vagina felt swollen, reaching out for you."

I ducked my head and blushed. I had never talked to Robert like that, and didn't know what else I should say, indeed, if I should say anything more. Trent saved me from making a choice.

"You felt different to me, too. You're right; I felt your muscles gripping me more than ever before. Your nipples were extremely sensitive tonight too. Whatever it was, it was fantastic."

We finally found a path to follow back to our building, and when we returned we found Susan sound asleep in her bed. Joan was lying on the floor watching Nick at Night. I couldn't believe what she was watching, 'Bewitched', a show I used to watch when I was her age. We sat on the floor with her, laughing at remembered scenes. After Samantha, came Mr. Ed, the talking horse. Our bones couldn't take sitting on the floor anymore, so we kissed her good night, and went to our room. We stripped, laid in bed, intending to watch the TV a bit, but I couldn't keep my eyes open. The next thing I remembered was the morning arrived.

Trent and I were really excited because we had a surprise for Joan and Susan. We booked both of them in that afternoon's children's swim with the dolphins. After breakfast we went to the current pool, and then had to drag the girls out for lunch.

"How come we have to have lunch, couldn't we just snack like yesterday?" Joan asked.

"No, you cannot." Trent hurried on when he saw the pout begin. "The reason you had to get out of that pool was so we could go over to the dolphin lagoon for your swim this afternoon!"

Susan and Joan were out of their chairs and had their arms around Trent in a flash. Both of them were shouting thank-you to us both, as they quickly left the pool and dried off. Lunch was eaten quickly devoured. In no time we were among the lucky few who were allowed onto the dolphins' beach for the opportunity of a life time. The three marine specialists were great with the children, clearly, carefully, and in a non-condescending manner, explained all about dolphins. They split into three groups; Joan and Susan were in a group with two other pair of siblings. They were the only Canadians in their group; the others were from Oklahoma and Idaho. Susan and Joan were the ones who surprised their instructor however. He told them he wanted to put their okoles in the water, and asked who knew what that meant.

Susan and Joan shot up their hands, and Susan told him, "It means your butt." He laughed and asked how she knew that. Susan and Joan combined to explain that some of their friends in New Mexico had lived in Hawaii for awhile, and used the word all the time. The kids were given dead fish, that they tucked into the straps of their life-vests, (a requirement), and slowly walked into the water, squatting so their okoles were wet. Their instructor gave a whistle and a hand signal, and a dolphin came right into to shore. He showed them the different parts of the dolphin, and allowed them to touch the dolphin. Susan took a step backward when the dolphin blew through his blowhole. Next, each of the children feed their dolphin.

Trent and I stood on the beach with the other parents, and watched in wonderment as our children fed fish to dolphins. The time flew by and their time with the dolphins ended. Susan and Joan could hardly wait to show their classes their video. We headed back to the pool to cool off and I told Trent that I wanted to swim with the dolphins.

"I'll go back over and sign us up, while you stay with the girls." I gave him a kiss and he turned back to the lagoon. The girls and I didn't stop at our chairs. We dove right into the water. The water was most refreshing after standing in the sun for an hour and a half. Twenty minutes later Trent joined us in the water.

"We're signed up, but I'm not sure if we'll be able to go. The program takes only a limited number each day, and they draw names. We'll have to keep our fingers crossed."

We were still in bed the next morning when the front desk phoned. They had good news and bad. My name was drawn for that day's swim with the dolphins, but not Trent's. When I let Trent know, he insisted that I go, and he'd try for the next day. I was torn. For many years I always put others before myself, and it was hard to take what I wanted. Others needs always came before mine, but I had to learn to acknowledge that I had wants as well. I had to drew a line in the sand somewhere. I decided to step over that line, and be selfish. Three hours later I stood in the water with my instructor, and found out that adults were actually allowed to swim among the dolphins. I adjusted my goggles and snorkel, and slowly waded deeper into the lagoon. Almost immediately, the dolphins swam up to us and circled us. Their faces showed an intelligent curiosity, that initially put distance between us, but when it was decided that we weren't a threat, they allowed us to swim side by side with them. I went to the surface, shadowed by a dolphin that rose ten feet into the air. She made a huge splash on the landing. I could have stayed there forever. My mind drifted, wondering what thoughts they had.

Out of nowhere I thought to myself, "She might be smart, but I bet she doesn't worry about her babies; where they are and how they are. All that concerns her is the here and now." The thought shocked me. Why should I complain? My here and now was pretty darn good: I had two wonderful girls, and a loving husband, great friends, and no financial worries. I didn't deserve to be unhappy; if that was the case, why did that thought come to mind? Our instructor gathered us together, and gave us fish to feed to the dolphins, as our time together drew to an end. When the last fish was eaten, my chief thought was for Trent. I was so sad that he didn't have the chance to share the experience with me.

Trent woke me early the next morning, and said that he had a surprise for me. He told me to put my bathing suit on, and to bring my snorkel equipment. I just followed him, since I didn't know what he had in mind. At first I thought we were going to the large pool, but he veered down another path, which we followed until we stood at the dolphin's lagoon. My instructor from the day before was there, waiting for us. I must have stood there with my mouth hanging open, because Trent stopped and explained.

"I really wanted to share the experience with you, so I made some arrangements yesterday, and we can swim with the dolphins for the next two hours."

I threw my arms around his neck, kissed him, and then got busy getting ready to go in. I didn't want to waste any time. This swim was comforting, and very sensuous.

We tried to duplicate the sinuous movement of the dolphins. We weren't successful, but it was fun trying. We helped the veterinarian and her staff, with their morning duties: physicals, blood work, training and bonding. We went from task to task, until we suddenly became aware of the gathering crowds on the bridges. The time had come to leave.

Trent and I walked arm in arm toward the launch landing, each of us trying to share our excitement about our morning. It wasn't until we were sitting in the boat that I thought to ask Trent how we were allowed to swim with the dolphins, and help out.

"I went and talked to the director of the program, and asked if she would consider it, if we didn't interfere with their morning routine. I also told her how impressed we were with their educational program for the children. I said that we thought it was great that the hotel brought in local kids, so they could share in the opportunity, that visitors experience. I offered to set up a fund that would allow them to expand their educational program, so that even more local kids could come." He stopped, and grinned at me. "I think that was the clincher. By the way, this afternoon I have a meeting with her, to get down to the details."

"That was a great idea, honey. Not just as a way for us to go for the swim, but I was thinking about that yesterday, when the girls were swimming. It didn't strike me as fair that only kids whose parents were wealthy enough to stay here could have the chance. Shall we have breakfast now, or do you want to see if the girls have eaten?"

"Let's phone them from the restaurant, and they can join us. Even if they've eaten, I want to tell them about the fun we had."

Five minutes later Joan and Susan were sitting at our table, ordering their breakfast. They wanted to know all about our swim. Joan teased me, because she knew about it the night before and I didn't. The rest of the day was very full. It was our last full day at Waikoloa, and we wanted to make sure we spent it doing all of our favourite things. We swam in the current pool, we played croquet, we slid down water slides, we swam under silvery drapes of water, we huddled in dark caves, and we lay in the sun. I took a break at the height of the sun, and retreated to the Spa.

I pampered myself with an hour-long massage that relieved the pain in my lower back. I indulged myself with a manicure and pedicure. The manicurist surprised me, when she mentioned the condition of my nails

"Clare, have you been changing how you eat the recently?" I was surprised by her question, and answered her in the negative.

"Why do you ask?"

"Your nails have ridges in them, and are very dry. I sometimes see this with clients who have begun strange diets, or, sometimes, when they are first pregnant."

I started to laugh at that suggestion, when realization dawned on me. I couldn't say for sure when my last period had been. I was sure it was over a month ago, in fact, I think it was in the middle of February. I also began to think of my little periods of extreme tiredness, and the odd nausea. I hadn't even considered that pregnancy was the cause, because it mostly happened in afternoon. With my other three pregnancies, although I wasn't sick often, it was always in the morning.

The manicurist looked up at my silence and asked, "Did I just diagnose another pregnancy?"

"I think you did; I've been so busy I didn't even think about it. Oh, I hope you're right!"

She told me that the drugstore off the lobby sold pregnancy test kits. That was where I headed the moment I was finished. I met everyone back at the pool, and convinced Trent to go for a swim with me. Susan and Joan were both reading, so we had some privacy. I led him into one of the grottos and thought about how to tell Trent. Finally I just started.

"Do you remember how wonderful we felt when we were making love the other night? I think I know why that was."

"That's great. Do you think we could do whatever it was, again?"

"I'm pretty sure that it will be like that for another seven months or so.", I told him in a matter of fact tone, and waited for the realization to sink in.

In a second, confusion and joy flit across his face. "Do you mean what I think you mean?"

"I'm not entirely sure, but we'll know for sure, tomorrow morning." I told him how I became aware of it. He laughed that someone I didn't know caught on sooner than I did.

Trent asked me, "Didn't you feel sexual changes, when you were pregnant with Joan and Susan?"

I ducked my head down as I felt the heat rise on my cheeks. I couldn't look at him, while I told him the truth.

"Robert wouldn't touch me once we knew I was pregnant, so I can't compare. He told me I repulsed him, that I immediately became a fat cow to him. He told me that it wasn't right to make love, with a baby growing inside me. Robert wouldn't even hold or kiss me. I guess he was the one who missed out, right?"

Trent's response was to hug me tight to him, and kiss the top of my head. The warm water swirled around our bodies, while the heat from our happiness, warmed our souls. I thought that it was the first day of the rest of a perfect life.

The next morning Trent and I both were awake early, and went into the bathroom. I provided the necessary sample, and Trent did the honours. At least this wasn't a difficult task for two scientists. Both of us had performed many tests over the years when we had to wait for results, sometimes over days, even weeks. But those time periods were fast compared to the two minutes it took for the pregnancy test to end. I couldn't look, I told Trent to tell me.

I had my back turned to him, I didn't want to let him down with my reaction, if the answer was negative. I felt Trent come closer to me, and I was sure he was going to break bad news. Instead he wrapped his arms around me middle, and caressed my naked belly.

"Hello, little one. Do you think this baby is a boy or girl?"

I was too happy to answer the question. I spun around, and threw my arms around his neck.

"I don't care what sex the baby is. I'm so happy that you and I are having a baby together. Do you think the girls are awake?"

Trent leaned into the doorway, and reported that the cartoons were already on, so we put our robes on, and went in to their room. We joined Joan on her bed.

"Susan, come up here with us. Dad and I have something we want to tell you." In no time Susan lay curved along my body, Joan contoured to Susan, and Trent formed the other bookend. He raised his eyebrow at me; I just nodded for him to go ahead.

"Yesterday Mom and I got a clue why she's been so tired lately, and this morning we found out that we were right. We're going to have a baby!"

I lay like a princess, receiving kisses from my children and husband. Susan wanted to know if it was a boy or girl, and was very disappointed that we didn't know. Joan wanted another specific; when was the baby due. I had to tell her that I'd have to wait until we were home and I saw the doctor.

"Do you have a general idea?" Trent asked me.

"I'd have to say sometime during the beginning of October, honey."

Joan was already planning how she'd help with this baby. "Mom, I can look after the baby after school. I could come straight home, and I could do the laundry, I'll do anything you want mom."

She was breathing hard, by the time she finished. I glanced over her head to Trent, who very helpfully shrugged his shoulders.

Joan and I sat on the edge of the bed, and I brushed her long hair, while I answered her. "I know you'll be a big help honey, but I don't expect you to change your life. You have lots of other things to do. We'll have fun spoiling this little one, won't we honey?" I could feel her body trembling a bit, while I continued to brush her hair.

"Mom, are you going to make a nursery, like Auntie Carol? If you do, can I help do some of the decorating?" I hugged her to me and fell back onto the bed with Joan in my arms.

"Of course you can help me honey." I barely managed to get that sentence out when Susan started telling us what she thought the nursery should look like.

We stopped talking long enough to get ready for breakfast. Once seated, Joan asked me if I was going to eat, and seemed surprised when I said of course.

"I thought pregnant women threw up in the morning." she told us.

"Not everyone does, and for those who do, it isn't all the time."

Trent and I decided that we'd have a substantial breakfast, considering the busy day ahead. We took full advantage of the breakfast buffet, especially the bread pudding. Trent discovered it earlier in the week and it was excellent. Joan and Susan wanted to go to the pool right away, but we made them come upstairs with us, so we could have them help with packing. An hour later we had our bags packed, and a new suitcase sitting at our feet. We bought it to carry our traveling clothes, which weren't needed until the end of the day. While the girls and I made our way to the current pool, Trent let the front desk know that our luggage was ready for pick up, and he also booked the special room, for those guests checking out. In too short a time, it was time to shower and change into our clothes, and pack our bathing suits. At four in the afternoon, we were driving down the driveway, away from bliss. We stopped at the Pizza Hut in Kailua-Kona, ate and went to the airport. An hour later we were in Honolulu, going from the inter-island terminal to international departures. During the hour and a half we had to wait for our flight, Susan fell asleep in her chair, and Joan struggled not to do the same. She just managed, if the flight hadn't been called she would have been sound asleep in minutes. Trent carried Susan onto the plane, Joan groggily followed him, and I brought up the rear. We settled into the same seats as on the way over, and Susan was back asleep before we even took off. Joan was next to the window, so

Trent and I sat next to one another, holding hands, wondered to one another about our baby.

CHAPTER 48

Within weeks of our arrival home, the labs were finished and we got down to work. We each had our own areas of expertise, and worked separately. What was really nice was being able to join one another for coffee breaks, (milk breaks for me) and lunch. I felt well, and didn't have any troubles with the pregnancy until I was in my sixth month. When I saw the doctor I complained of extreme fatigue, and restlessness while sleeping. She told me to stop working for at least a month. I did as I was told. For the first few days all I did was sleep. I didn't get up in the morning to see the girls off. I didn't even get up to eat. I just didn't have the energy. It took a lot of effort to get out of bed and get dressed, so I'd be ready when Joan and Susan came home from school. By the end of the week, I didn't even bother dressing for them. One afternoon, Susan came into my bedroom complaining that there weren't any snacks in the house. I shocked myself and I shocked Susan when I yelled at her.

"I don't care if there aren't any snacks in the house. You always want everything right now. You didn't complain like this when we moved to Lethbridge. I had to make do without lots of things. Go away!"

Susan's eyes, widened, as she stared at me with her mouth hanging open. She didn't say another word, she just slowly backed out of the room, her eyes never leaving my face. She came to an abrupt halt when she backed into Joan, who'd come to see what was wrong. She stared solemnly at me, and silently spun Susan around, and marched her down the hall. I could hear Susan crying. I didn't feel any sympathy for her; in fact I was mad at her, at Joan, and at Trent. The big problem was that I couldn't say why I was angry. I wanted to be left alone. I didn't want anyone expecting anything from me. Everyone always wanted me to do something for them. I wanted to run away and indulge myself and be utterly selfish. The anger I felt bubbling to the surface must have given me enough energy to get out of bed. I phoned the Calgary Inn to see if there were any vacancies. There was and I booked a room. I threw some clothes in my suitcase, dressed, and walked to the garage without a word to Joan and Susan. I could hear them talking softly behind Joan's door. The minute I backed out of the driveway I began to feel free.

Checking in only took a short while, and within half an hour of leaving the house, I was sitting in a cozy chair, wrapped in a thick, soft robe. I ordered something to eat, opened a book, and held it open at the same page. The arrival of room service startled me out of my trance. I ate, without tasting the food, and crawled into bed. I didn't keep up the pretense of reading. Instead, I decided that it was the perfect night for a movie marathon. I watched four movies before I decided it was time for sleep. I don't think I moved all night, since I was so stiff when I slid out of bed. A bright sun poured into the room when I pulled the drapes back. In that light I looked at the clothes I brought with me, and realized that I hadn't packed very well. It didn't even dawn on me that I could phone someone to bring me clothes. I also didn't even think about calling my family to tell them where I was. I stood holding the one cool dress I'd brought, trying to decide what to do. Finally I phoned the concierge and asked him to arrange for a taxi to take me to a maternity shop; which company I left to him. I didn't have the strength to decide. There I was, surrounded by shops, but I didn't want to go into the mall. He told me that he'd have a cab ready for me in fifteen minutes. I pulled my dress over my head, ran a brush through my hair and went downstairs. When I was in the taxi, I heard the doorman give the driver instructions as to where to take me, and to wait until I was finished, and to bring me back. The doorman, told me the fare would just be added to my room charges. I never said a word to the driver. I was barely aware of the traffic, only when I heard the car door slam, did I shake myself to some form of alertness.

A saleswoman came over to see what I was looking for, and I think I startled her when I told her that I needed everything. I bought underwear, dresses, a bathing suit, shorts and tops, flip-flops and nighties. I was literally exhausted by the time I was finished. I had enough strength to sign the bill, and walk out to my taxi. The sales woman and the taxi driver put all my bags in the car, and then another trip passed in a fog. The concierge ran to my side when I walked in, and took the parcels from the driver. He handed them off to one of the doormen, and helped me to my room.

"Mrs. James, are you all right? Do you want me to call the doctor for you?" He stood over me, as I sank onto the bed, and I probably frightened him, with my answer.

"Thank-you, but I think I'm okay. I just need to rest."

"If you're sure Mrs. James, I'll go now. Please give the front desk a call if you need anything, good-night."

I felt great. Someone was fussing over me. I didn't have to worry about anyone, instead, there were people waiting here to give me anything I needed or wanted.

I stripped and stood naked in front of the mirror. My belly was the biggest it had ever been. I slid my hands over it, caressing my baby, talking to my baby. I told the baby that I'd always protect it, and that no one else but me would look after him. I looked at my breasts that were swelling in size; beyond what they did when I was pregnant with Joan or with Susan. I slipped my hand underneath them, and felt the heaviness. I knew that I would have lots of milk to give my baby. I was all he needed.

With complete suddenness, fatigue hit me. My legs supported me long enough to crawl under the covers. When I woke up, I had no idea what time of day it was. I pulled open the blinds, and saw the sun low in the western sky, so I knew it was late. I padded over to the bureau and found my watch. It was nine in the evening. I had slept the day away. I didn't care. I could sleep when I wanted, and do what I wanted, when I wanted. That realization gave me energy enough to order dinner. Thirty minutes later, my meal was being laid out on the table. I ate while I flipped through the television stations until I found a comedy. I laughed my way through an episode of MASH. Once I was finished eating and the show was over, I decided that I should get out of the room. I picked up my new bathing suit and went to the top floor spa. While I floated the water supported my aching back, and my belly poked high above the water. There wasn't anyone else at the pool, and I drifted in silence. I turned over and swam a few lengths. Another woman slipped into the pool. She was pregnant too. After awhile we began to talk, when we each stopped for a break. Annie was with her husband who was in town on business for three weeks. This was their first baby, so there wasn't any reason for her not to join him. Annie and I shared all sorts of pregnant women talk. I startled myself when I heard myself fabricating a story for her. I heard myself tell her that I was in town from Lethbridge, and that I came to Calgary when my husband kicked me out. I basked in her sympathy. By the time we were shriveled like prunes, we decided that we'd get together the next day, and go to Princess Island park. When I was back in my room, I didn't really think about what I told her. I was just happy to have someone to talk to; someone who was concerned about me. Unbelievably, I was tired enough to go to bed at a normal hour.

Annie and I had a great time during the next week. We had lunch together, and then we'd go to the park, or go for a swim. I panicked at the thought of going into the downtown malls, although I didn't know why. Each day saw me add another layer to the life I had created for Annie. Each layer brought more sympathy. Anger would suddenly bubble to the surface, and I'd have to fight not to drive away my new friend. When I was alone, I'd puzzle over the anger. I couldn't even say what made me angry, I could just feel my body go rigid from it.

Annie and her husband kept inviting me to go to dinner with them, but I didn't want to leave my cocoon at night. . I did go to the Owl's Nest with them for their last night in Calgary, and we had fun. We exchanged addresses. I wasn't truthful and gave her my old Lethbridge address. I didn't want to see her again; not after all the lies I told her. Later that night, when I lay in bed I shocked myself by not even being sorry.

I went back to severe cocooning the next day. The room service waiter and I became on a first name basis. He brought me food at least a couple times a day. I finally finished my book, and got enough energy to get dressed and go downstairs, and buy another couple of books. I watched the hotel movies, I watched TV, except for the news. I didn't want to know what was wrong in the world. All that mattered was my baby. I didn't bother to dress, other than throwing on a robe when Andy delivered my food. I wanted to look at my belly, run my hands over my belly, and watch my belly jump with the kicks of my baby.

The next day, I was surprised when it wasn't Andy at the door with my lunch; instead, it was the restaurant manager. He introduced himself to me as he set the table and put my meal on the table. An hour later I was surprised by a knock on the door. I dragged myself out of bed to see who it was. I peeked out and saw the hotel manager, Mr. Frame, so I opened the door.

"I was just up on this floor, and thought I'd drop by. First I wanted to see how you are enjoying the hotel. When we have long-term guests, I like to meet them, and make sure that all their needs are being met. Is there anything that we can do for you?"

"I'm as happy as can be. I don't have to cook; all I do is pick up the phone and Andy brings what I've ordered."

"Please let me know if there is anything that you need. Have a nice afternoon, Mrs. James."

I decided that I would have an indulgent afternoon. I phoned the spa and booked a facial, a manicure, a pedicure and a massage. My body and my spirit relaxed during the pampering. It was hard to leave. However, it wasn't as if I was going somewhere that I had to switch gears for. Back in my room, I paced around wondering what I wanted for supper. The realization hit me that I wanted to eat at one of the restaurants, instead of in my room. I wasn't going as far as eating in the Owl's Nest by myself, but I did go to the grill. I took my latest book with me, and settled into a booth. I felt protected; I had both privacy and a good view. I read while I waited for my food, and while I ate I watched the people going by in the lobby below. I closed the day by curling up in bed, and watching a movie. The TV was still on when I woke in the morning. The sun streamed into my room the minute I opened the drapes. It was a day that cried out for me to join it outside. I pulled on shorts, a top and sandals. I pulled my hair into a ponytail, washed my face brushed my teeth and headed outside.

Although it wasn't lunch time, a steady stream of people was already headed to Princess Island Park. I walked along the pathways until I found a bench in the sun, facing the river. I didn't read, I didn't watch the joggers; I simply starred at the river. After a time, I began to see the river not as a mass of water, but rather as many separate little streams. The streams didn't flow in a straight line; they bent around obstacles, they burbled over rocks, creating turmoil and music. Each stream held its own course for a portion of its journey, but inevitably, it would join the other streams, gathering strength. Together they had enough strength to flow smoothly over the rocks, together the streams created the riverbed and together they pushed their way along, through the city.

My tears began their own streams down my cheeks. I could feel them curve along the sides of my nose, collect there, and then run down my cheeks. I didn't stop them; I let them fall and with each rivulet I admitted to the pain I carried. Yes, I was thrilled to be pregnant, but this pregnancy could only remind me of Patrick. I couldn't be selfish and do what other mothers did every day. I couldn't bring him home with me. No one forced me to give him up for adoption; I forced myself. I deprived him of his mother and his sisters. I deprived myself of my son, and deprived Joan and Susan of their brother. I think I also gave them something else. I must have given them doubt. If I didn't bring home Patrick, what would I do if I got mad at them? I gave myself torment; torment that I couldn't examine for more than minute slices of time. Where is my son? Is he healthy? Is he happy? Is he mad at me? Does he know that I exist? Does he know that he has two sisters? Did I do the right thing? How could not keeping your own child be the right thing?

I slowly became aware of the anger that I could finally acknowledge. I was mad at Trent! Yes, while I was pregnant, I'm sure it reminded him of Nina, of when she was pregnant with Julia. Yes, he suffered from their loss. But it wasn't his choice. They were taken from him, in an instant, and it was an instant that he did not have any control over. He didn't plan their loss. I had to live through a pregnancy, feeling Patrick kick and move inside me. I had to fight my greatest urges. I loved babies, I loved looking after them, I wanted to look after my baby, like any other mother. Instead, while I feeling his life inside me, I was planning for his loss. I inflicted the pain upon myself. The act of leaving your child to strangers must be the closest thing to suicide that the living can experience. At that point I could no longer control myself, and the quiet tears gave way to sobbing. I was aware enough to hope that no one was close enough to hear. My wish was not to be granted.

"Clare, here is a Kleenex." I turned to the voice, stunned to see Carol standing at my side. I couldn't even speak. I took the Kleenex, and began to sob once again. Carol sat calmly next to me, not uttering a word; she held my hand. When I needed another tissue, she silently handed me one. I thought I had cried all my Patrick tears in Lethbridge, and it frightened me to realize that I had only just begun. My body emptied itself of tears, it began to force itself to take long, deep breaths. Only then did Carol begin to speak. She didn't expect me to answer her, she just told me how the last few weeks had been.

"I'm am so relieved that we were able to find you! No one is mad, and I think we are all a little ashamed. I know Trent is mad at himself. He didn't stop to think that this pregnancy would bring such difficult feelings to you. He's mad that he didn't help you through this. He's not mad at you. I came so I could let you know how everyone is feeling; so that you know we are beginning to understand the conflict you must be feeling. You're probably wondering how we found you. Trent didn't do anything for the first two days, except call Ann, Lora and Lena. They are all concerned, in fact Lena said she was going to fast, pray and go for a sweat, all for you. Trent didn't know what else to do so he called the police. They've been searching. Detectives went to all of the hotels downtown, and when one went to the Calgary Inn, he got lucky. The hotel staff: the doorman, the concierge and a waiter recognized you. That was the other day, just before the manager went to your room, to make sure that it was you, and that you were okay. Trent didn't want to rush you, or make you feel trapped. We thought it best if you were outside when one of approached. I'm sorry, but I've been waiting in the lobby and when I saw you this morning, you looked well, and I decided to follow you here. I could hardly keep my tears inside while I watched you starring at the river. Your pain is sitting at the surface now.

No, don't pull away; it's good that we can see this pain. Now we can reach it, and help ease it. I hope you'll let us."

Carol fell silent and we sat in silence. I wasn't sure if I could trust myself to speak, so I didn't. A wind came up, and shivers cooled me off.

CHAPTER 49

Carol noticed, and used that to motivate me to leave. "Why don't we go back to your room, pack your things up, and we'll go back to my house. You don't have to worry about seeing anyone, until you're ready."

I simply nodded. I knew I didn't want to be alone any more, but I wasn't sure that I could talk with anyone yet either. Within the hour, I was sitting in Carol's den. I didn't turn the lamp on I just sat. I could hear Carol's voice coming from the kitchen. I knew she was on the phone to Trent, and a sense of dread came over me. I was sure that I destroyed my life once again. How could I face Trent? How could I face Joan and Susan? What could I possibly say? I heard the phone being hung up, and I sat stiff with fear. I was afraid that Carol was coming in to say that Trent was on his way over. Instead I heard Carol on the phone again, but I couldn't make out who she was talking to. It wasn't long before she was back, with a tray of tea and cookies. Carol poured the tea for each of us, handed me the cookies, and sat down before she spoke.

"Trent wanted me to tell you one thing. He loves you. I think he knows that you're not ready to see him right now, he just wants to make sure that you know how much he loves you." I must have relaxed, so Carol took advantage of the opportunity to ask me something.

"I bet you are having trouble imagining what you'll say to him or when you see Joan and Susan, right?"

"What can I possibly say, except that I'm sorry for worrying them, for leaving them?"

Carol smiled at me, and told me that the worst part of having an argument, for her, is trying to figure out a script in her head. The hard part is that when you write a script you have to write all the parts. Since we can't possibly know whatever the other person is going to say, it is impossible to do.

"I had a feeling that you'd feel like that, so I called a friend of mine. In fact, you met her, Dr. Wright, when you picked me up at a meeting last year. She's a psychiatrist, and I think she'd be very helpful for you, for Trent, Joan and Susan. This is too big for you to deal with on your own, and you all love on another too much to destroy your family, because you don't want to accept help. She told me she's able to clear her afternoon tomorrow, and come over here. She wants to see you, and then Trent. Then she'd want to talk to you together. From there, she'd decide what would be the best course. Would you like me to call her back and tell her that you'd like her to come over tomorrow?"

"Yes, thanks Carol. Aren't you getting tired of coming to my rescue?"

Carol stopped on her way to the desk phone, "I'm not rescuing you, I'm just helping you get over a big hill." I heard her set one o'clock, tomorrow for Dr. Wright visit. My body suddenly collapsed into itself, and I could barely keep my eyes open. Carol helped me to the guestroom, pulled the blinds while I undressed and crawled under the covers.

"I'm not going to wake you for supper. When you need to eat, you'll wake up. If you need anything, come and get me. Don't worry about disturbing anyone, I shooed my family over to your house for the night."

I didn't hear another thing. I fell asleep instantly. I woke some time during the night and tried to stare through the blackness, but it was complete. Instead I saw visions of the morning. What was I going to say to Trent? How could I possibly explain what I did to him? If anyone didn't deserve to be hurt it was Trent, and I know I hurt him. I was afraid when it dawned on me that I hadn't even thought about Trent, Joan or Susan all the time I was gone. What kind of mother was I, what kind of wife? Maybe I deserved to be punished by having to give Patrick up. Did I deserve to be happy now, when I did such a terrible thing? No matter how hard I tried, I could only see Trent and I sitting opposite one another, but that was all I could picture. Exhaustion pulled me back into a deep sleep. I was woken by Carol's knock on the door.

"Sorry to wake you, but I thought you'd want to shower and have some breakfast before Angela gets here. I put out some fresh fruit and croissants for you. The tea is made and if you want anything else, help yourself. I'll pop into the shower while you eat."

I wasn't really hungry, but I knew I needed to eat, so I managed to eat a little something. I stood under the pounding water, hoping to stall for time, but Carol thrust reality upon me. She opened the door and told me it was ten-thirty. That left me half an hour to get dressed and compose myself. I managed to get dressed in that time, but by the time I sat on the couch, I failed with the composure part. I didn't know what to do with my hands, I didn't know how to sit, in fact I felt like I was going to jump out of my skin. I almost did when I saw a car pull into the driveway. I saw a tall, slim woman come to the door; I heard the bell. I couldn't say anything; Carol came into the foyer, opened the door and greeted her friend. I could hear them coming into the living room, and stayed seated. The doctor was a noise in the forest; she could have been a wild animal coming to harm me, or, she could be the rescuer. I didn't know which; what was the right response? Fight or flight? Indecision trapped me into immobility. I looked down on the scene from the advantage of the ceiling. Dr. Wright held out her hand when Carol introduced us and I saw myself making the appropriate response. Of course I had to be appropriate. I heard Carol ask if I wanted her to stay for awhile. I forced myself to give an answer contrary to what I really wanted, but I knew I had to face Dr. Wright by myself. Carol left us alone, and went upstairs. Now what? I'd never done anything like this before.

Dr. Wright smiled at me, leaned forward to put her tea down, and said, "Clare, I just know a few details about what you've been going through, so I don't know too much. You don't know too much about I do, so let's learn from one another, okay?"

"I feel really embarrassed, and I think I might have just ruined my life with my husband and my children. I've always been the responsible one. What do you want me to tell you?" I asked her. She had a calm voice and manner, and I began to relax a bit.

"Probably the best way to begin is for me to ask you some basic questions, so I can get a clear idea about your life over the past six years. How does that sound to you?"

I grabbed the paddle offered. I felt I could answer questions, but if I had to form the story, I wouldn't be able to at that point. "Yes, that sounds like a good idea to me."

"I understand that you met Carol while you were going to U of A. When you finished university you moved to Westlock, right? Can you tell me about why you left Westlock?" was the first question that Dr. Wright asked me. What a first question, when you think of all the ground covered by the answer.

"I left Westlock because my husband left me, and because I finally decided that the girls needed to get away from their father." I took a deep breath and continued. "I found out that I was pregnant the day he left. I didn't have a chance to tell him. I helped him pack his things, he drove off in his car, I made my mind up, called Carol. We escaped Westlock for Lethbridge." I told her.

"You sound very matter of fact about it. Can you remember what feelings that you had that day?"

"I think I probably had ever emotion that existed. I surprised myself when I was calm when he told me. Then I shocked myself when I realized that I was happy he wouldn't be in our lives anymore. Then I felt ashamed that I stayed with him, that I allowed him to keep abusing the girls and I. I was proud that I could organize a plan." I stopped at that point for a breath, and a pause for remembrance.

"Clare, it is amazing that you were able to cope with all of that in one day. Most women only have to deal with one issue at a time, and often they find that over whelming. It sounds to me that you were very strong. I'm sure you were happy to have such a good friend to help. Clare, you know what a lot of people have told me, and I'll admit that I'm still surprised when they say they resent it when friends help them. I'd like you to tell me what you think about that."

"I prayed that the Carol I remembered from university still existed. I had to have a starting point for the new life I was thrown into. Both Carol and Chris gave me the support that allowed me to begin again. I don't know how they did it, but they were always able to judge how much help was enough, and when I needed extra support. I remember being surprised at the bond that formed between Chris and I. I can honestly say I hadn't been friends with a man before. I could talk to him as easily as I could Carol. I wondered why I was so lucky to have Carol in my life again, and the bonus was Chris."

Angela asked me, "Why didn't you have any men as friends in your life before?" My response was to tell her what my growing up years were like, and then the domination of my life by Robert. It wasn't until I finished that story that I realized something.

"I just realized that Robert was jealous. Whenever we were at a party, if I was talking with a man, he'd make sure to join us, and almost all the time, he'd put his arm around me; his fence; his ownership." Angela sat quietly and allowed me to think about what I had just revealed. I did have value as a person; I wasn't the stupid woman that my husband kept on talking about. I was an interesting person. If I wasn't then others wouldn't want to talk to me when I did get out socializing.

"How do you feel about what you just said? Surprised?" I nodded slowly.

"I'm shocked that I didn't realize that before. It was so obvious; I wonder how I missed it?"

Angela described the cycles that abusers went through. She talked about how they systematically tore away at their spouse's self-esteem, and then used that to isolate that person from friends or family, who would try to build it up again. Once a person is trapped in that web, it can be almost impossible to step back far enough, to get a clear picture. I sat there looking through my mind catalogue of pictures, when Angela startled me with a direct question about the present.

"Why do you always feel responsible for everything, Clare?"

"I don't know." I sat across from her twirling my rings around my finger, waiting for her to say something. Finally, when she didn't say anything, I figured she wanted more from me. I tried again. I know my mom was responsible for me, but she couldn't do very much. My dad did the best he could to make me a servant in the house, I don't think he ever looked after me. I don't remember him playing with me, helping with my home work, I don't remember him doing anything except order me around. If I wanted anything I had to figure out how I'd do it."

"Didn't you repeat that pattern?"

I sat silently, staring at the carpet, staring at its pattern, to avoid acknowledging mine.

"Clare, look at your marriage. Who budgeted for everything, who made sure that everything ran smoothly, and most of all who took the blame if something went wrong?"

"I did." The silence stretched until I looked up at Angela and finished the rest of my thought. "Just like my mother. And to think I used to blame her all the time. I wondered why she didn't rescue me. I'm glad I never said anything to her."

CHAPTER 50

Angela suggested that we take a stroll around the garden; that we give ourselves a break. I eagerly agreed, and a minute later we were warmed by the sun filling the back yard. I pointed out the flowers that Carol and I had planted, and showed her where the path to my house started. Angela asked if I'd like to stay outside in the sunshine and I eagerly jumped on the suggestion. She told me, "I think we should talk a little now, about what has happened to you over the past weeks."

I felt my cheeks redden; I bent my head forward, so my hair would cover my embarrassment. "I can't believe I did it. I couldn't help myself. I had to leave. I'm ashamed. I've ruined everything. Trent isn't going to want to talk to me. The girls must hate me!"

"Clare, I want you to listen to me. Did you know that there are a lot of women suffering like you are? Professional people over the past fifty years have done a horrid disservice to birth mothers. It is hard to believe how callously birthmothers were treated. They weren't given all their options, they were made to feel ashamed, they were told that their grief was a punishment. They were told not complain about the punishment, because they deserved it. First they 'sinned' by getting pregnant, and then they gave their babies away. They did as they were told, but then were punished by those same people who counseled them, for doing something so 'unnatural.' Most often when birthmothers returned to their homes after delivery, they weren't allowed to talk about their baby, or their feelings. They got the message that in order to be accepted back into their family, they had to pretend that they had never given birth, that they weren't bleeding to death on the inside. To somehow survive, many learned to push their feelings deeper and deeper, until they could no longer find them. It is only in the last year or so that society is willing to hear the pain that birthmothers have suffered, and continue to suffer from. One of the reasons we are hearing more and more about birthmothers and their stories, is that they are now married and having children with their husbands. It is impossible to pretend with your doctor that you've never had another child. You have to dredge that up, so the doctor can look after the new baby in the best way. Birthmothers have to decide if they are going to tell their husbands about their past, and most importantly, share all those feelings that they didn't deal with, which were waiting to be acknowledged."

By the time Angela got to that part, I could barely see her through the blur of my tears. I tried to protest. "But I did cry then. I told Trent about Patrick. I did the best I could."

"Did you hear what you just said? You couldn't give in entirely to your emotions, you were on your own, responsible for Susan and Joan. When you re-met Trent, you didn't tell him for some time, about Patrick. You thought his grief was more 'legitimate', right?" I just nodded. "Don't you see, that you really haven't spent the time you needed to grieving over your loss?" Angela asked me.

I could only choke out, "But I did it myself, I made the decision. I don't deserve to feel any pain. I caused it!" I must have raised my voice, because the next thing I knew, Carol was sitting next to me holding my hand. I felt a Kleenex being pressed into my hand, but my tears weren't to be stopped so easily. I didn't have time to worry about not being able to see through my tears, I was too busy trying to gulp a breath of air. I had to spend every bit of energy I had just to breathe. Slowly I could pay attention to the voices that I heard, Carol and Angela. I followed their directions, and was slowly able to take slightly deeper breaths, until finally I felt like I actually had a lung full of air. I became aware of the rest of my body. My eyes were still streaming tears, and my nose was running. I found that I had doubled over, my hands holding my stomach protectively. My hands were trying to hold in a pain that was no longer buried. I stayed as I was, and rocked back and forth.

I heard Angela. "Look at what you are doing, Clare. Look! You are trying to comfort yourself, by holding that part of you that hurt then. Your body is in pain everywhere, because it isn't just the pain you felt at childbirth. You carry it with you every day! Now that you are pregnant again, your body is responding to the familiarity of pregnancy. While you have been busy in your mind, trying to deal with all the pain you carried, your body was betraying you. I think that last week your body asserted itself, and you just couldn't cope.'

I listened to her, but was suddenly so exhausted I couldn't talk. Both Carol and Angela realized that what I most needed right then was rest. Carol folded the lounge chair down, and led me to it, lay me down and covered me with a light blanket. The sun was comforting, and almost instantly I was asleep. How long I slept, I don't know, but as I slowly became aware of my surroundings, I could hear a low babble of voices, from the house. I froze, when I realized that one of the voices belonged to Trent. The time had come. Could I make myself walk to him, and listen to his judgment of me? Apparently I still had some small reservoir of strength left. I stood up, and on shaky legs took the steps into the house. I saw Trent in silhouette. I heard the voices stop. I couldn't go any further. I stayed where I was; waited for Trent to turn around and pass sentence. I couldn't look at him when he did. I closed my eyes. I didn't hear his voice. I slowly became aware of his cologne. I felt him come to a halt, a hair's width away. Then I felt forgiveness, when he slipped his arms around me, and drew me into the safety of his being. I knew then that we'd continue our journey together, together as husband and wife. Together as parents to Joan and Susan and the little being whose arrival we eagerly anticipated. What we wouldn't do is forget or ignore the other member of our family, Patrick. He wasn't physically with us, but his being would forever influence each of us. His being was a member of our family.

Angela and Carol withdrew, and gave Trent and I some time on our own. We didn't speak. We silently held hands, and walked around the backyard, looking at the flowers, and at the trees in the ravine. Angela appeared in the French doors, and called us into the house. I resumed my seat in the living room. Trent began to sit next to me, but Angela motioned him to a chair next to her. I wanted to touch him; hold his hand. I looked at Angela, and she answered my unasked question.

"Clare, I want you to use words to tell Trent how you've felt. I want you to depend on words to tell him how you hurt. You have spent too much of your life being silent. Now is your time to talk." She turned to Trent. "You can ask a few questions to clarify, but I'd rather that most of the time you listened." Angela looked me in the eye, "Begin Clare."

After the emotional day, I started off confident that I'd be able to tell my husband how I felt, without falling apart. It was false confidence on my part. Angela held out an arm to stop Trent from going to me. Somehow, I finished and when I dared look at Trent, he looked as drained as I felt. He glanced at Angela, came over, knelt on the floor and pulled me down to him. The silence drew over the three of us, broken when the school children ran past the house on their way home from school.

"Clare and Trent, I like to see you both tomorrow, and then the next day I'd like you to bring Joan and Susan with you. Clare, do feel ready to see the girls tonight?"

I felt panicky when she asked me because I knew the answer was no, but I made myself answer truthfully. "Good, I'm glad you answered that way, because I don't think you should see them until at least tomorrow night. I also think it is important that they need to have their dad at home tonight. I think it will be good for you both to have some solitude for reflection this evening. It will help with the work we have to do. I'll see you both at my office, tomorrow, at one o'clock, if that works for you." Trent and I both nodded. Angela stood up, called good-bye to Carol and left.

Trent and I looked at one another shyly, waiting for the other to speak. He took the plunge.

"I think I should go home now too. Joan and Susan will be home, and they made me promise to come home right away after I saw you." He walked to the back door, and started across the lawn toward the path, when he thrust his hand into his pocket.

"They'd be really mad if I forgot to give these to you. They made them all by themselves. It was their idea." He handed me two handmade cards. I struggled to read them through fresh tears, they simply said, I love you mom.

I could only whisper my thank-you before he walked away, toward our house.

In the afternoon, Trent and I met at Angela's office, and began learning about the work that I had to do individually and what Joan and Susan had to work through. Trent wasn't left out. He had suffered a loss, and filled his void with love, but he chose to love us. We loved him back with all our might, but we had caves within, caves that we learned to avoid. We were afraid of the dark, and we were afraid of lighting those caves. If there was light then we'd have to look too closely. We were afraid of what we'd see. The hardest thing for me to look at that afternoon was the faces of my daughters. I could imagine their faces when I saw them that night. Earlier, Angela had Trent and I play acted different scenarios that we could imagine.

Reality was so different than I imagined. I could see Joan and Susan's faces looking over the fence, watching for us to come down the path. I actually saw them first, and stopped abruptly. The evening sun slanted over the hill, layering light upon their hair. Joan's face wasn't calm or excited. Instead her introspection was plainly visible. I was afraid that I gave her something of mine that I shouldn't have; taking responsibility for everything. Susan wasn't still. Her head was swiveling in every direction, and a sunny smile was shone everywhere. Their pull was magnetic, overwhelming my fear. Susan saw me first.

"Mommy, mommy! Hurry! Joan, they're here!"

I took the easy route, and scooped up my ray of sunshine, while I was hugging and kissing her, I snuck a look at her sister. Joan's face crumpled, and she threw her arms around me, and let her tears stream down her face. I could hear her murmur, "I love you, mom."

We were able to just squish through the French doors, as we kept our arms around one another. I guided them over to the chesterfield, where we collapsed in a heap.

"I love you both so much." I murmured over and over.

Once we all composed ourselves, I asked Joan and Susan to listen carefully to me.

"I just told you both that I love you more than I can possibly tell you." I took a deep breath. "That is why it has been so hard for me since I found out that I was pregnant. It brings back all the memories of when I was pregnant with Patrick. It is because I love you both that my heart feels like it is breaking when I think of Patrick, and the decision I made. I didn't put him up for adoption because I didn't love him, just the opposite in fact. I can't imagine my life without either of you, but I made the decision to live without Patrick. Part of me kept telling myself that I don't deserve to feel all the hurt and pain that I do, because I caused it. When a woman is pregnant her body makes special hormones, and they really affect your feelings. I didn't do either of you any favours, when we didn't talk very much about Patrick. Both of you suffered a loss, too, your little brother."

I could see tears pooling in their eyes, so I rushed to finish. "We're all going to do something, together, so we can help ourselves feel better."

With my arms around their shoulders, and their dad sitting at their feet, we told them about Dr. Wright. It was time to lighten the mood.

"Let's go out to see my garden." Nature certainly is insistent telling us that no matter what, life proceeds. Plants had matured, and some were already beginning to form their flowers. Each step had to be attained before the next stage could begin. I suppose that was what we had to accomplish. Soon it was time to leave for Dr. Wright's office.

CHAPTER 51

Both Joan and Susan were comfortable with Dr. Wright, particularly when they didn't have to spend a lot of time just talking to her. Almost right away, she gave the girls their own sketchbook, and pencil crayons. She asked them to draw pictures about our life in Lethbridge. They worked in her outer office, while she worked with Trent and me, focusing this time on the death of Julia and Nina. When Trent finished recounting the morning they died, Dr. Wright asked him to verbalize his emotional state. Then she asked him to look at his emotional pain in a different way; as if he was responsible for it, responsible for their deaths. He looked aghast, as he struggled to find the words. In his silence, Dr. Wright intervened. "That gives you an idea of the depth of emotion laying beneath the pain that Clare has been living with. Her pain is deep, real, visceral, but she couldn't admit that it existed, because it was her decision that created the void, the pain."

Trent reached out for my hand, and held it tightly, as he spoke. "I can't believe that I've been so blind to not have realized the difference. You're right. It was horrid, it was unfair, they shouldn't have died that way, but I didn't have any control over it. It boggles my mind if I try to think of planning on not having them with me. Honey, I thought I had a good idea of what you went through when Patrick was born, but I didn't. I want you to feel free to tell me when you're having a bad day, and share your feelings with me if you can. I know that this pregnancy must bring those memories back very strongly. I don't blame you if it brings back negative feelings, or confused feelings. I don't think I can say we'll get over this, because Patrick will always be a part of you, a part of the girls, but we can learn to support one another."

While he was speaking, hot tears trickled over my cheeks, and found their way to my chin, and dripped down onto to my clenched hands. We sat quietly while composing ourselves and then Dr. Wright opened the door for Joan and Susan. They shyly handed over their drawings to Dr. Wright, who then showed them to us. Dr. Wright turned to Joan and asked her to tell us all about her pictures.

"This is mom, Susan and I in front of our house. Over here is my friend's house, and there is my school. It is when we first moved to Lethbridge. In this picture mom is in the kitchen, and she looks fat. She has tears in her eyes, I guess she is cutting onions. Here I drew about a picnic we had down by the river, with Auntie Carol and Uncle Chris. I scribbled over the sun; at first I remembered a sunny day, but then I thought I was wrong, so I drew some rain drops."

"I really like your pictures Joan; I think you're a pretty good artist. Can you remember any feelings that go along with the pictures?" Dr. Wright asked Joan. Joan just sat quietly, and shook her head no. "I want you to do me a favour this week. I want you to take these home, and hang them in your room, and look at them each day. In this book, I'd like you to write down how you feel looking at them. Okay?"

Joan looked at me with relief, and nodded yes. Susan went over and stood next to Dr. Wright.

"Did you see my pictures, did you like them?"

"I certainly did like them. Why don't you show them to your mom and dad, and tell us about them?"

"I was just little when we moved there, so I drew a picture of me in a crib. This is mom. I made her really big, because that is what I remember. This is me in a crib and Patrick is with me."

"Can you remember how you felt about the time of these pictures?", Dr. Wright asked Susan.

"Not really, except that I was really excited when mom told us that she was going to have a baby. I wanted to help look after it."

"I'm going to ask you to write in this book, just like Joan's going to. Okay?"

With the agreement from both Joan and Susan to use their journals, we finished with Dr. Wright for the day. Everyone was through the door, except me, when Dr. Wright asked where I was going to spend the night. I looked at her in surprise. "At home of course." Then I laughed when I realized that just the day before I was afraid to go home. "It feels like the right thing to do."

"Just remember that we've just started. Don't try to force anything, deal with things as they come up. I'll see all of you in two days. Good-bye."

The summer sun was still high in the sky when we walked to the car. It was a perfect evening to get some ice cream and enjoy a stroll. My suggestion was met with enthusiasm, so we stopped at the ice cream parlor along Kensington Road, across from the river. We joined the long line of people snaking along the sidewalk, and eventually stood in front of the freezer, re-evaluating our flavour choices, picked outside. We had to decide quickly; there were too many people waiting for their turn. We left the store with double cones. We decided to do the only sensible thing, and crossed the street to join half of Calgary walking along side the river. It wasn't just humans on bikes and skateboards we had to watch for, the Canadian geese had joined the crowd, in search of goodies. We just walked content to be once again in each other's company. By the time we got in the car for the short drive home, we all had streaks of ice cream around our lips and down our chins.

I enjoyed the night-time rituals. When Joan emerged from the shower I combed her long hair, and marveled at my daughter who was no longer a little girl. I sat on the floor next to the tub, while Susan enjoyed the mounds of bubbles. When they finally burst I shampooed her hair, and we had fun reverting to an old game. I'd trace a letter on her back with my finger, and let her guess which I had printed. Both Joan and Susan must have been worn out from their emotional day, they both appeared in front of Trent and I, already in their baby dolls, and announced they were going to bed. We both went with them and settled them in their beds.

Trent and I went to the family room and sat side by side, holding hands. For some reason, it reminded me of when we 'became' a couple. He told me that the end of the school year schedule was out for both Joan and Susan. They were both finished the next week. Joan had final exams on Friday, Monday and Tuesday, and then on Thursday was their elementary 'graduation'. The parents were invited to the school, for the presentations, and then all the kids were going to the Winter Club. The parents had rented the pool and the bowling alley for the afternoon. Susan's class was going to Bowness Park for their end of year picnic. Trent told me that we were marked down to supply Rice Krispie Squares.

I must have looked surprised, because he told me, "I thought I'd be cooking, so I suggested something I knew I could make, and that every kid loves."

"Do you know how nice it is to be sitting here, talking about everyday things?" Trent nodded and then drew me into a hug and ran his hands over my belly.

"I'm tired honey, let's go to bed."

Trent stood and pulled me to my feet. We went from door to door, checking that they were locked, before we went down the hall to our room. We peeked in on the girls, and both were sound asleep. I undressed, and stood in front of the bathroom mirror, trying to get the elastic from my hair. My arms were so tired, I wasn't having much luck. Trent appeared behind me, and gently loosened the elastic from the tangle I had made, and put it on the counter. He slid his hands around my belly, and then up until they supported the weight of my breasts.

"Our baby must be getting big. Your breasts feel so much heavier now. Your skin is like velvet; I just love the feel of it under my hand."

He kissed the side of my neck, and I could feel myself tensing - I wasn't sure I was ready to make love. He didn't say anything, just led me to bed. We lay side by side, feeling the warm breeze. I heard him whisper that it was hot, and could we just lay touching one another? Once again Trent showed his love for me, and tried his best to anticipate my needs.

The next week was hectic. Not only were there the end of year school activities, but every day I had to remind the girls that they had to write in their journals. It was easier for Joan, because she remembered more clearly than Susan, and she had the skills to write what she wanted to say. Trent worked with Susan, who didn't seem troubled by talking about her pictures, but didn't know how to write everything down. Dr. Wright had told us not to discuss the journal entries until we met with her again.

Thursday evening we again met with Dr. Wright. The first thing she wanted us to do was discuss the journal entries the girls made. Joan sat beside Dr. Wright.

"I wasn't really sure what to write the first day, so I kept looking at my pictures, until finally I wrote this. I remember liking our new house, even if it was smaller than where we lived before. I liked the quiet. I liked just having mom and Susan. I was really happy that my friends lived so close to me. I'm not sure I remember mom getting bigger, but I drew that, so I guess I did. Maybe when I saw mom crying I didn't know why. I don't like the picture of the picnic. I can't decide if it was sunny or if it wasn't."

"That is a really good start Joan." Dr. Wright told her. "Can you tell me what else you wrote about your pictures?"

"I think that mostly I thought about that picnic. We always had fun with Auntie Carol and Uncle Chris, but I don't remember going for a picnic when it wasn't nice out. I drew Susan with a smile, so I guess we were having a good time." Joan turned and looked straight at Dr. Wright. "How come I drew everyone else with frowns?"

"Why don't you think about that while we see what Susan wrote. Did your dad help you Susan?"

Susan jumped right in, in her usual way. "Daddy had to help me, because I don't know how to spell all the words. But he promised me that he wrote them just like I said."

"May I read what he wrote for you, Susan?" Susan was nodding so hard, that her blond curls swung back and forth. Dr. Wright read, "This is my baby brother, and I'm going to help mommy look after him. But now I feel sad, because he didn't come home to sleep in my crib. I think mommy is sad."

"You did a very good job Susan, thank-you."

Dr. Wright turned to Joan, "Have you figured out why you made everyone frowning?"

"Right now I think I remember everyone happy for awhile, but then they weren't. That is all I remember now."

"Susan, why do you think your mom was sad?"

"I heard her crying one night."

"That's great girls. I'd like you to draw again for me tonight okay? When you're finished you can show us your new pictures."

Once Joan and Susan had left the room Dr. Wright asked Trent and me about how our week had gone. We told her that it had been such a hectic week that we all just had minutes to spend together, but that time had been very comforting.

"I felt very safe. It was almost like the beginning of winter and the first snowstorm arrives, and you feel like you're snuggling into your home for the rest of the winter. Joan was getting her swimsuit and towel ready for school, and I was able to casually mention that I wonder if Patrick likes the water as much as his sisters. Joan looked at me funny: I think she was waiting to see if I'd get teary. When I didn't, she laughed, and told me that she could picture him in his bathing suit, with his little tummy poking out. Suddenly, Joan startled me by asking if I thought we'd ever see him again. I told her that I didn't know, but that I'd love to. She seemed satisfied with that answer, and we continued with our chores. It was a relief to share a quick little moment like that, where we said what we wanted to say, but didn't let it weigh us down."

"Trent, how about you? How did you feel about the week?"

"Like Clare said, it was really hectic, but I didn't feel pressured. I remember feeling relief when I thought about asking Clare if this was like when she was pregnant before. I didn't think about it forever, instead I just asked. Clare and I went around the garden while she talked first about her pregnancy with Joan, then Susan and then Patrick. She told me about concrete things, instead of how she felt. It is funny though, because I think she was more relaxed after that. It was a good week."

CHAPTER 52

Carol and Chris were indispensable to us. Whenever either of us needed another ear, they were there for us. A couple of evenings they had the girls for sleepovers, giving Trent and I some quiet time. I needed to be with friends who knew the whole story; I certainly didn't have the energy to tell it to anyone.

Dr. Wright told us to start with small details that were non-threatening, and when our comfort level rises, we move to the next level. Gradually we will become comfortable talking about anything surrounding Patrick. Susan knocked at the door; she was anxious to share her artwork with us. This time she had drawn a big building with a lot of windows. High up in one of the windows was a baby, floating in air. Susan confirmed our guess that she had drawn the hospital, and that it Patrick in the window. When asked why he was floating, Susan said that he wasn't, that I was holding him, but I was invisible. Joan's picture again reflected a picnic – this time she painted half of the picture in sunlight, with happy people. The other half was drawn against a stormy sky, and everyone is huddled on a blanket. She didn't want to talk about it, so Dr. Wright reminded Joan and Susan to write in their journals. We made an appointment for the end of the following week.

The summer became very busy. School ended, and our visitors arrived. As planned the summer before, the Martinez family returned for the Stampede. Trent drove out to the airport to pick them up. Susan and Joan were pacing the sidewalk, waiting for their arrival. When I heard the girls' squeals I knew they had arrived. Mansi and Kele looked wonderful. Mansi looked particularly serene, and when I held her at arms' length after our hug, she grinned and nodded yes to my unspoken question. I didn't have a chance to say hi to the kids; they disappeared into the house. Trent and Kele hauled all the bags downstairs to the guestrooms, while Mansi and I went into the kitchen to get us all something to drink.

Mansi looked at me and said, "Surprise!" I laughed and demanded to know when this baby was arriving. Mansi told me that February 4 was her due date. "We really missed Martha when Maria took her home, and now will have another little one in the house. Kele is very happy; he loved cuddling Martha, and was really good with her when she got fussy. Emily is thrilled that she is going to be a big sister, and Neil says he's glad he'll have a baby to cuddle. He's just like his dad. How are you feeling? You look wonderful."

"I'm feeling better now than I have for the last few months. I am getting awfully big though. I hope this summer isn't too hot." I told Mansi the truth about how I was feeling. I didn't want to load everything on her the minute she walked through the door. Later, when the two of us had a good amount of private time, we'd have a heart to heart talk. Of course while we were talking, we had organized the drinks and snacks.

We were just heading out to the deck when Kele and Trent came into the kitchen and relieved us of the trays. Thankfully the sun was low enough in the sky that the deck was finally in shade. We spent an hour or so catching up before the kids joined us. Sure enough, when I looked at my watch, suppertime was approaching. With kids these ages, you really don't need a watch to tell you when to start cooking. All that I really had to do was light the BARBEQUE and wait for it to heat up. Earlier in the day I'd made a rice salad, the garlic bread was ready to pop on the BARBEQUE, and the salad sat in the fridge, just waiting to be served. I brought the steaks out to Trent and left him in charge of cooking them, while I supervised the kids as they set the table.

While we sat eating, Trent and I outlined what our schedule was for the next few days. The Stampede Parade was the next morning, and we had reserved seats. That is why when we told them we'd have to be up at five o'clock in morning they were surprised. When we explained that there hundreds of thousands of people trying to get downtown, they began to get an idea of what we were talking about.

The next morning we herded everyone through showers, breakfast and dressing. Thankfully our company wouldn't look like tourists; they wore their well- worn jeans, their boots and scuffed up hats. Mansi and I used our pregnancies as an excuse not to dress western. We loaded the cars with the necessary supplies: drinks, food, change of clothes, wet wipes, umbrellas and sunscreen. Kele and Mansi looked at us like we were nuts. "You guys don't know Calgary; if you don't like the weather, stick around five minutes. It has only rained on the parade once, but it has rained before and after. It has snowed. People have broiled in the heat. If you go to the parade, plan for all of the above."

We drove over to McMahon Stadium, to catch the shuttle busses that were running downtown. We joined the throng of people oozing toward the busses, and finally boarded. The Martinez family was amazed at how much the city seemed to cater to the parade; streets were closed, sidewalks were blocked and people thronged down streets toward their destination. We moved along with the crowd until we reached our seats.

By the time we were settled all along the top row, the sun broke through the early morning cloud to bathe 9th Avenue in brightness and warmth. The strip began. Our fellow waiters began to shrug off jackets, and the last of the coffee was finished off. It wasn't long before I passed the sunscreen down the row, with instructions that everyone should make sure not to miss any spots on their necks and faces.

I think Kele and Mansi thought the time would drag, while we waited for the start, but soon they were engrossed in conversation with fellow tourists who sat around them. They were shocked at how far away people came for the Stampede: Australia, Sweden, Germany, Italy, Japan and New Zealand were all represented in our section. There were even some fellow Americans, not from the north-west as they expected, but from New York and New Jersey. The crowd's noise suddenly faded as it became aware that the time had come.

A high pitch whistle was heard, and then the bands began. We waited for five minutes or so before we had our first sight of the parade. The Parade Marshall rode a beautiful Palomino. I held my breath, waiting to see Kele, Mansi, Neil and Emily's reaction to the Blackfoot Indians from Standoff. I didn't say a thing, but watched their faces. I swear that Neil and Emily sat just a little straighter, while they watched the men, women and children approach on horse-back. The men were just riding past us when I heard my eldest daughter.

"Halona! Halona! Over here, it's me, Joan." She was standing and waving while she yelled. Once Halona looked up and saw her, Joan was on the move. The rest of the kids followed. They walked along the edge of the street, while they talked to Halona, who was trying to remember to ride, smile and wave. "How come you didn't call when you came to town?"

"We just got in last night, and I thought I'd call you once I knew where our tipi is so you can find us. Are you going to be home tonight?"

"We'll probably be home late, but call whenever, with directions. Just leave a message on the answering machine. These are my friends from Albuquerque. See you."

Three hours later the last horses went past us, and the 'official' signal that the parade was over, came into sight: the street sweeper. We sat for awhile, since there wasn't any use in trying to move, so we stayed put. The street in front of us was a mass of humanity whose only movement was a slow shuffle. Kele and Mansi had incredible expressions on their faces. Mansi turned to us.

"I can't believe it. I've never seen such a wonderful parade. I didn't think it would be so long, or have floats and bands from so far away. It's great that a band from Albuquerque was here. I just loved all the Indians in their traditional wear. The colours were great; the little kids looked so cute, perched in front of their mom or dad, on the saddle. Emily told me they were going to meet that friend of Joan's at the Indian Village. "Where is that?" Kele asked.

Trent explained that Indian Village has always been part of the Stampede grounds.

"We'll go tomorrow, and then you'll be able to meet Halona and her family, and go inside their teepee. Throughout the day there will be dancing that we can watch. Right now though, I think we'd better get over to the buses that are going to the Stampede grounds, so we'll be there in plenty of time for the rodeo."

We waded into the thinning crowd, found the buses and within half an hour we were going through the entrance gate. Stampede wouldn't be Stampede if we didn't eat junk food for lunch. We grazed from booth to booth: corn dogs, pizza, cake donuts, candy apples, and candy floss. The trail led us to the grandstand, where we quickly found our seats. The Martinez's were very familiar with all the events, since there are numerous rodeos in New Mexico. We cheered for all the cowboys – Canadian and American alike. Everyone had regained some of their energy by the time the rodeo ended, and the kids clamored to go on the rides. I draw the line at rides; I can't even watch them without getting dizzy.

CHAPTER 53

Mansi shared my problem, so after arranging a meeting spot and time, we headed into the barns. We strolled up and down the rows, looking at the horses and the other animals. I think having something else to look at made it easier, whatever it was, as Mansi and I admired the livestock, I began to fill her in on what my life had been like over the past few months.

"Now I understand why you didn't hold Martha very much, and why the girls were around her so much. I hope that you didn't think we'd condemn you because of your decision to put Patrick up for adoption." Mansi stopped suddenly, grabbed my arm and gaped, "Oh my God, I just remembered all those things I said to you the day Martha came to us. How could I have done that? I'm so sorry. Can you forgive me?"

"Mansi, you had no way of knowing. You couldn't have known the effect of your words on me. In fact you probably don't have any idea how much you helped me. The decision to move to Albuquerque enabled us to start a new life. If we had been totally on our own, I don't know what it would have been like. Having your friendship made all the difference in the world. You and Kele were so thoughtful and of course it was Kele who helped Trent and I meet once again."

We hugged in the middle of the aisle surrounded by horses and people. We agreed that it was definitely time for a rest and found a stand selling fresh lemonade. We collapsed on a bench under the shade of a tree, and slowly renewed our energy. Everyone showed up at the right time and in the right place and we made our way home. No one felt like cooking that night, so it was a fast food night. The kids went to bed early, not only were they tired, but they were planning on being up late the next night. We didn't last much longer.

In the morning Trent and Kele took the kids up to the club so they could swim, and we could relax. By mid-afternoon we were once again on our way to the stadium, to catch our ride down to the grounds. The kids had time to go on more rides and then we slowly made our way to the grandstand for the evening show. I told Kele and Mansi that the Young Canadians were well known across the country, and always put on a good show. All of our guests were excited about seeing their first chuckwagon race. They started off the evening's entertainment. As one, the Martinez family sat on the edge of their seats, yelling and cheering as loudly as everyone around them. When the first race was over, they were delighted to realize that there were still eight heats left to go.

The Young Canadians performed for the grandstand crowd. The grand finale of the show was the fireworks. They were spectacular as always, and signaled the end of that portion of the day. We sat for awhile letting the crowd leave, since I can't stand having to go up and down stairs while being pushed by impatient people. Once we were outside the grandstand, we went straight to Indian Village. I had the directions to Lena's tipi and without a wrong turn we were standing in front of it.

Joan knelt at the closed door, and scratched at the closed flap. Halona's bright smile greeted us all and Lena called out for us to come in. Before we did I made sure to tell everyone to remember to only walk clockwise, as is tradition. I also mentioned that everyone should take their cue from what they observed.

Some of the elders still prefer that men and women were on opposite sides of the fire. Before Trent and I went in, I made sure that he had the tobacco in his pocket where he could reach it easily. Once inside I was glad that I gave everyone a quick lesson, since Lena's mother and grandmother were with her. The men walked to the right before they sat down, with the other men. The girls, Mansi and I continued around the circle until we came to the empty space next to Lena.

Once we were all seated Lena began talking to her grandmother in Blackfoot, telling her who we were. Then Trent walked to the center place at the fire, and presented the tobacco to Mrs. First Rider. Lena told her mother and grandmother that the Ramirez's were from New Mexico and were part Indian. Both Mrs. First Riders were interested in what type of ceremonies they practiced, and were disappointed that they didn't know very much about their traditional lives.

While the adults were talking the girls were quietly talking in the background, when Halona stood and walked to her grandmother's side, knelt, and asked if she could show her friends all the things in the tipi. With the okay from her grandmother, Halona began to take things down from the lodge poles. She showed them her father's head dress that he wore while competing in the Men's Traditional category.

Halona showed us all the backrest that was her father's. Each of the children tried it, and all of them said it was very comfortable.

I thought that we should most likely go, since it was getting late, but all the First Riders insisted that we stay for the inter-tribal dancing. Just then, Julius poked his head in to retrieve his outfit. We filed out, so there would be room for him to change. Before he went in we had a short visit and promised we'd visit later in the week. Halona and the girls came out of another tipi, and Halona was already in her jingle dress, and Joan was braiding her hair.

I helped her with her barrettes and feathers. Susan was bending down fastening her leggings. Emily was right next to her, looking at the design on Halona's moccasins, and tracing them with her finger. Soon it was time to find a seat to watch the Grand Entry. First the flags of Canada and the United States were brought in, and most importantly, the flags of the Blackfoot and Sarcee Nations flew beside them. Elders were the flag bearers, and an Elder of distinction carried the Eagle Staff.

Behind the flags, representatives of the RCMP formed an honour guard. First came the male dancers; the traditional, the grass and the fancy dancers. The women followed; the traditional, the shawl, the fancy and the jingle dancers. Each participant of the Grand Entry danced one full circle around the dance ground, and then gradually formed ranks. Once all had entered the circle, an Elder offered a prayer in Blackfoot.

When he was finished the first of the dances began. I never tire of watching the dancing, and our guests had their eyes glued to the dancers. They had a hard time deciding where to focus their eyes; the feathers and the bells of the grass dancers, the hypnotic sway of the buckskin fringe that fell from the traditional women dancers, the energetic swirling of the young men in the grass dances, or the compelling rhythm of the jingle dancers. Soon the competitions began, and Kele and Trent went down to snap picture after picture.

Between categories there were inter-tribal dances and a friendship dance; people from the audience were invited to participate. Joan, Susan and Emily ran down, found Halona and stood with her. While they waited for the drumming to start up, Halona gave Emily a quick lesson. After their first turn around the circle, Emily began to get the hang of it. Mansi was thrilled to watch her daughter join in a heritage that she was part of.

"You know last year there was something called, The Gathering of Nations, at home. I wasn't sure exactly what it was or if we belonged. Now I know, and next year we'll be there. Do most of the natives here speak their language?"

It was hard to be truthful, but I told her. "I hate to admit it, but when there were residential schools, kids were punished for not speaking English, so a lot of them lost their language. It was real problem when they went home during the summer and they had to talk to their families who didn't always speak English. But over the past few years those people are beginning to realize what they lost and are really making an effort. A lot of the elders still speak Blackfoot, pretty much all the time and they are being invited into the schools to teach both native and non-native children. I know Halona speaks Blackfoot quite a lot, but I think she understands more than she can speak."

We stopped talking and watched as our children danced together; Blackfoot, White and Hopi. This was what Martin Luther King meant when he talked of his dream. Did their difference mean anything to the four girls as they danced to the ancient beat of the drum? I am sure that the girls saw their differences as opportunities to do different things and eat different foods. Their differences didn't interfere with their friendships.

"I can't believe all these little kids are still awake and active at this hour. My kids at that age would be awfully cranky by this time. I thought a lot of the older people would have left a long time ago."

"I know that I was surprised the first time I went to a pow wow, but that is what happens. Speaking of cranky, I'm getting very tired. Are you ready to head home?"

"I sure am, all we have to do is find our husbands and kids, and then we can go."

The girls were not happy to leave, but they cheered up when we promised them that we'd bring them down to the grounds the next day. Lena had invited them, and Neil to come down in the afternoon and stay with them in the tipi overnight. That way they wouldn't have to miss any of the dancing.

The walk to catch the bus seemed to have doubled in length, but finally we were all collapsed on seats. I struggled to keep my eyes open until we were back. I failed. Trent woke me when we arrived at the stadium and we all trudged off to the cars.

CHAPTER 54

Mansi and I were very lucky ladies: both of our husbands were up early and made breakfast for everyone. All we had to do was sit and eat. We were both so tired still that it was an effort even talking, so Trent and Kele volunteered to take the kids for a swim, and then down to Indian Village. They packed a small bag for the kids to take, and then they were off. We sat in companionable silence. Now was the time. I began to tell Mansi how I felt and what I had done. She did me the courtesy of sitting quietly throughout my tale. Rather than speech she used touch to show her support. After I told her that I was still feeling ashamed for running away, I came to an abrupt end. Mansi sat next to me, holding my hand.

"You don't have to feel that way. You did the only thing that made sense to you at the time. I think you needed some time to protect yourself from your sadness, before you could talk about it. You know, I remember my grandmother telling me of a ritual that used to be practiced for women.

A holy woman led this ceremony for her after her second baby died the day she was born. I don't remember the details, except that all the women in the village gathered together to pray for the baby and most importantly to pray for my grandmother. She told me that they prayed she would accept her tears and her pain, so that she could continue to look after her little boy who was just over a year old. Together they decided on a name for the little one, and dressed her in traditional clothes, so that she would remain a part of them, even in death. When the prayers were over, the men of village came to express their grief and offer support to both of my grandparents.

She told me that although she was very sad, she was able to continue her daily routine because she knew everyone knew of her tragedy and would help her if she needed them. Her mother-in-law made her special food and her mother made her a new dress: both symbols that life continues despite our pain. But their offerings also were a symbol of their grief for her, and the little one. I think it was the sharing that made the pain easier to bear. You were the only adult in your house, and were the caregiver for Joan and Susan. Who was your caregiver?"

I tried to protest, for how could I ignore Carol and Chris? "Actually, I was very lucky, that Carol and Chris were both my lifelines."

"I know that they were wonderful, but when you lay awake in the middle of the night, no one was there to take you in their arms. No one was there to tell you that it was alright to cry, to tell you that you were right to feel the pain of losing Patrick. Those people you worked with didn't publicly talk with you about how you felt. All the messages that came your way pointed in one direction and that was denial."

We sat in the cool silence, until I asked Mansi, "Why do you think it is so different in you culture and mine? Babies aren't given to strangers forever, someone in the family looks after them until they can go back to their mother. Death is talked about and mourned by the community. We do totally the opposite. Young girls are shamed because they are having the most precious thing in the world. Often they are abandoned by their families, when they most need support. When a loved one dies, some friends of the bereaved don't visit, don't offer their support, because they don't know what to say, and they want to avoid feeling awkward. I can't figure it out."

Mansi sat sipping her tea, and then said, "My people have always lived in a very harsh climate. There is heat, there is cold, there is water and then there is none. The heat can kill, the cold can kill, the waters may rage and kill, and it kills even more often when it is absent. We see death daily. Animals die in the desert, their death site marked under a circle of buzzards. As we live, death is always around us, if not animals than plants. Death isn't a stranger to anyone, young or old. I don't think I understand why there is such a difference about babies. I don't know, maybe death makes each life even more precious. All I know is that I get so mad when I think of what you went through."

We sat immersed in our own thoughts, until I glanced at the clock. "I'm going to do some weeding in the garden before it gets too hot." Mansi stood up and walked behind me out through the patio doors. "You don't have to work you know, you're on holidays."

She giggled, "This isn't work. This is quiet time with a friend, on a beautiful summer morning." We picked weeds from among the flowers, transplanted a few hostas that were already spreading themselves a little too vigorously, and then we watered the flowers. Mansi choose the flower beds, while I watered the hanging baskets. She delighted in the flowers that were unfamiliar to her and was amazed that we gave our plants so much water. "Back home these would have to live on what fell from the sky or formed as dew in the morning."

"I was thinking about what would to do this afternoon, and I thought if you're interested we could pack a picnic supper and drive out to Elbow Falls. It doesn't take long to get there, and there are cool spots even on hot days. We could even dangle our feet into the water. What do you think?"

"That sounds great – cool and relaxing, which is exactly what I want today." Mansi told me. Once we finished watering, we cleaned up and went to the grocery store. We picked out a rotisserie chicken, some salads, bread and fruit.

At home we organized our supper; cut the chicken, washed the fruit and packed everything up. Trent and Kele showed up by three-thirty, and half an hour later we were on the road. I think we all felt the freedom of not having the children in tow. We savored the freedom since it wouldn't be long before we were all, once again, parents of a newborn.

Most of the traffic was going in the opposite direction; young families with tired children heading home. We easily found a parking spot right behind the picnic spot that we chose. There was both sun and shade, and the river stormed over the boulders right next to us. We decided to view the falls from the top of the trail, and Mansi and I slowly walked up the side of the hill, until we were above the falls, looking down on them. When you first see the river it is hard to imagine that the falls would be of any consequence. That impression is swept away when you see the horseshoe shape the falls have carved out of the mountain.

It is easy to see where the river once plunged downward and onward. Kele and Mansi stood leaning against one another, breathing in the moist air, letting the spray cool them off. Trent stood behind me, his arms around my belly, nuzzling my neck. We too appreciated the spray that landed on us. We all managed to rouse ourselves and walked back to our picnic site. Kele spread the table with a tablecloth and Trent started a fire, while Mansi and I went to all the trouble of taking our supper out of the cooler, and placing it on the table. The evening sun was still high in the sky.

Kele was laying on his back looking up at the sky, "I can't get over how long it stays light up here. Did our early evenings surprise you when you guys were in Albuquerque?"

"When we first got there, it was strange that kids were all in their backyards so early. We take for granted that summer means being able to play baseball, soccer, golf or anything until fairly late at night. To me the days seemed too short." I told him. "Somehow to me summer means everyone out late at night; kids playing in their backyards, families walking along the river or a path, or just sitting enjoying the soft evening air."

Mansi looked at her watch, "I guess the dancing will have started by now. I bet Neil has already taken a million pictures. He and Emily were so excited about spending the night with Halona."

Trent added, "I'm sure they've already joined in one inter-tribal dance. I wonder if this is something that they'll want to do once they're home."

"I know that Mansi and I hope so. They haven't been too enthusiastic about their culture in the past. That is probably our fault. When we were growing up I don't remember anyone doing our traditional dances, except some of the old women and old men. I wonder where we'll have to go to find someone to teach them, and to make their outfits. You know, I remember when I was in elementary school, another boy asked me if I was a wetback, I wasn't sure what that meant, but I sure knew it wasn't good. He had a horrible leer on his face. I hate to say it, but I knew enough not to tell him that I was Mexican, instead told him that I was Italian. I'd forgotten about that."

"I've been thinking a lot about Halona and her mom the last few days, and how accepting they were of the girls and me. No questions were asked, what was happening at that moment was what was important. I remember feeling very restful when we were together."

We lapsed into silence and listened instead to the rushing water, the aspen leaves as they trembled in puffs of air. I'm not sure if we all heard the rustling in the trees at the same time, but almost as a group we swiveled our heads. First a coal black nose was seen, and then chestnut brown eyes peered over a branch. The nose and eyes materialized as a female elk when she decided that it was safe to walk through our picnic area. She was followed by her calf, and three more mothers with calves at their sides. We sat as still as possible, barely daring to take silent breaths. The adults stood at the river's edge guarding their young, who were having their bedtime drink. Time became indefinite – it was impossible to say how long we sat as statues. I began to hear a roar from the top of the parking lot, and when the motorcycle stole the silence, the elk bounded away, as if they had never been.

"You know I've always hated it when motorcycles came up next to me when I'm driving. It never fails that it at that exact time when you're trying to hear something on the radio. And obviously the elk share my opinion." At least that was what I claimed.

Mansi and Kele were amazed at how close they had been to the animals, and for more than a quick glance. As we watched the sun slide down toward the highest peak, I told them about the fox I had seen in the river valley, in Lethbridge. To this day I don't know why it behaved the way it did: she jumped out of the bushes, onto the path, looked at me, and then, rather than going back to the safety of the bushes, she slowly ran down the path in front of us. It was almost as if she was issuing an invitation to follow. When I finished that tale, the sun made its last call, with a bow that was breathtaking. A saffron glow emitted from behind the mountain, shading the sky and the clouds in all of its tones. It was impossible to leave that beauty behind, so we maintained our vigil, until midnight blue inked over the sky. It took just a moment to pack up our picnic site, and soon, we were headed back to Calgary.

A cooling wind came up while we were driving home, so the house welcomed us into coolness. We went straight to bed, and I think I was asleep before my head hit the pillow. I woke in the morning to quiet, and luxuriated in it. I rolled over and slept once again.

We took advantage of our childless state and slept in and then leisurely made breakfast. Trent and Kele just finished the morning clean up when the kids phoned. Joan sounded like she was still asleep.

"Yes, I'm tired mom; we didn't go to bed until dancing was finished and the prizes were awarded. I don't know if you remember me mentioning a girl named Anna that I went to school with in Lethbridge, but she's here as Princess of the Peigan Tribe. I was really surprised to see her. I didn't know she was Native. She is a Jingle Dancer. I loved her dress. It's black and white, and the silver jingles looked neat against those colours."

I took advantage of her pause for breath.

"How did Emily and Neil like the competition and staying with the First Riders?"

"Mom, even Neil tried dancing in some of the later inter-tribals! Halona introduced him to some of her guy cousins. They hung out together; checking out the girls, watching the men's games and when they showed up after awhile, we were shocked when we saw Neil dancing with them. He didn't look too bad!."

'Do you want us to come down and pick you up now?"

"No!" was the shrieking answer I received. "I'm not even dressed yet and we want to visit some more. Besides, Mrs. First Rider asked me to invite you guys down for supper tonight."

After a few more minutes of chat it was arranged where and when we would meet. I turned to my audience and passed on all the information.

CHAPTER 55

"I think you guys are going to be busy when you get home. It sounds like your kids have really caught the bug as far as dancing goes. Obviously Neil has one of the basics down - checking out the girls. I think a lot of boys go to pow wows just to check out the girls."

We dressed and then went over to the university. Trent and I were anxious to show off our new labs and fill in Kele on some of our projects. We were like the proud parents of a newborn - sure that no baby was as fantastic as ours.

"Kele, do you see how we organized this section; does it look familiar?" Trent asked Kele over in one corner.

"This looks just like John's lab at home."

"You're right. So many lab assistants commented how easy it was to work in it that I spent quite some time in there just observing the arrangement, the flow. At first I wondered at the placements of different instruments, but it worked. I figured, why mess with a winner, so I didn't."

I was showing off my lab to Mansi, and explaining how I used my research in New Mexico as the basis to open a new avenue of inquiry. She knew a lot about Kele's work, so she wasn't bored, and asked some insightful questions. By the time we wandered back to Trent's lab, they were still in the middle of things, so I decided to take Mansi over to the day care centre. I unlocked the door and flicked the lights on; stood back and waited for her reaction. She slowly made her way from section to section, saying nothing, but looking and touching everything. Suddenly she whirled about and faced me from the opposite side of the main room.

"Fantastic! I sort of envisioned what you had in mind, but this is incredible. Everything is here. This is what every work site should have."

I crossed the room and joined her, steering her into the nursery section.

"I love this room. Look at these chairs. If a mom or dad comes in to give their little one a bottle they can do it in comfort. I would have loved a chair like this when the girls were babies."

Mansi agreed, and decided to try one out for size. I plopped into the one next to her. We sat in companionable silence. I could see Mansi scrutinizing the room and she had a concentrated look on her face. I just waited, she'd tell me soon enough.

"I'd just love to be able to do this down home. I don't think I'd be able to organize it though. I could see myself running the day to day operations though."

I grinned to myself, because I half hoped she might say that very thing.

"While I was setting this up, I had it in the back of my mind that I'd like to see the idea implemented elsewhere. Of course at that time, I was really thinking of just the city, but why couldn't we do it in Albuquerque? I actually made things more simple for myself while I was in the middle of it by making copious lists and notes. I haven't had time yet, but it was my plan to set those into a business set-up plan. There are an awful lot of rules and regulations that you have to follow, and approval has to be obtained from almost every government organization and department. But, once you know what the sequence is, the hard part is done. I imagine that you'd have to do research down there, since things vary from city to city in this province, so obviously that would be the case between countries."

"I could phone all the appropriate people and by the time this baby is born, at least have all the information to really decide if it would be a good idea."

We remained in the nursing chairs while we tossed the idea around some more, until we heard male voices. I felt proud when I heard Trent telling Kele that I was responsible for the idea and the implementation of the day care.

"Clare, you had a great idea. I swear that every day at work someone is worried about their child-care. Remember Blair? After his wife had their first baby, they searched and searched for day-care, and just before she was going back to work they found a day-care that was in the right price-range, even if it was half an hour away from home, and in the opposite direction from work. Their little guy wasn't there for more than three months when they took him out. He had a horrid case of diaper rash. It was pretty obvious that he didn't get changed often enough. Then they took turns taking vacation days, until her mom could get up from Florida. She stayed for a month before they found a day home for the baby. Neither of them is totally relaxed about it though, after their first experience. Then there is the problem of what to do when a child is sick. Your program would take care of all their problems. At least one of them would be able to see their baby throughout the day. I wish the university had this program."

I glanced at Mansi and nodded to her. I saw her take a deep breath and make her decision.

"Kele, Clare and I were just talking about that. She told me that she envisioned, right from the beginning, of expanding this all over Alberta. We decided there wasn't any reason that it couldn't work at home. She already has most of the information and procedures listed. I was thinking that once we were home I'd make some phone calls to see what government regulations we'd have to deal with. I think we'd have to put together a proposal for the university."

Mansi suddenly glanced up at Kele.

"You'd help me with that part wouldn't you? I've never had to do anything like that."

Kele moved over to Mansi stood behind her and laid his hands on her shoulders.

"You know I will, baby."

Trent laughed and told me that I had just turned Mansi's life upside down. He also told her that if anyone was qualified to set up the program it was her. She had devoted much of her married life to raising her children, and other children of her extended family. Even though she only worked for a year before Neil was born, her university degree worked in her favour. She had her degree in Education, with a specialization in elementary school.

We went up to the club for lunch, and stopped at Co-op for some groceries to take down to the grounds. We also had to buy some more tobacco. I wanted to make sure that we had enough in case we visited with other elders. I was beginning to get the hang of what to buy when invited for supper. It had to be something that would be seen as an extra. It would be insulting to arrive with the main part of the meal; you don't want to imply that there won't be enough food. I usually stuck to desserts, fruit and drinks. Luckily we had been told to park down behind Indian Village, so Trent and Kele didn't have to carry everything too far. The kids must have seen us coming; they appeared almost as soon as the groceries were set down, and they tore open packages of chips and cookies, said hi and disappeared. Lena laughed.

CHAPTER 56

"Isn't it wonderful to be appreciated for you company? Do you think they'd ever appear if we didn't keep providing new food?"

"Probably not." I answered.

"I'd like to take you visiting some of the other tipis. A lot of elders met your children last night and they wanted to meet you."

Lena looked at us, and we nodded, but I asked her to wait just a minute. I had Trent locate the tobacco, and we split it between us, so it would be handy. Lena led us over to a tipi two over from hers.

She called out, "Auntie, I brought Joan and Susan's mom and dad, and Emily and Neil's parents."

We heard a soft voice telling Lena to bring us in. Lena and I were around the same age, so I wasn't expecting her auntie to be very old. The woman who welcomed us into her lodge had lived through many changes, over a very long time. Her skin was the colour of wild mushrooms, and the lines reminded me of velvet, softly bunched. When I presented the tobacco to her, the touch of her hands laid softness upon mine. She invited Mansi and me to sit on either side of her. We lowered ourselves to the ground and Lena gave us each backrests. Her auntie began talking to her in Blackfoot.

Lena told us, "My auntie is really my great-great aunt, and she would like to know if you'd mind if she spoke Blackfoot. She understands English and can speak a little, but she's more comfortable in Blackfoot."

Mansi and I nodded and smiled at the old woman. We heard the soft murmur of her words, and then Lena began to translate.

"Auntie wants to tell you that your children were raised very well. She was surprised to find them so polite. She thinks too many children today don't have any manners. She was very surprised when Neil offered her tobacco. She made me ask Neil why he did, his answer was that she seemed to him to be the mother of all the family there, and that she reminded him of his grandmother.

He is a very good boy, and smart too. He will be important one day - important to his people."

She reached over and took Mansi's hand in hers and slipped something into it. She held Mansi's hand around the object and chanted a prayer. She gently held Mansi's hand closed when she went to look at what she held.

"Auntie wants you to wait until you leave." Lena told Mansi. I felt auntie's hand on mine, and turned so I could see her face more clearly. She began to speak.

"Auntie wants you to know that she sees something very special for both of your girls. She is telling me that when she touches Joan, that she feels deep emotion, that one day she'll use and somehow that will have something to do with our people. She thinks Susan too will always be connected to us, but in a way totally different than her sister."

With that the woman whose eyes no longer saw clearly, pressed two small bags into my hands. Lena told me that they were for the girls, the rough one, with some bead work was for Joan and the smooth bag for Susan. Auntie, for that is what she asked us to call her, invited Trent to sit by her. He sat quietly while she looked at him slowly, and then spoke. Lena, once again translated.

"You have looked after your family well, and you must continue."

Trent responded. "That is my most important job. I will Auntie."

It was Kele's turn to sit with Auntie. He was told that his daughter had a special fire, one that burn brightly. Auntie gave him a beaded necklace to give to Emily.

We sat quietly watching the flames of the small fire flicker against one another, and onto the new wood that Lena added. The flames wrapped themselves around the sticks, until they too were on fire. I glanced at Auntie and thought she looked tired. When I caught Lena's eye, she nodded, and told Auntie that we were going to check on the children, and that we'd see her later. Trent and Kele helped us pregnant ladies up and then we filed out. We blinked in the bright sunshine and what seemed to be a different time. Once again we were in the middle of a frenzied Stampede grounds. We walked without speaking, until Mansi asked if it was alright to look at Neil's gift. Lena answered yes, and Mansi opened her hand revealing an arrow head threaded onto a thong.

Lena thought we'd find the kids at her brother's tipi. Sure enough we could hear the girls giggling and boys trying to shush them. Lena poked her head in through the open flap, saw there was still room, so we piled in behind her. She introduced her nephews and nieces. Our girls were occupied with her newest nieces - twins who were just six months old. One of Lena's nephews, Blair, was sitting next to Joan, and seemed intent on keeping close by. My daughter looked up at her dad.

"Dad, when the babies' mom comes back in a few minutes, we thought we'd like to go to the midway. I need to get some more tickets."

Trent grinned at Lena and said, "They need us for food and money!" Trent and Joan went outside where he handed her enough money so she could get a lot of ride tickets, and had left over for snacks for everyone. He reminded her that we were going to have supper there. Not long afterward, Wilma, Lena's sister was back and the kids cleared out, moving as one toward the midway. Lena introduced us and we spent time getting to know Wilma. She was a nurse who worked at the hospital on the reserve, and was currently on maternity leave.

During the rest of the afternoon we went from tipi to tipi and from group to group of people. I'm sure we were introduced to everyone staying in the village. We watched some of the afternoon dancing. Late in the afternoon the kids showed up again, ready, of course for supper. Mansi and I offered to help Lena, and she gratefully accepted. Indian tacos were the main course and those I knew how to make. Lena already had some fry bread ready and we continued frying more. I made a small one for Mansi. As soon as it was ready I took it out of the pan and sprinkled it with cinnamon and sugar. She thought it was as good as promised. We chopped tomatoes and onions, and shredded mounds of cheese. We finished as the dancing ended. Lena's extended family began to drift our way.

As other family members settled the elders in their chairs, Lena reminded us that after the blessing we would serve the elders their meal. Once that was done, then it was help yourself for the rest of the family.

Lena's grandfather gave the blessing in Blackfoot, and it startled us to hear our names mentioned. Afterward Lena told us that he was welcoming us and that he was sure that this was just the first of many times we'd be together.

Halona, Joan, Emily and Susan were put to work after supper washing up the dishes. Neil and Blair put them away. Soon it was time for everyone to get ready for Grand Entry. Joan, Susan and Emily helped Halona with her dress. With the Grand Entry completed, another evening of competition was underway. It was hard to drag the kids away, but we had to be on our way home. Lena and I promised Halona and Joan that we'd arrange a visit for them later during the summer.

Too soon, Kele, Mansi, Neil and Emily were on their way home. It took the four of us a while to relax. While we did, we reflected on the impact of their stay. I felt better having been able to talk with Mansi about Patrick, and about my flight from reality. I know Trent had long conversations with Kele that left him serene afterwards. I'm sure that the biggest impact on their family was the exuberant, positive exposure to Native culture, up close and personal. Mansi came away from the visit with a changed agenda for her year. I know she was truly interested in opening a day-care centre based on our model. It will be interesting to see if she does more than think about it. It would create a lot of changes in her life; but then change isn't necessarily bad. Her children won't be home forever. If this works for her, it would let her begin a new career, based on her education and her experience, all the while not worrying about her own child-care arrangements.

Joan was affected by their visit. She may not have stayed down at the village as much as she did, and in that case she wouldn't have become friends with Blair. He seemed to be a nice young man. Lena said that her brother, Blair's father raised horses, and that Blair was the child who was most interested in working with them. I knew that was probably one of the key attractions to Joan. She was becoming horse mad. It was something I wouldn't discourage, because I was as well, but didn't have the luxury of indulging in it. Of course the fact that Blair followed her around like a puppy and tried to please her certainly helped create a positive feeling in Joan. Blair was very quiet, but listened to everything said. I'm sure that she'd be spending time with Blair as well as Halona, on the reserve. We had already issued an invitation to Halona to join us in Calgary for the first week in August.

Susan was still enthralled with the babies, and wanted to go with Joan, to the reserve, so she could help with the twins.

CHAPTER 57

The rest of the summer flew by. We were busy with everyday things. We were busy with planning for the baby's arrival. We worked hard with the therapist, opening up, talking about all those things we had reined inside of ourselves for so many years. Joan struggled and struggled with pictures that couldn't decide if they were happy or sad. One day, shortly before our appointment I heard Joan in her room. Her head was on her knees, covered with her hair. She was quietly crying. I didn't know if I should interrupt her or not and just stood in the doorway. Joan has my sense of people moving near and looked up at me. I was surprised to see a smile bracketed by tears.

"I know why those pictures were mixed up. I want to wait until we are at the office to say though. Is that okay?" I just nodded and smiled and went to our room. Trent was changing and I told him what Joan said.

He thoughtfully listened and said, "She is so much like you, always wanting to do things the right way for others. That is wonderful, but we sure know that it can backfire. I think that is something she'll have to see unravel in you and then allow herself the courage to say she's important."

"It is hard to hear that I had modelled a damaging pattern for her. But you are right."

Thirty minutes later we were all in the car and on our way to hear Joan's revelation. Joan told Dr. Wright what she now knew.

"I always loved going down to the river for a picnic and so that why I drew a sunny day and had everyone smiling. Now I know why I changed the picture and blotted out the sun, and made everyone frowning." She looked steadily at me, took a deep breath and continued her story. "Mom, that was the day you told us that we wouldn't have Patrick at home with us."

She paused and I felt everyone's eyes on me. I closed my eyes and could once again feel that hot sun beating on my back. I heard the soft rustle of aspen leaves. I kept my eyes closed. I had to say the right thing for Joan and for myself. Only the truth was possible.

"Joan, you could pick up on my feelings so well, that it must have been confusing for you to see me smiling and talking about not bringing Patrick home, without sounding or looking really upset. I was just trying to keep it together for you and Joan. It wouldn't be fair to put all my doubts and fears on little girls. I certainly didn't plan to deceive you and I don't think that you are saying that I did. I just wanted to give you information that you could handle." I paused.

"Think of all the choices that I made. I made them quickly, and didn't look back. On the whole I knew my choices were right, except of course, Patrick. Did I make the right choice not to tell your father? Yes, absolutely. He wasn't a father to you two, I had no expectation that he would change. His decision jolted mine into action; I knew I didn't want him around in any shape or form. Did I make the right decision keeping Patrick's existence a secret from you as long as I did? Did I really make the decision to give my baby up? Did I think about every possible choice? Did I do the right thing; not just for me, but for Patrick and for you Joan and you Susan. Were those the right decisions?"

You could hear everyone's soft breathing in the safety of that room.

THE END

ABOUT THE AUTHOR

Frances Yancey represents almost the entirety of the adoption cycle. She herself is adopted, she and her husband adopted a First Nations child, she and Wayne had a biological child, she became a birth grandmother, and a grandmother

Frances found and contacted her daughter's birth family. Overnight her daughter became a member of a very large extended First Nations family. A very respected family elder will soon conduct a naming ceremony for all her children.

She also found and met her birthmother, as well as her half-brother and an aunt. She has waited over 20 years for her half-sister and her other half-brother to know of her existence. Frances' birth family was directly opposite that of her daughter's family. She was feared and not wanted.

Frances lives with her husband Wayne in Covington, Washington. Together they are joyfully raising their eldest grandson, and their two youngest grand-daughters. Her daughter lives minutes away. Her daughter's other two sons were adopted and live in the area. The family isn't traditional, but these children are loved by their mother, grand-parents, uncle and adoptive parents.

Frances and Wayne' son remains in Calgary with his little boy. Until she met her birthmother, her son was the only person in the world to whom she was biologically related. Now her grandson is one more precious link in a very small chain.

Any scientific ideas within the manuscript are from the author's imagination and she is solely responsible for all the errors within.

The author drew on her experiences living in Calgary, Alberta, Edmonton, Alberta, Kailua, Hawaii, and Lethbridge, Alberta to paint pictures of the locales featured in this story.

People of many cultures shared their intense and private experiences with the author. No disrespect is meant for any of the cultures represented within. She is totally responsible for any errors, misrepresentation or omissions.

ACKNOWLEDGMENTS

I am indebted to my best friend, Bonnie Neuman, who has consistently supported me through each life crisis and stages . She also never doubted that there was a book to be written.

I am thankful to Scott and Troy Mason who have opened their hearts to our family, as their family continued to grow through adoption. Their support when days seem very long has been invaluable.

I am thankful to Cheryl Burke, who was my first friend in a new city. Cheryl and her husband Dan have invited us into their lives. They welcomed us into their family home at Lake Chelan. She openly shares her artistic knowledge with me. Dan and Cheryl are our favorite couple to get lost with.

I am thankful to Betty Johnson, who moved in next door and became a dear friend. She listens to what is being said and hears what isn't.

I am thankful to Chris Hoey, whose family therapy helps our unusual family manage, what are at times, very rocky roads. She is also extremely thankful that he took the time to read this book and react with such positive comments.

I am thankful to the many people I have encountered over the years: birth mothers at support groups, members of the adoption circle as they organized, and parents and children in times of crisis. Each have their unique stories and perspectives which have expanded my life's understanding.

I appreciate the honesty from my editor Phil Jack.

CPSIA information can be obtained at www.ICGtesting.com
Printed in the USA
BVOW011229280912

301668BV00004B/56/P